Innovation and Internationalisation

T0298887

This book provides a comprehensive examination of the many factors that influence the internationalisation of SMEs into China. SMEs represent more than 50 percent of the economic activity and employment in China. This book explores the experiences of SMEs that have internationalised to China from Australia. Australian SMEs are at the forefront of foreign SMEs in China with over 5000 Australian SMEs currently operating in China and a long history of association. The book is unique in that it presents a multidisciplinary perspective of the subject, considering seven different discipline perspectives (internationalisation, innovation, entrepreneurship, networks, resources, human resource management and barriers and liabilities). This makes the book one of the most comprehensive treatments of internationalisation to China so far. Each chapter in the book deals with a different perspective and includes its own separate analysis. The chapters commence with a consideration of the current knowledge on internationalising to China for each perspective, analyse the interviews of representatives of 35 SMEs operating in China and then draw conclusions which are relevant to students, scholars and professionals. Each chapter includes extensive examples from the interviews. This integrated book is particularly useful for small business owners, international business management consultants, instructors and students.

Stuart Orr is Professor of Strategic Management at Deakin University, Australia and has published over 100 articles and books on strategic and international management.

Jane Menzies is Senior Lecturer of International Business at Deakin University, Australia. Her research interests are the internationalisation of Australian businesses to China, and innovative SME internationalisation.

Connie Zheng is Senior Lecturer of Human Resource Management (HRM) at Deakin University, Australia. She has published her work in various international journals such as *Asia-Pacific Journal of Management*, *Personnel Review* and *International Journal of Manpower*.

Sajeewa 'Pat' Maddumage is a Doctor of Business Administration (DBA) student in the Department of Management at Deakin University, Australia, and is studying SME internationalisation to China.

Routledge Frontiers of Business Management

For a full list of titles in this series, please visit www.routledge.com/series/rfbm

Innovation and Internationalisation

Successful SMEs' Ventures into China

Stuart Orr, Jane Menzies, Connie Zheng and Sajeewa 'Pat' Maddumage

Routledge
Taylor & Francis Group

LONDON AND NEW YORK

First published 2018
by Routledge

2 Park Square, Milton Park, Abingdon, Oxfordshire OX14 4RN
52 Vanderbilt Avenue, New York, NY 10017

Routledge is an imprint of the Taylor & Francis Group, an informa business

First issued in paperback 2019

British Library Cataloguing-in-Publication Data
A catalogue record for this book is available from the British Library

Library of Congress Cataloging-in-Publication Data
Names: Orr, Stuart, author. | Menzies, Jane, author. | Zheng, Connie, author.
Title: Innovation and internationalisation : successful SMEs' ventures into China / Stuart Orr, Jane Menzies, Connie Zheng and Sajeewa "Pat" Maddumage.
Other titles: Innovation and internationalization
Description: First Edition. | New York : Routledge, 2018. | Series: Routledge frontiers of business management ; 16 | Includes bibliographical references and index.
Identifiers: LCCN 2017039937 | ISBN 9781138638952 (hardback) | ISBN 9781315630571 (ebook)
Subjects: LCSH: Small business—China. | Joint ventures—China. | Management—Technological innovations. | Personnel management—China.
Classification: LCC HD2346.C6 O77 2018 | DDC 338.8/8851—dc23
LC record available at https://lccn.loc.gov/2017039937

ISBN: 978-1-138-63895-2 (hbk)
ISBN: 978-0-367-37560-7 (pbk)

Typeset in Galliard
by Apex CoVantage, LLC

Contents

Figures

Tables

Foreword

Doing business internationally is a topic of perpetual interest to scholars, business people, politicians and anyone with an interest in the world around us. For most of us, international business in China would be at the top of this list. And little wonder; the tremendous number of opportunities that are available, the rate of change and rapidly growing importance of China to the world's economy and foreign investment in developed and undeveloped countries alike, makes it a fascinating subject.

However, despite the global interest in China, detailed studies of the experiences of foreign businesses, especially small and medium-sized enterprises (SMEs), in China are still relatively few in number. Yet, SMEs generate more than 50 percent of GDP in China and are a large source of employment and, indeed, innovation. Therefore, this book is a very welcome contribution to this area and greatly expands our detailed understanding of how foreign SMEs can succeed in China.

The book is particularly interesting because it considers a range of important different perspectives, including the internationalisation process, innovation, entrepreneurship, human resource management, resources, networks and barriers to success. It also focuses exclusively on foreign (Australian) SMEs which have been established in China. Also, it brings the story to life as the 35 interviews on which this book is based paint many interesting and detailed stories about the 'real life' experiences of the managers in these organisations. These have been collected from companies along the east coast of China from Shanghai, Guangzhou to Hong Kong in a diversity of sectors, ranging from agriculture to manufacturing, building and construction and mining to wholesale and technical, business and property services to biotech and business types, from importers and exporters to wholly owned foreign enterprises and entrepreneurial start-ups.

One of the most fascinating things about China for scholars is the rate with which business and cultural practices in the country are changing. Practices and regulations are constantly evolving, creating both challenges and opportunities for foreign enterprises trying to learn how to develop and maintain their businesses. Unquestionably, it is an environment where entrepreneurs can excel, which is probably the reason for the very large number of local and foreign SMEs which have established themselves there. This book provides an excellent description of the experiences of the managers of these sorts of businesses as they faced challenges and developed their own solutions.

The book contains many lessons for business managers considering entering China, or expanding their Chinese operations. For scholars, the book explores the validity of a number of contemporary management theories in the Chinese context and helps to answer the question of whether these theories explain the internationalisation of developed country SMEs to China, or whether the Chinese context, such as its culture, economics and business practices explains differences in this organisational behaviour. This is an important area for academic research, which has continued to divide opinions for many years. For everyone else, the book provides a fascinating insight into the interplay between foreigners trying to adapt to the Chinese environment and their Chinese customers and partners.

I recommend this book to all those who are engaged in Chinese studies and research, managers who are planning or operating businesses in China, those who have experienced living and working in China and those with an interest in the tremendous opportunities China offers the world. Enjoy!

Professor Chris Rowley
Kellogg College, University of Oxford
Editor, Asia Pacific Business Review
Editor-in-Chief, Journal of Chinese Human
Resource Management

Acknowledgements

The authors would like to acknowledge the financial assistance provided by the Australia China Council (ACC), Department of Foreign Affairs and Trade to the value of $28,000 to conduct the research to which this book is based on (ACC2013-14043).

The authors would like to thank all the editorial staff at Taylor and Francis who helped us so much along the journey from developing the initial concept to submitting our final draft. We would also like to thank the editing and production team at Taylor and Francis who transformed our plain text files and content into the attractive and polished publication you have in front of you. We would especially like to thank Prof Chris Rowley of Kellogg College, Oxford University for reviewing the book and preparing the foreword. It was a great endorsement. Finally, the authors would like to thank the (blind peer) reviewers who contributed their time and talent to review the chapters. They provided many useful insights and helped us to prepare a thoughtful analysis of the issues.

1 Introduction

Introduction

China's strong economic growth over the past decade has provided the motivation for tens of thousands of foreign businesses to establish successful Chinese operations. The opportunities in China have attracted both large and innovative small to medium foreign enterprises (SMEs). Understanding the unique challenges experienced by these foreign SMEs as they internationalise to China is important for their survival and success. They have not, however, received the same attention as large organisations internationalising to China. Identifying the mechanisms behind foreign SME's experiences in China will improve not only our understanding of the way they internationalise, it could also identify concepts of importance for the internationalisation of large organisations as well. Developing a theory and understanding of 'how' foreign SMEs utilise innovation to internationalise to emerging economies, such as China, is an important contribution to the Chinese research literature. It is particularly important to identify how such organisations respond to both the rate of change in the Chinese business environment and the current convergence of Western and Eastern management styles in China. This book examines these issues from a range of management perspectives. It has practical relevance for managers considering internationalising China, as it describes the practices of successful SME Chinese market entrants and the issues that they experienced.

China offers opportunities in many industries, particularly for innovators, entrepreneurs and companies seeking rapid rates of growth (Boyd, 2016). Operating a foreign business in China also has a much higher level of attendant risk than operating a business in a developed economy. Factors such as sudden regulatory changes or theft of intellectual property are constant challenges. Boyd (2016) argues that SMEs are generally less risk adverse than large organisations, however, and better able to respond to the risks experienced in China. It is important to understand how foreign SMEs can utilise this capability to improve internationalisation success rates in emerging economies such as China.

China's growth and economic development has cooled off somewhat between 2010 and 2017, relative to its double-digit economic growth between 2000 and 2010 (except for the GFC period). In the last three years, China's growth has settled down to around 7% per annum (Department of Foreign Affairs and Trade, 2017). Subsequently, the context for SMEs in China in today is markedly different to the way it was ten years earlier. According to a 2017 McKinsey report, the four key characteristics of the business context in China are a slower economic growth, competitive challenges for foreign enterprises, demographic challenges resulting from the aging population and unequal economic growth across regions and trade disputes between China and the US, due to Trumpism effects (Orr, 2017).[1] The ageing population is due to the long term effect of China's one child policy on birth rates.

Trumpism offers advantages for non-US foreign companies in China as the trade relationship tensions between the US and China create opportunities for companies from other countries. An anticipated flattening of wages growth in China may also provide further benefits for foreign businesses, however, this will be balanced out by a reduction in economic growth and the housing market, which are likely to reduce opportunities for foreign businesses in China (International Monetary Fund, 2017). Orr (2017) predicts that economic growth will drop below even 6% in the future. In addition, difficulties with maintaining adequate raw material supplies due to trade restrictions and tensions between China and other sovereign governments could also restrict foreign business opportunities in China (Orr, 2017). The ageing populations in key cities such as Shanghai and tougher commercial laws in China will also introduce some of the issues to the business environment in China that many companies from developed countries experience in their home market. These factors will create a slow-down and increased complexity in the Chinese economy and increase the challenges for foreign business, especially SMEs, in China.

Over the past decade, however, China has offered a range of opportunities to foreign enterprises that they do not have at home. These include opportunities for increased rates of growth, much larger markets than most SMEs would experience in their home country, including large numbers of consumers who wish to buy healthy and safe agricultural products, as well as innovative new and branded products (Orr, Menzies and Donnelly, 2017). The appearance of health problems more common in the West, such as obesity, has also created a range of new business opportunities for foreign enterprises in China. These opportunities have driven foreign companies to pursue the Chinese market since Deng Xiao Ping's "Open Door" policy was introduced in 1978 (Tian, 1986). The results, however, have been inconsistent, and both successes and failures are common. Evidence regarding the experiences of SMEs in China, however, is much less limited, and experiences may be quite different to that of larger companies. This book and the research which has been conducted for it has been driven by the need to identify the factors that affect small-business internationalisation in a rapidly changing foreign market context.

The research findings in this book address a range of different perspectives on the process of SME internationalisation to China. The data was collected from Australian SMEs because large numbers of SMEs from this country have been taking advantage of the opportunities in China since China first opened its doors to foreign operations and, particularly over the last 10 years as China's growth has created a large and attractive domestic market. In 2014, approximately 5400 Australian SMEs had operations in China (Keating, 2014), making it the country with the largest number of foreign SMEs operating in China since the Cultural Revolution. The length of history and number of Australian SMEs in China suggests that these organisations will possess the most comprehensive and detailed body of knowledge regarding foreign SME experiences in China. In addition to the ability to provide a more longitudinal perspective, these organisations are also more likely to have developed a greater understanding of the issues, more sophisticated responses and more developed communication with other SMEs through local dedicated associations. In a complex and rapidly changing environment such as China's, it is important to collect data from the most informed sources.

Participants representing 35 Australian SMEs with current business operations in China (exporting, importing, wholly owned foreign entities (WOFEs) and entrepreneurial start-ups by Australian firms in China) participated in the research. A range of individuals from these SMEs were interviewed, which included owners, managing directors, senior managers, executives, managers and consultants familiar with the company's business activities in China. Each chapter in the book analyses this data to identify constructs in a different theory domain that relates to internationalisation. The findings are then compared with the extant literature to extend the SME internationalisation literature. The individual chapters analyse the data from the perspective of internationalisation, innovation, entrepreneurship, human resource management, liabilities theory, network theory and resources theory. The conclusion chapter integrates these findings into a typology of SME internationalisation, for which the constructs are based on a multidisciplinary perspective comprising the above theory domains. The book also considers the practical aspects of SME internationalisation and each chapter describes the implications of these findings for the management and development of foreign SMEs in China. The conclusion chapter also includes recommendations for approaches that SMEs should take to develop their operations in China.

SMEs in China

SMEs are now a very significant segment of the economy in China, as they are in the US and the EU. Although they had been a smaller portion of the economy in China in the past, by 2007, China had over 4.3 million registered SMEs, of which 95 percent were privately owned and which constituted 60 percent of GDP at the time (Asia Pulse, 2007). Today SMEs make up 98 percent of all registered companies in China, contribute 60 percent of China's industrial output and create 80 percent of China's jobs, own 54 percent of total assets, generate 68 percent of total revenue and 64 percent of total profits (China statistical Yearbook, 2016; Urbach Hacker Young, 2017). Over the period 2011 to 2015, China's 12th five-year plan specifically focused on support for SMEs with the objective of their numbers growing over that period at an annual rate of 8 percent (China Economic Review, 2011). This initiative generated massive investment in an already burgeoning SME sector in China. For example, in the relatively small city of Shenzhen in southern China, just the publicly listed SMEs now have a combined market value of over 600 billion USD (China Business News, 2014).

By inference, this suggests that the most representative area of the Chinese economy on which to focus when investigating international business establishment in China is the SME sector as it is the most representative sector by sales volume, number of organisations and economic effect. Findings drawn from research examining the behaviours of foreign SMEs investing in China will not only be important for the development of the international SME literature, it also reflects on internationalisation into the most important sector of the Chinese economy. This factor, combined with the apparent capability of SMEs to utilise their innovative capabilities to enter new markets is the reason for the focus on SMEs in this book.

Importance of China in international business

China is a critical trading partner for the US, Europe and most developed countries, including Australia. China established a free trade agreement with Australia (2015) and also has free trade agreements with Korea, Switzerland, Singapore, Pakistan and several other smaller countries (China FTA Network, 2017). The EU is seriously considering a free trade agreement with China (European Commission, 2017). Whilst the literature has investigated the trade between China and most developed countries, the research investigating internationalisation to China from developed countries is much less extensive and conclusive. SME internationalisation in China has potential to represent a significant level of Foreign Direct Investment (FDI), particularly from smaller developed countries, such as Australia. Understanding the patterns of FDI in China, especially in light of the rapid increase in China's economy and the opportunities for investment in China is important for both economic and international business theory development.

China's growing middle class

China's middle class has been growing for more than 20 years and now includes 300–400 million of China's 1.35 billion in population (Fukyama, 2013). By 2020, the Chinese middle class will constitute over 75 percent of the total population (McKinsey, 2013). This is a very dramatic increase from representing only 4 percent of the population in 2000 (Iskyan, 2016).

Chinese middle-class income has also increased significantly. In 2013, the income of 75 percent of China's urban communities was around 8000–30,000 USD per year (McKinsey, 2013). The Chinese middle class now has approximately the same purchasing power (corrected for the price of goods in China) as the middle class in most developed countries. Unsurprisingly, the increased buying power of the Chinese middle class has not only created new business opportunities for both foreign and local SMEs, it has also increased both the sophistication of customers and the demand for innovative products. The creation of new business opportunities has been particularly significant. For example, it has led to an increased demand for non-traditional Chinese foods such as wine, red meat and dairy products, and demand for supply from foreign sources offering high quality food and food safety, such as Australia (DFAT, 2014).

China's increased urbanisation

China's population is also becoming more urbanised as the Chinese move from agricultural to commercial employment (China Development Research, 2013). In 2015, 56 percent of the Chinese population lived in urban locations (China Statistical Yearbook, 2016), compared to 80 percent in developed countries (Anderlini, 2014). This urban growth is an important development for SMEs and particularly for foreign SMEs in China. The increasing concentration of markets simplifies the logistics associated with getting goods and services to the market. Logistics is a significant barrier in China where rural infrastructure including road and rail transportation are limited and difficult to manage. Operating in an urban environment with more developed infrastructure and in close proximity to markets is particularly important for foreign SMEs which lack the local knowledge and contacts that local companies would use to larger scale distribution networks.

Urbanisation will continue to increase in China over the foreseeable future. Currently, China's government plans for the transfer of a further 100 million people from rural to urban locations, which will increase the percentage of urban population to 60 percent by 2020 (Anderlini, 2014). This plan includes the development of transportation networks, urban infrastructure and residential real estate. By 2030, it is projected that the urban population will be 70 percent of the total population, or approximately 1 billion people (World Bank Group, 2014). The increased urban concentration is also likely to generate demand for further new and innovative products and services making it a logical focus for foreign innovative SMEs.

Increased demand for innovation in China

The Chinese government has planned for the economy to shift from a focus on manufacturing and export, to include innovation and services for the last 10 years (Macquarie Bank, 2017). The development of an innovation based economy (and society) was one of the key goals of the Government's 2011 five-year plan. There is already evidence that innovative products and services are becoming increasingly attractive industries in China (Abrami, Kirby and McFarlan, 2014). Some of the measures which have been put in place by the government to increase innovation include the establishment of high-technology business zones, the attraction of foreign investment in the wind turbine industry (which has made China one of the global centres of wind turbine production), the introduction of caps on importing technology (to stimulate local technology product development) and increased investment in research and development in key industries.

As part of the current 13th five-year plan, the Chinese government has focused on development of innovation in biotechnology, energy-efficient technologies, equipment manufacturing, information technology and advanced materials industries (KPMG, 2016). This policy is intended to keep the skilled people in China to develop new innovations and products (Macquarie Bank, 2017). This is a dramatic change in policy from earlier five-year plans where the focus was on technology importation and the development manufacturing and export capability. In the past, the government had encouraged innovation in selected industries, but through structural arrangements which tended to drive technology from the top down, at a slow pace (Abrami, Kirby and McFarlan, 2014). The result has been that China has demonstrated an innovative capacity in industries such as consumer electronics and construction equipment, but not in industries such as the pharmaceutical or automobile industries. This investment is forecast to generate between one and 2 trillion USD in the Chinese economy by 2020 (Roth et al., 2015).

The development of an innovation based economy offers clear advantages to innovative foreign SMEs. These government initiatives will develop the infrastructure necessary to support innovative SMEs in China and the market, particularly the urbanised middle class, will develop a taste for innovation as more innovation becomes available. These initiatives may, however, also result in a challenge for foreign innovative SMEs. As local SMEs develop their own innovations with the support of government initiatives, innovation based competition will increase. The potential for the development of innovation based competition may require innovative foreign SMEs to both focus on staying one step ahead of the industry and be flexible enough to change markets when competition becomes too intense.

Environmental sustainability in China

China is progressing quickly down the path of becoming environmentally sustainable. The 2011 five-year plan included an objective of becoming a sustainable and environmentally responsible country (Li and Woetzel, 2011). The government focus on the environment in the current (13th) five-year plan includes environmental sustainability governance, investment and technology and will provide many opportunities for foreign SMEs (KPMG, 2016). The accelerated rate of environmental development incorporated in this plan will create a strong level of demand for environmental services and innovations, as well as testing the existing capacity in China in this area, which could be expected to generate substantial opportunities for foreign SMEs with capabilities in this area. SMEs from countries such as Australia with well-developed environmental management profiles are likely to experience a particular advantage.

Effect of trade on foreign internationalisation of SMEs to China

Australia was one of the first developed countries to establish a free trade agreement with China – this outcome reflects one of the reasons for the large number of Australian SMEs that have invested in China. The China Australia Free Trade

Agreement (ChAFTA) was the result of a 10 year negotiation between the two countries and came into force in December 2015 (Austrade, 2017). The free trade agreement was a product of the level of trade between the two countries in the decades prior. Whilst the volume of trade between Australia and China is much less than the level of trade between China and the US or EU (European Commission, 2017), China has been Australia's number one trading partner since 2007 (Uren, 2007).

Australia exported 70 billion USD in goods and services to China in 2015–2016, and imported 55 billion USD of products from China (DFAT, 2017). This was an increase of 10 percent from the total trade between the two countries between 2016 and 2013 (DFAT, 2014). Australia's exports to China included iron ore, coal, gold and wool products, whilst China's exports to Australia included telecom equipment, computers, furniture, games and sporting goods (DFAT, 2017). In addition, Chinese investors have invested in Australian mining, agriculture and real estate. Australia's investment in China was 60 billion USD, whilst China's investment in Australia was 70 billion USD (DFAT, 2017).

The introduction of the FTA in 2015 further stimulated and increased the volume of trade and FDI between the two countries (Austrade, 2017). The level of trade between the countries and Chinese investment in Australia provided the connections and familiarity with China which was an important foundation for the motivation for Australian SMEs to enter China. It also created the context for the Australian government to promote the involvement of innovative SMEs in China (in Asia) through major initiatives (Australian Government, 2012).

The study

The data was collected in late 2013 and early 2014. Interviews were conducted with senior representatives of each of the participant organisations using a structured questionnaire which was made available to the organisation one month prior to the interview. The objective of the research was to identify the factors which influenced the internationalisation of the SME in the following areas, internationalisation process, innovation, networks, entrepreneurship, resources, barriers and liabilities and human resource practices.

The study was supported by a grant from the Australia China Council (ACC). The study was also indirectly supported by the Australia China Business Council (ACBC), AustCham (Australia China Chamber of Commerce) Shanghai, AustCham Hong Kong and AustCham Guangzhou. Each of these Chambers of Commerce assisted with making contact with potential participants. Ethics approval was provided through the Australian National Ethics application process. The criterion for inclusion in the study was that the business employed between 1–200 staff (definition of an SME according to the Australian Industry Classification Scheme), the owners were Australian and the business was located in China. Candidates were contacted by e-mail (which included a plain language statement explaining the project) and invited to participate in the study. Non-respondents were followed up with phone calls.

Once individuals had agreed to participate in the study, the aims and background of the study were explained, and confidentiality and anonymity was assured. A time was then made to conduct the interview. Interviews were conducted in Melbourne (if the organisation representative travelled to Australia), Shanghai, Guangzhou and Hong Kong. Interviews lasted approximately one hour. The interviews were recorded and transcribed by a professional transcriber. Three participants wished not to have their interviews recorded, and notes were taken instead. Interviews were conducted with representatives of 35 SMEs operating in China.

Research method

The debate in the literature regarding the development of theory for organisations in China (Witt and Redding, 2013; Zhang, Zhou and Ebbers, 2011; Alon et al., 2011; Deng, 2009) was used to derive the research method for this project. In line with this literature, this research has assumed no a-priori knowledge or theory. Subsequently, a grounded theory approach was adopted in which an inductive method has been used to identify the theories which apply to contemporary internationalisation to China. Grounded theory was developed by Glaser and Strauss (1967) and suggests that the development of theories should be grounded on data collected from the phenomena, especially in the interactions and social processes of people. The grounded theory approach was most appropriate for this book because the intention was to "generate or discover a theory" for a phenomenon which was considered sufficiently different to the context for which existing theory has been developed (Corbin and Strauss, 1988: 107; Creswell and Poth, 2017). According to Creswell and Poth (2017), ideal participants have experienced the phenomenon personally, as they will be best able to support the development of a theory that explains practice. A strong grounded theory can be expected when the data has been collected from participants who have experienced the process (Creswell and Poth, 2017). Grounded theory requires the researchers to develop an overall explanation of a phenomenon, informed by a reasonably large number of informants (Creswell and Poth, 2017).

The design of the instrument was based on a constructivist approach, as recommended by Charmaz (2006). Using this approach, the theory development results from a co-construction process dependent upon the interactions between the researcher and the participants. The project also included the following features (Creswell and Poth (2017):

1   A focus on the process of internationalisation of the innovative SMEs in China.
2   The development of theory as an explanation of how or why the process occurs.
3   Utilisation of the data provided by the participants to identify emerging theories or constructs which guided the collection of the data. This required returning to the participants for further information and then extending the

evolving theory with the new data. This continued until no further ideas were identified from the data.

4   The use of inductive processes and thematic analysis, including the identification of the category which is the focus of the theory and the relationships with the other categories identified as the theoretical model is constructed.

The findings were independently coded by three research team members. The results were then compared and the final coding determined by consensus between the researchers. Specific themes for each of the areas of SME internationalisation examined in this book (internationalisation, innovation, entrepreneurship, human resource management, liabilities theory, network theory and resources theory) was then identified with the assistance of the computer software NVivo. The themes and specific findings for each of these areas is presented in each of the chapters.

The coding commenced with the thematic coding of the data into the major categories. This open coding was used to identify the core category and the remaining categories were organised around this category. The core category was selected on the basis of representing either causal conditions, strategies, intervening conditions that influence a strategy or consequences (Strauss and Corbin, 1990). The model represented by this coding was then utilised to develop the propositions that represented the relationships between the categories within the model, for each of the research domains included in this project. These domains were internationalisation, innovation, entrepreneurship, human resource management, liabilities theory, network theory and resources theory. These propositions were augmented by diagrams (Morrow and Smith, 1995) and examples to provide contextual narrative (Strauss and Corbin, 1990). This enabled the representation of the complexity of the environment and the presence of different perspectives in the findings (Charmaz, 2006).

The sample

The basic characteristics of the sample, including industry, entry mode and location are provided in Appendix 1.[2] The sample consisted of businesses from the property industry (12 businesses), manufacturing (7), biotechnology (5), construction (4), wholesaling (2), mining (2), technology (1) and agriculture (2).

The forms of business adopted by the participants were importers (3), exporters (4), wholly owned foreign entities (WOFEs) (18) and Australian entrepreneurial start-ups in China (10).

A number of the SMEs had operations in several locations in China. The locations in which the participants operated included Shanghai (21), Guangzhou (5), Hong Kong (5), Mongolia (1), Nanjing (1), Newcastle (1), Beijing (4), Suzhou (4), Xian (1) and Shenzhen (1). The average number of staff employed by these organisations was 57. The most common number of employees was six. Further descriptive details of these organisations is provided in Table 1.1.

Table 1.1 Summary of the organisations involved in the study

Case number	Industry type	Main entry mode	Employee size	Pseudonym	Locations in China
1	Wholesaling and Retailing	Import	40	Furniture Co	Shanghai, Suzhou
2	Manufacturing	Import	25	Rubber Co	Shanghai
3	Manufacturing	Import/Export	12	Chemical Co	–
4	Technical Services	Export (services)	42	Security Co	Xian, Shanghai
5	Manufacturing	Export (services)	6	Man Control Co	Shanghai
6	Manufacturing	Export	180	Pneumatic Co	Beijing
7	Biotechnology	Export	65	Biotech Co 3	All over China
8	Biotechnology	WOFE (partnership)	400	Biotech Co 1	Mongolia, Nanjing
9	Biotechnology	WOFE	6	Biotech Co 2	Shanghai
10	Biotechnology	WOFE	72	Biotech Co 4	Shanghai/Suzhou
11	Business and Property Services	WOFE	100	Recruitment Co	Shanghai and Beijing
12	Business and Property Services	WOFE (license)	40	Accounting Co	Shanghai
13	Business and Property Services	WOFE	100	Vehicle Co	Shanghai
14	Business and Property Services	WOFE	10	Office Co	Beijing and Shanghai
15	Mining	WOFE	200	Resources Co	Shanghai
16	Mining	WOFE	684	Processing Co	Shanghai and Beijing
17	Building and Construction	WOFE	50	Metal Frame Co	Shanghai
18	Building and Construction	WOFE	180	Build Co	Shanghai and Beijing, Suzhou and Harbin
19	Building and Construction	WOFE	50	Architect Co 1	Shanghai and Shenzhen

20	Building and Construction	WOFE	70	Architect Co 2	Guangzhou
21	Manufacturing	WOFE	100	Box Co	Suzhou
22	Manufacturing	WOFE	60	Medical Equip Co	Shanghai
23	Manufacturing	WOFE	80	Print Co	Guangzhou
24	Agriculture	WOFE	30	Milk Co	Shanghai
25	Agriculture	WOFE (export)	5	Meat Co	Hong Kong
26	Business and Property Services	BIC	25	HR Consult Co	Shanghai
27	Business and Property Services	BIC	32	Social Media Co	Shanghai
28	Business and Property Services	BIC	3	Consult Co 1	Shanghai
29	Business and Property Services	BIC	5	Consulting Co 2	Shanghai
30	Business and Property Services	BIC	1	Finance Co	Shanghai
31	Business and Property Services	BIC	1	Arbitration Co	Hong Kong
32	Business and Property Services	BIC	10	Marketing Consultants Co	Hong Kong
33	Business and Property Services	BIC	5	Investment Co	Hong Kong
34	Building and Construction	BIC	200	Architect Co 3	Shenzhen
35	Wholesaling and Retail	BIC	8	Shop Co	Guangzhou and Shanghai

Structural characteristics of the data

In addition to the thematic analysis of the data for the specific theory areas investigated by this project, the data was initially examined to identify the most frequently identified terms. The wordcloud in Figure 1.1 presents the frequencies of the 25 most frequent words found in the interview transcripts. It shows a predictably frequent occurrence of the words China and Chinese and a proportionate, but lower frequency of the words Australia and Australian in the responses. Interesting terms identified in this group included innovation, market, development, different, make, deal, government, time and know. The maximum count was for the word China which was identified 1400 times, representing approximately 2 percent of the total transcripts. The least frequently identified term was Australian, which was identified 350 times or constituting approximately 0.5% of the total transcripts. Each of the words was associated with a synonym. Although the word Australia was only associated with the country, the word Australian was associated with a number of terms that reflected Australian culture.

Figure 1.1 Word cloud of interview data

The term China was also associated with Taiwan, which was an interesting finding as it was not also associated with Singapore, despite Singapore's significant Chinese population and investment in China (Mathew, Krishnamurti and Sevic, 2005). Similarly, the term Chinese was also found to be associated with the term Taiwanese. A number of the identified words were associated with competitiveness. They included innovation, make, deal, market, different, development, product, clients and find. Cumulatively, these terms represented 6 percent of the total number of words in the transcripts. The next most common word group included organisational descriptions including people, company and government. These terms jointly represented 3 percent of the total number of words in the transcripts. Other words more personally oriented to the entrepreneur's experience included call, pay, look, help and trying. These constituted 3 percent of the total number of words in the transcripts.

These findings suggest that the interview responses focused very strongly on competition cultural identity, followed by competitiveness, organisational and then personal/entrepreneurial considerations.

A cluster analysis of the terms presented some similar and interesting findings. Figure 1.2 shows that entrepreneurial terms resulting in business development

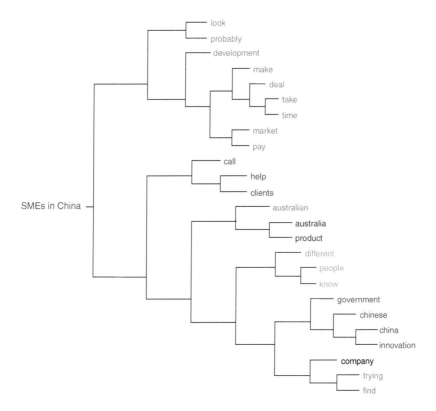

Figure 1.2 Cluster analysis of interview data

formed one cluster. These terms included words such as development, deal, time, market and pay. The other major cluster was very sequential and incorporated identity terms such as Australia, product, people, government, Chinese and company. Interestingly, innovation was associated with this cluster, rather than the other cluster which contained the entrepreneurial terms. The word *different* was also associated with this cluster, rather than the more intuitive connection it would have had with the entrepreneurial cluster.

Structure of the book

The book commences the analysis with an examination of the internationalisation process of the participants. This analysis takes into account the various stories and practices which describe the context for these organisation's internationalisation processes, as well as the details of the approach that they took. This analysis is provided in Chapter 2. Chapter 3 analyses the role of innovation and how innovation was used in the internationalisation process by the SME participants. This chapter considers the types of innovation utilised by the SMEs, whether these approaches were successful in the Chinese market and whether the Chinese context influenced their contribution to the internationalisation process. Chapter 4 analyses the role of networks in SME internationalisation and discusses how these networks are established, their function and how they affect the internationalisation process.

   Chapter 5 analyses the role of entrepreneurship in the internationalisation process of these SMEs. The focus of the analysis then shifts to the resources and capabilities that these organisations utilised in the internationalisation process and how they were utilised. This is discussed in Chapter 6. Chapter 7 examines the barriers, liabilities and costs faced by innovative SMEs in the Chinese Market, in particular the liabilities of foreignness (LOF), liabilities of smallness (LOS), liabilities of outsidership (LOO) and the barriers that the participants experienced when internationalising. Chapter 8 analyses the HRM practices and issues that the participants experienced in the Chinese market. This chapter considers the HRM practices that the participants adopted, the issues associated with them and strategies for managing human resources in the Chinese market. The conclusion chapter brings the constructs from the preceding chapters together and presents an integrated perspective of internationalisation process for innovative SMEs entering the rapidly developing Chinese market in the form of a typology. This chapter also considers the practical implications of these findings and offers recommendations for SMEs considering or already operating in the Chinese market. Directions for future research are also included in this chapter.

Conclusion

This book provides a detailed examination of the process of innovative SME internationalisation to China. The book has adopted a grounded theory approach to analysing this data. It analyses data from 35 innovative SMEs that have internationalised to China and data from seven different and relevant theory domain perspectives to extend the existing SME internationalisation literature. The book combines findings from each of the theory domains into a single combined set of constructs. These constructs represent the four principal approaches through which innovative SMEs internationalise to China and are presented in the conclusion chapter in the form of a typology.

SME internationalisation is an important area for research as increasing numbers of SMEs internationalise from both developing and developed countries every year. It is also an area of research which is underdeveloped and lacks constructs which are suitable for both the nature of an SME and the types of foreign country environments, such as China, which they are entering. Innovative SMEs are a special case and especially warrant attention as the extent literature does not provide relevant constructs for this business context. From an internationalisation perspective, the entry of foreign SMEs into China is a subject of particular interest because the majority of businesses operating in China are SMEs. Chinese SMEs are responsible for much of both the innovation, as well as the development of new industries in China. The entry of foreign SMEs, particularly where the entry involves partnership and cooperation with Chinese enterprises, may become one of the principal mechanisms through which Chinese business practice becomes integrated with the business practices of the rest of the world. This book responds to both of these topics by developing constructs which represent the process for innovative SME internationalisation into China and by explaining how these organisations operate in the Chinese environment and cooperate with local Chinese organisations.

The quotation "Search for stones to cross the river" (Linong, 2006) is attributed to Deng Xiao Ping, the creator and driver of the economic reforms in China. Deng Xiao Ping's analogy represented the search for momentary resting places as China makes its transition from a centrally planned economy to a modern-day market economy, integrated with the world economy and politics. Deng Xiao Ping's advice is equally applicable to innovative foreign SMEs planning to enter the Chinese market. Increasingly, governments such as the Australian and British governments recognise that supporting the entry of SMEs into environments such as China is a critical path for the development of trade relations, as well as ensuring joint economic prosperity (Economist, 2014; Austrade, 2017).This book considers each of the theory perspectives as one of these 'stones' and suggests a pathway comprised of these stones, through which successful internationalisation into a rapidly developing business environment, such as that of China, can be achieved. It is hoped that this book will provide guidance to the reader for achieving success and prosperity in the Middle Kingdom, *Zhongguo*.

Notes

1 Trumpism effects refers to discriminatory and adversarial United States policies directed towards different countries of the world, which may cause strained relationships.

2 Only basic characteristics were provided to protect the anonymity and confidentiality of the participants.

References

Abrami, R. M., Kirby, W. C., and McFarlan, F. W. (2014). Why China can't innovate, https://hbr.org/2014/03/why-china-cant-innovate, retrieved on 20 March 2014.

Alon, I., Child, J., Li, S. M., and McIntyre, J. R. (2011). Globalization of Chinese firms: Theoretical universalism or particularism. *Management and Organisation Review*, 7:2: 191–200.

Anderlini, J. (2014). China's rebalancing requires more investment of the right kind, *Financial Times*, www.ft.com/content/f8ed7dd8-841d-11e3-b72e-00144feab7de, retrieved on 20 April 2017.

Asia Pulse. (2007). China's number of registered SMEs tops 4.3 Mln, *Asia Pulse*, October 22.

Austrade. (2017). China-Australia Free Trade Agreement (CHAFTA), www.austrade.gov.au/Australian/Export/Free-Trade-Agreements/chafta, retrieved on 26 April 2017.

Australian Government. (2012). Australia in the Asian century, www.defence.gov.au/whitepaper/2013/docs/australia_in_the_asian_century_white_paper.pdf, retrieved on 20 April 2017.

Australian Government. (2016). Global innovation strategy, https://industry.gov.au/innovation/GlobalInnovationStrategy/index.html, retrieved on 25 April 2017.

Boyd, T. (2016). Risk takers and growth makers look to China, www.afr.com/brand/chanticleer/risk-takers-and-growth-makers-look-to-china-20160315-gnjm2s, retrieved on 26 April 2017.

Charmaz, K. (2006). *Constructing Grounded Theory: A Practical Guide Through Qualitative Analysis*. Thousand Oaks, CA: Sage Publications.

China Briefing. (2012). Foreign law firms in China, *China Briefing*, www.chinabriefing.com/news/2012/02/07/foreign-law-firms-in-china-2012-listings.html, retrieved on 28 March 2012.

China Business News. (2014). Number of companies listed on China's SME board up 19 times in 10 yrs, *China Business News*, May 26.

China Development Research. (2013). *China's New Urbanization Strategy*. Florence: Taylor and Francis.

China Economic Review. (2011). China to boost number of SMEs. *China Economic Review*, September 27, 2011.

China FTA Network. (2017). *China FTA Network*, http://fta.mofcom.gov.cn/english/, retrieved on 22 July 2017.

China Statistical Yearbook. (2016). *China Statistical Yearbook*, National Bureau Statistics of China, www.stats.gov.cn/tjsj/ndsj/2016/indexeh.htm, retrieved on 22 July 2017.

Corbin, J. M., and Strauss, A. (1988). *Unending Work and Care: Managing Chronic Illness at Home*. San Francisco, CA: Jossey-Bass.

Creswell, J., and Brown, M. L. (1992). How chairpersons enhance faculty research: A grounded theory study. *Review of Higher Education*, 16, 41–62.

Creswell, J. W., and Poth, C. N. (2017). *Qualitative Inquiry and Research Design: Choosing Among Five Approaches*. Thousand Oaks, CA: Sage Publications.

Department of Foreign Affairs and Trade. (2014). *China Economic Fact Sheet*, Department of Foreign Affairs and Trade, http://dfat.gov.au/trade/resources/Documents/chin.pdf, retrieved on 25 April 2015.

Department of Foreign Affairs and Trade. (2017). *China Economic Fact Sheet*, http://dfat.gov.au/trade/resources/Documents/chin.pdf, retrieved on 25 April 2017.

Economist. (2014). Foreign entrepreneurs in China: Small is not beautiful, *The Economist*, 413:8909, 66.

European Commission. (2017). Countries and regions, *European Commission*, http://ec.europa.eu/trade/policy/countries-and-regions/countries/china/, retrieved on22 July 2017.

Fukyama, F. (2013). China's middle class gets political, www.afr.com/p/lifestyle/review/china_middle_class_gets_political_2XgpFfpKDawuA4dugkl9gN, retrieved on 16 August 2013.

Glaser, B. G., and Strauss, A. L. (1967). *The Discovery of Grounded Theory: Strategies for Qualitative Research*. Chicago: Aldine Publishing Company.

International Monetary Fund. (2017). A shifting global economic landscape, *International Monetary Fund*, www.imf.org/external/pubs/ft/weo/2017/update/01/, retrieved on 24 April 2017.

Iskyan, K. (2016). China's middle class is exploding, *Business Insider*, www.businessinsider.com/chinas-middle-class-is-exploding-2016-8?IR=T, retrieved on 26 April 2017.

Keating, E. (2014). Australia-China Free Trade Agreement finalised: Winners and losers revealed. *Smart Company*, November 17, www.smartcompany.com.au/finance/economy/australia-china-free-trade-agreement-finalised-winners-and-losers-revealed/.

KPMG. (2016). The 13th five year plan – China's transformation integration with the world economy, *KPMG*, October 2016, www.kpmg.com/cn, retrieved on 23 July 2017.

Li, G., and Woetzel, J. (2011). What China's five-year plan means for business, *McKinsey Consulting*, www.mckinsey.com/insights/economic_studies/what_chinas_five-year_plan_means_for_business, retrieved on 28 March 2014.

Linong, Z. (2006). *China Business: Environment, Momentum, Strategies and Prospects*. Singapore: Pearson Prentice Hall.

Macquarie Bank. (2017). How high tech innovation is reshaping China, www.macquarie.com/au/corporate/expertise/how-high-tech-innovation-is-reshaping-china/, retrieved on 26 April 2017.

McKinsey (2013) Mapping China's middle class, McKinsey Quarterly, https://www.mckinsey.com/industries/retail/our-insights/mapping-chinas-middle-class.

Mathew, M., Krishnamurti, C., and Sevic, Z. (2005). A survey of Singaporean Chinese investors in Mainland China and their knowledge of the Chinese language. *Cross Cultural Management*, 12:1, 46–59.

Morrow, S. L., and Smith, M. L. (1995). Constructions of survival and coping by women who have survived childhood sexual abuse. *Journal of Counselling Psychology*, 42, 24–33.

Orr, G. (2013). What's in store for China in 2013, www.mckinsey.com/global-themes/china/whats-in-store-for-china-in-2013, retrieved on 26 April 2017.

Orr, G. (2017). What can we expect in 2017 in China. McKinsey & Company, www.mckinsey.com/global-themes/china/what-can-we-expect-in-china-in-2017, retrieved on 26 April 2017.

Orr, S., Menzies, J., and Donnelly, M. (2017). Born in China: A new type of Australian business, *The Conversation*, June 28.

Roth, E., Seong, J., and Woetzel, J. (2015). Gauging the strength of Chinese innovation, www.mckinsey.com/business-functions/strategy-and-corporate-finance/our-insights/gauging-the-strength-of-chinese-innovation, retrieved on 26 April 2017.

Strauss, A., and Corbin, J. (1990). *Basics of Qualitative Research; Techniques and Procedures for Developing Grounded Theory* (2nd ed.). Thousand Oaks, CA: Sage Publications.

Tian, X. (2007). *Managing International Business in China.* Cambridge: Cambridge University Press.

Urbach Hacker Young. (2017). China's declared backing for SMEs may open doors to foreign investors. *Urbach Hacker Young International Limited*, www.uhy.com/chinas-declared-backing-for-smes-may-open-doors-to-foreign-investors/, retrieved on 22 July 2017.

Uren. (2007). China emerges as our biggest trade partner, *The Weekend Australian*, May 5.

Witt, M. A., and Redding, G. (2013). Asian business systems: Institutional comparison, clusters and implications for varieties of capitalism and business systems theory. *Socio-Economic Review*, 11:2, 265–300.

World Bank Group. (2014). *Urban China: Toward Efficient, Inclusive, and Sustainable Urbanization.* Washington, DC: World Bank Group.

Zhang, J., Zhou, C., and Ebbers, H. (2011). Completion of Chinese overseas acquisitions: Institutional perspectives and evidence. *International Business Review*, 20:2, 226–238.

2 Internationalisation of innovative SMEs to China

Introduction

Internationalisation is broadly seen as a way that firms progressively increase their activities and resource commitments to foreign markets (Johanson and Vahlne, 1977, 2009). There are a wide range of theories and approaches adopted in the literature to explain and justify the internationalisation of firms. In this chapter, we focus on two approaches, which includes the 'stage approach', where the internationalisation of a firm is a dynamic, gradual and staged process that occurs over time (Bilkey and Tesar, 1977; Johanson and Vahlne, 1977; Johanson and Wiedersheim-Paul, 1975) and the international new venture (INV)/born-global approach, where the firm rapidly expands to international markets close to the inception of the business (Oviatt and McDougall, 1994; Knight and Cavusgil, 1996). The applicability of these approaches is considered for the internationalisation of the innovative small and medium-sized enterprises (SMEs) examined in this book and utilising a range of different entry modes. In this chapter, we examine how these firms internationalise and what is interesting about it.

An examination of the literature reveals that internationalisation in general has been a well-researched topic, however the literature on how innovative SMEs internationalise has been less examined, with most of the studies on this topic looking at the role of innovation, exporting activities and the performance of the firm (Love and Roper, 2015). Most of the studies reviewed by Love and Roper (2015) have looked at the relationship between innovation, internationalisation and performance. The general conclusion is that if a firm is innovative, it would be likely that the firm is involved in exporting, and subsequently the firm would achieve better performance outcomes in terms of profits and productivity. For example, if a firm develops a new innovation through research and development (R&D), such as a product or service, it may wish to sell those products in foreign markets to gain more income with more profits which increases the firm's performance. In addition, most of the literature has looked at innovative firms, exporting and SMEs, but not other forms of internationalisation such as importing, wholly owned foreign entities (WOFEs) and entrepreneurial start-up firms or born in China (BIC) firms.

Based on this we ask the following research questions: "how do the innovative SMEs internationalise?" and "what approaches do they follow to internationalise their businesses? Would they be more likely to follow the stage approach, or the INV/born-global approach?" These questions are important to investigate as there are many SMEs out there who are struggling to internationalise, as they do not know which way to go about it, and need guidance on how to do it. Therefore, this chapter has some practical applications. For academics they will know whether the internationalisation theories are relevant for these innovative SMEs, and practitioners will have a better idea about how these might be done. We now review these theoretical perspectives.

Theoretical perspectives on internationalisation

Stage theory

The first theory we examine is the stage theory (Johanson and Vahlne, 1977), which states that internationalisation is a sequential, gradual and evolutionary process (Rodrigues, 2007). It may be described as a stepwise process of increasing involvement and commitment with overseas markets (Rodrigues, 2007). Stage theory was initially developed by Johanson and Vahlne (1977), and it suggests that as knowledge and understanding of internationalisation increases, the firm will make larger resource commitments to internationalisation. It assumes that the internationalisation of a firm is a dynamic, gradual and step-by-step process that occurs over time (Johanson and Vahlne, 1977; Johanson and Wiedersheim-Paul, 1975). As the firm grows, they will increase their level of internationalisation and commitment from exporting to other activities such as foreign direct investment (FDI). They are able to do this because as firms spend more time in the market, they gain more experience and knowledge of internationalisation and foreign markets. One concept associated with stage theory is "the liability of foreignness (LOF)," (Zaheer, 1995), which means that when a firm first starts off internationalisation they will lack understanding of the foreign country, which can be characterised as a liability or cost, which limits the organisation from being successful in the market place, also from devoting more resources to the country, however as their knowledge builds and their liability decreases, the firm may wish to make further investments, and devote more resources to the venture.

The stage theory is reasonably generic, and hence could be applied to innovative SMEs. However, one issue that may impact on the SME making further commitments to the market is the small size of the SME, and their lack of resources, which we refer to as the liability of smallness (LOS) (Hannan and Freeman, 1984; Stinchcombe, 1965). Organisational size is a central topic in the study of the internationalisation of SMEs, as previous studies have established that smaller organisations behave differently from their larger counterparts (Anderson, Gabrielsson, and Wictor, 2004; Coviello and McAuley, 1999; Gomes-Casseres, 1997; O'Cass and Weerawardena, 2009).

In addition, the firms' past international experience is important for increasing their international expansion. Apart from the stage theory, introduced by

Johanson and Vahlne (1977) in the 1990s, Oviatt and McDougall (1994) introduced the concept of INVs, or what is referred to as born-globals (Knight and
Cavusgil, 1996).

International new ventures (Born-Global firms)

The second theory, or rather group of theories, states that the whole process of
internationalisation is an ever changing, fast paced and evolving process. Companies may start overseas activities in a shortened period of time, either by-passing or
leaping over some or all of the logical steps of increasing foreign market commitment (Oviatt and McDougall, 1994). INVs are defined as a business organisation
that, from inception, seeks to derive significant competitive advantage from the use
of resources and the sale of output in multiple markets (Oviatt and McDougall,
1994). The business typically begins with a proactive international strategy but
does not necessarily engage in FDI (Freeman, 2000). The emergence of INVs, or
born-global, has been one of the defining features of twenty first century global
capitalism (Knight and Cavusgil, 1996). More open markets, lower communication and transport costs, and the availability of staff with more international experience have created opportunities for smaller players to enter global markets. As
a result, more companies are now born-global with an explicit vision to draw a
substantial portion of their sales from beyond their home market. However, born-
global firms faces a triple threat when they enter foreign markets (Sapienza et al.,
2006). Not only do they have to cope with the LOS and the liability of newness
common to all entrepreneurial ventures, but they also must overcome an additional LOF that adheres to all ventures entering foreign markets (Zaheer, 1995).

The extant literature shows considerable differences of opinion regarding the
speed required to be defined as a born-global firm. It is seen to range from
two years from inception (McKinsey and Co., 1993) to three years (Knight and
Cavusgil, 1996), to eight years (McDougall, Shane, and Oviatt, 1994). The factors that lead to this rapid process of internationalisation have dominated born-
global analysis. The drive, vision, experience and ability of the entrepreneur have
been considered to be a key driver in the pace of born-global firm internationalisation (Autio, Sapienza and Almeida, 2000; Knight and Cavusgil, 2004; Oviatt and
McDougall, 2005). In particular, the ability of entrepreneurs to identify, assess and
act on opportunities is considered vital (Oviatt and McDougall, 2005). Linked
to the influence of the entrepreneur is the development of an innovative culture considered unique and essential to born-global development. As Knight and
Cavusgil (2004: 127) explain, born-globals are inherently "entrepreneurial and
innovative" firms with a culture that facilitates the acquisition of knowledge, and
capabilities that engender early internationalisation. In an attempt to link the
entrepreneurial literature with the forces that influence the pace of firm internationalisation, Oviatt and McDougall (2005) propose that entrepreneurs act as
interpreters to both the enabling and motivating forces of accelerated internationalisation. Enabling forces are embodied in faster and more efficient shipping
and airline routes, as well as improvements in digital technology, which enable
firms to have enhanced forms of communication and increased transportation

efficiencies for their products. Motivating forces encourage entrepreneurs to enter markets quickly, either to capitalise on technological opportunities, or react to the presence (or potential presence) of competitors. Entrepreneurial decisions based on these forces influence the speed of internationalisation by interpreting these enabling and motivating forces and acting upon them.

Early research revealed that born-global firms often have a weak domestic base from which to launch their international efforts (Knight and Cavusgil, 1996). Research by Ibeh (2003) found that if small firms possess an entrepreneurial orientation, as is common with born-globals (Rialp, Rialp and Knight, 2005), they are more likely to enter international markets sooner when faced with a hostile domestic industry. Fan and Phan (2007) conclude that the larger the size of its home market, the less likely it is that a born-global firm will choose to go international at inception, and they are more likely to enter international markets sooner when faced with a hostile domestic industry. Considering that Australia, the focus of the current study, is a small domestic market, it would be expected that Australia would have a high proportion of firms targeting international markets.

McDougall, Oviatt and Shrader (2003) state that born-globals target niche market gaps so that they may remain competitive, while their success is frequently attributed to entrepreneurs who have the vision and drive to avoid following a slow, evolutionary path to internationalisation. Although this research expands the born-global literature, the emphasis is on comparisons to traditional process or 'stage' theories of internationalisation. A more fundamental issue has been explored, but still remains largely unresolved, as we do not clearly know which factors distinguish the born-globals from other rapidly internationalising firms (Crick, 2009; Kuivalainen et al., 2007; Lopez, Kundu and Ciravegna, 2009). Although the pace or speed of internationalisation is seen as a unique and defining characteristic, true born-global firms can be identified by using some different strategies in addition to their speed and pace of internationalisation (Kuivalainen et al., 2007).

Some researchers argued that born-global firms do not appear to present a challenge to the 'stage' models in theoretical terms when management factors are taken into consideration. The study conducted by Rodrigues (2007) revealed that nearly half (44%) of the surveyed companies engage in international activities within five years of creation. The companies also started international activities in a similar fashion; the manager and the company gain experience and develop contacts. There are barely any significant discrepancies between the strategies followed by SME managers from the five countries surveyed by Rodrigues (2007). According to Rodrigues (2007) the manager is the key decision maker in the internationalisation of the SME and managers engage in overseas activities for different reasons. There are push drivers, internal stimuli at the company or home country level and there are also pull drivers, external stimuli coming from the target country. The most frequent is the attraction of growing overseas markets and following customers that go overseas is the second reason (Rodrigues, 2007). Rodrigues (2007) found that the most common push driver is to exploit full production capacity and the second is a shrinking domestic market. To grow their organisations, SME managers want to escape from their mature markets and increasing competition at home, and choose to look at growing international markets (Rodrigues, 2007). Most of these born-global companies are in the service sector and more than half have fewer than 50 employees (Rodrigues, 2007). According to the survey results, they have much more intensive international activity than the average surveyed company and all the born-global companies receive income from overseas, compared with just under half of surveyed companies as a whole. They rely to a great extent on their own patents and consider them as one of the most important factors of their international competitiveness (Rodrigues, 2007). All of the organisations were of a young age and, given the innovative nature, there are firms which seek knowledge and technology abroad; a knowledge-seeking motivation is also present (Rodrigues, 2007).

Opposed to the above view, other researchers are of the opinion that the emergence of the INV presents a unique challenge to the stage theory (Oviatt and McDougall, 1994). This implies that established theories are less applicable in an expanding number of situations where technology, specific industry environments and firm capabilities are rapidly changing (Oviatt and McDougall, 1994). Thus, the stage theory of firm internationalisation is increasingly incongruent with recent developments, and a large scale operation has become one, among many ways to compete internationally (Oviatt and McDougall, 1994). Wicramasekera and Bamberry (2003) undertook a study to explore the phenomenon of born-global firms within the Australian wine industry and the findings indicated three major reasons for acceleration of the internationalisation process within the wine industry: (1) ready market for products (for example Australian wine has ready markets in foreign countries due to its quality and reputation), (2) domestic market issues (the taxation regime in Australia is an impediment to domestic market expansion and is a reason for tapping into export markets) and (3) networking – the importance of "building relationships" and "access to contacts" as an important driver in achieving rapid internationalisation (Wicramasekera and Bamberry, 2003). The survey findings showed that a significantly high proportion of managers in the born-global firms had previously worked for a company that had exported or imported goods (Wicramasekera and Bamberry, 2003), suggesting a role for previous international experience similar to the stage theory. The findings also highlight the importance of having international and industry experience of management (Harveston, Kedia and Davis, 2000) and access to networks (contacts) for rapid internationalisation (Welch and Luostarinen, 1988; McGaughey et al., 2002).

In summary, the pace of internationalisation occurs due to the entrepreneurial drive of the founder(s) as well as the small size of the domestic market. Born-global firms did not rely on low-commitment entry modes to the same extent (Knight and Cavusgil, 2004); instead, the most appropriate entry mode was determined by the firm's product and its ability to meet client needs (Taylor and Jack, 2013). More recent literature has looked at how opportunity based issues impact on firm internationalisation (Dimitratos, 2016). In particular, Dimitratos et al. (2016) looked at how entrepreneurs mould and shape the characteristics of

SMEs to gain opportunities in foreign markets, and in particular examined issues such as risk attitude, market orientation and networking orientation, in respect to time to internationalisation, entry mode and market presence.

Internationalisation process of Australian innovative SMEs to China

The results of the current study indicate that SMEs followed either the 'stage' or the 'born-global/INV' form of internationalisation approaches when they internationalised to China.

Stage model approach

Of the 35 SMEs interviewed for the study, 21 SMEs had expanded their business activities into the Chinese market by way of an approach similar to 'stage' internationalisation as discussed in stage theory (Johanson and Vahlne, 1977). Those that are categorised into the 'stage' approach had spent significant time developing their business activities domestically and for some internationally, before involving themselves with the Chinese market. For these SMEs they had operated more than five years before entering the Chinese market, and notably one SME had operated more than 50 years prior to entering China, as the following quotation indicates:

> There was a big discussion here along the lines of our customers keep telling us we're going to China, you should come and set up here with us and they'd been just talking about it for a couple of years. I guess at some stage they said we need to get on with this, the event that triggered it I guess was the desire to get offshore and that was when things were still very buoyant in the market so I guess it was confidence, we can go and do this exploration and get established.
>
> (Case 6: Pneumatic Co)

Domestic and international experience

The results indicated that all SMEs spent significant time in domestic markets, some of them involved with international markets too prior entering to China. Out of the 21 SMEs categorised in the 'stage' internationalisation approach, 11 SMEs had international experience in another country prior to entering the Chinese market, with 10 having no experience. For those who did not have international experience, they did have a long running business experience in the domestic market in their market sector. In addition, for some SMEs who did not have international experience, their managers had prior international experience including exposure to the Chinese market with their previous jobs.

As per Johanson and Vahlne (1977)'s stage theory, SMEs involved with export-ing and importing activities in the first phase of the internationalisation process prior, had then devoted more resources to their international venture, and had established WOFE operations. Of the 10 SMEs having no prior international experiences, five of those were in the first phase of the internationalisation pro-cess and involved in importing (Furniture Co, Rubber Co and Chemical Co) or exporting activities. This indicates that those SMEs had waited a longer time and had not moved to the next phase in the Chinese market for some reason, which possibly led to less exposure to international markets.

Eleven (11) SMEs in the 'stage' form internationalisation category had inter-national experiences in other countries prior to entering the Chinese market. Most of those SMEs were exposed to Asian and Middle Eastern countries, and few had business operations in the USA, Europe and Africa as well. The inter-national experience and knowledge possessed by the SMEs had affected their decision making to internationalise to the Chinese market. The SMEs who had prior international exposure acted with confidence entering China and eight out of 11 of those SMEs established WOFEs, which indicates that they assume less perceived risk.

Those 10 SMEs that internationalised to China without prior international experience developed the necessary knowledge and gained the necessary expe-rience in their domestic market by conducting their business operations for a longer time (six to 15 years) prior to expanding to China. This knowledge and experience in the domestic market, coupled with opportunity in the Chinese market had triggered these firms to internationalise to China. The manager's knowledge and previous experience had positively impacted on internationalisa-tion of their businesses to China as well.

Eleven SMEs had internationalised to China as a result of knowledge and expe-rience they earned gradually by operating in domestic and international markets. The quote below demonstrates the SME's use of international knowledge and experience before deciding on establishing their China operation model, making the China operation more successful:

> The business model for us long term in China would be significantly differ-ent than how the Institute operates in other countries in the region. So for example, we have offices in Lao and Burma and so on, and in these countries we still operate in a fairly traditional aid and development context. Whereas in China what we're hoping to do is successfully commercializing our first product.
>
> (Case 10: Medical Co)

SMEs in the 'stage' category had also gradually built their business and opera-tional knowledge in the domestic market (Australia) and some also internation-ally in other markets. This knowledge and experience, alongside opportunity, had then motivated them to internationalise to China. The qualitative comments demonstrated that internationalisation of a firm is a dynamic, gradual and stage process that occurs over time, as the following quote indicates:

> Effectively we were looking at China for our supply chain, and lo and behold eventually we decided let's start a manufacturing organization here (China) to essentially help us get a global footprint into a lot of low cost markets.
>
> (Case 21: Box Co)

The quote below provides evidence for the SME using China as one of their key international destinations, which was a result of a gradual process of internationalisation:

> We absolutely are in pretty much all of the markets around the world except Latin America and Africa. Why China? We've been here now 15 years. So it's a one stop easy shop and our biggest market is in Asia, Japan, South East Asia, China and Hong Kong because of that reason.
>
> (Case 14: Office Co)

However, Johanson and Vahlne's (1977) stage theory further states that once knowledge and understanding of internationalisation increases, the firm will make larger resource commitments to internationalisation. Therefore, it is possible that when the firm grows to a considerable size, it may move its level of internationalisation from exporting to other activities such as FDI, by setting up either a joint venture or wholly-owned companies or it may even build a global firm directly in overseas markets as the evidence will show in the next section.

Born-global firms

For the other 14 SMEs considered in the study, they had followed a 'rapid' internationalisation approach when entering the Chinese market. The firms categorised into this 'rapid' approach had spent a short period of time developing their business activities in Australia before involving themselves with the Chinese market. For these 'rapid' approach SMEs they had operated a maximum of four years before entering Chinese markets and they looked for international markets due to domestic market limitations:

> Australia only has 200,000 babies every year so we looked at that and said our demographic is this niche organic segment of those 200,000 babies. So we had to say let's look international, and this coupled with 100s of email enquiries for our [product].
>
> (Case 24: Milk Co)

This firm did not have prior international experience, and internationalised rapidly to China, as Chinese demand increased significantly in the wake of the melamine milk scares. Therefore, a rapid approach may be triggered by the opportunities that are on offer in the foreign market.

Ten of the SMEs in the 'rapid' category were considered to be 'born in China' (BIC) firms as they had commenced business activities for the very first time in China by Australian nationals. Out of the 35 SMEs investigated in this study, there were 14 SMEs that had commenced their China operations within a short period of time after they had established their business domestically in Australia (less than three years) (four SMEs) or they had directly entered the Chinese market without operating the business previously in Australia (10 SMEs). It was evident that the SMEs that were rapidly internationalised had spent less than four years' time with local and/or international operations before entering the Chinese market. Some were also classified as being BIC. As a result, this meant that the internationalisation process to China for these SMEs was a rapid process and they had no adequate time to gain knowledge and experience operating as a domestic business and/or an international business prior to entering China. The results are closely in line with the findings by Knight and Cavusgil (1996) who argue for a possibility of SMEs to be born-global despite their short period of time operating in the domestic markets.

The results further indicated that owners/managers of seven out of 10 BIC firms had prior knowledge and experience in China. Some of these managers/owners had worked in China for long periods of time, for example the longest was up to 30 years for one (Shop Co) and some were Australian Chinese, for example they were either born as Australian Chinese or were Chinese background and grew up in Australia. The following quote indicates that the manager had international experience in China and his knowledge and experience impacted on him creating a business in China:

> I looked at our industry and I've actually been dealing with China for pretty close to 30 years now. In a previous life I was managing a factory for a family business and we started importing from Taiwan 40 years ago although they didn't become cost effective so the Taiwanese companies started moving to China to build plants over here and we started dealing with China then.
>
> (Case 35: Shop Co.)

The above quotation highlights the importance of experience in China for rapid internationalisation. Previous research by Wicramasekera and Bamberry (2003) identifies that a significantly high proportion of managers in the rapid or born-global type firms often had previous international working experience, and the results of the current study support this finding.

One more notable aspect of the study results is that seven out of the 10 BIC SMEs were in the service sector, which may suggest that it is easy to rapidly internationalise when an organisation is a service sector organisation, as they do not require the capital investment that non service sector firms might need, and hence it is perceived to be low risk (Menzies and Orr, 2014), and managers can use their experience, skills and knowledge as the key resources for this internationalisation.

According to Rodrigues (2007) most 'rapid' or born-global type companies are in the service sector. The cases suggest that managers or partners commenced a majority of these service type SMEs mainly employing their skills and knowledge as the key resources.

Entry modes and types of internationalisation

Given the lack of examination in the literature of 'how' this internationalisation occurs for different entry modes, we aimed to examine whether internationalisation patterns varied by entry modes, across the importing, exporting, WOFE and born-in-China SMEs. Each entry mode and its respective internationalisation process will now be discussed.

Importing and internationalisation

There were three SMEs that operated as importers, which were either manufacturing firms (Rubber Co and Chemical Co) or wholesalers in the case of Furniture Co. For the manufacturing SMEs, their main business in China was to purchase materials for their production facilities in Australia. The SME's main driver for internationalisation was the cost advantages that China can offer, for example these firms can make savings associated with sourcing key materials required for their products for a cheaper price in China. In addition, the shipping costs and delivery times did not pose a problem to the SME due to the existence of efficient and economical shipping and freight forwarding services between the main cities of China and Australia. As a result this situation promotes importation from China to Australia:

> We import products that we can't produce ourselves. If we can produce it ourselves we usually will, but the market in Australia isn't big enough to support endless capital investment. For instance if we have got to spend two or three million dollars on a production line for a market that's only going to return around a couple of million a year in turnover, it's illogical to make any investment. Obviously the Chinese market is looking for very competitive pricing.
>
> (Case 2: Rubber Co)

The above quotation suggests that China has a specific purpose for the organisation, which is to save costs on produced items, and to sell those products to the Australian market. There were no plans for further internationalisation. In addition to importing, one of the importers also exported their products to China and another country such as Malaysia. Three importers had spent significant time in their local and international operations; one of them did indicate that they had no intention of committing more resources to overseas (China) operations as indicated in the below quote:

> Probably our future strategy for China is trying to focus on getting an alternative market to China. This is probably our strategy moving forward. Now

whether that's achievable or not I'm not 100 percent sure. The cost of China is going up.

(Case 1: Furniture Co)

But all in all, these firms had appeared content with their 'form' of internationalisation, and business, and were not looking to establish their business in China at a later point in time:

We just export and import, though nothing (official) has been set up there yet. We use agents as well as we communicate locally directly, and we have no plans for further expansion.

(Case 3: Chemical Products)

This suggests that 'firm strategy' and what the firm wants to achieve may be the influencing factor in whether a firm further internationalises through the stages model (Johanson and Vahlne, 1990), and that it is not necessarily that a firm has more experience and knowledge, so it makes further commitments to the market. Similarly, it was interesting to note that none of the importing firms were what we classified as born-globals or INVs because these internationalisation types did not lead to sale presences in international markets (Knight and Cavusgil, 1996; Oviatt and McDougall, 1994). Based on this we developed the following propositions for future researchers to test:

Proposition 2.1a: Innovative importing SMEs are less likely to internationalise further when they are satisfied with the status quo of their international activities.

Proposition 2.1b: Innovative importing SMEs are more likely to internationalise using the stages approach when they detect opportunities in the foreign environment.

Proposition 2.1c: Innovative importing SMEs are less likely to follow an 'INV' or 'born-global' approach.

Exporting and internationalisation

This study investigated four different exporters (Security Co, Man Control Co, Pneumatic Co, and Biotech Co). All of these firms were service organisations, with some products/hardware for sale and provided consultancy type services to clients in China, on a project-by-project basis and they did not have offices in China. One of the SMEs who was involved in exporting had some prior international experience and had been involved in other Asian and Middle Eastern countries before entering the Chinese market in the same manner (on a project basis). When asked if they intended to make more commitments to the Chinese market, two of them had indicated their intention of establishing a WOFE in China soon. On the other hand, others were satisfied with the way they have currently been operating as indicated in quote below:

We don't have any activities in China but we do have a number of clients who are Chinese businesses so we don't have any physical business in China.

So the business that we run is based in Australia, and we provide services to our Chinese clients from Australia, and we don't have any plans at the moment to change this model.

(Case 7: Clinical Trials Co)

This SME had entered the Chinese market for the purpose of opportunity seeking due to the limited market in Australia for their specialised service, where they only had a very narrow market segment and hence a lack of opportunity for growth. These SMEs tried to cut costs associated with their entry strategy, which is probably characteristic of the very small SMEs, who experienced the LOS, 'resource poverty' and had very limited resources, which may be a factor that influences the choice of entry mode. The qualitative comments of the SMEs in this group had indicated that some were also involved with importing out of China, and had experience with other international markets prior to entering the Chinese market and some do not. According to stage theory (Johanson and Vahlne, 1977), importing and/or exporting are the first steps of the internationalisation process, and as a result it is not likely that these SMEs will have prior international experience or knowledge involving this first step of internationalisation.

The results of the exporters did provide some mixed results that two out of the three had no indication of committing more resources to China moving on to the next step of internationalisation stages (export/import to FDI or WOFE), however, the other two SMEs (both exporters) indicated their willingness to establish a WOFE type business in China and to devote further resources to a high commitment venture. A lack of adequate resources was a key reason for why SMEs preferred not to make further commitments to the Chinese market. Therefore, and again 'resource poverty' had limited these SMEs in their further expansion:

The reason we looked to China is because in Australia we have a lack of funds for what we do, lack of investment capital, and we have a lot of good research so there's big opportunity to commercialise that research and get it into China with Chinese capital.

(Case 22: Medical Equipment Co)

However, the difficulty of building a partnership in China may hinder further investment in research and prevent sufficient resource commitment. As an interviewee from an equipment service provider company who provided industrial automation services to the equipment manufacturing industry in China commented, the SME had been involved with the Chinese market since the early 1990s, however was still waiting to establishing a significant partnership with a Chinese firm. As a result, the firm appears to not be following the stage theory to move up to the next level, as the quote suggests below:

We sub-contracted in and out of China for the 90s and up until 2009 and we were really just working for other companies within China. In 2009, we saw the opportunity but there just hasn't been the demand for automation and I think until we actually develop a significant partnership with a Chinese company then we probably won't be establishing an office until that time.

(Case 5: Equipment Co)

The above quote provided some evidence that SMEs do not always follow the stage approach and commit more resources to the market just because they acquire market knowledge and experience, and still they experience resource restrictions and do require partnerships to access resources that they need. To summarise the findings of the exporters the following is proposed:

Proposition 2.2a: Innovative exporting SMEs who develop knowledge and experience of the international market will be interested in internationalisation, however they would be more likely be constrained by a lack of resources to progress through to higher commitment modes.

Wholly Owned Foreign Entities (WOFEs)

An analysis of the results suggested that 14 of the 18 SMEs in the 'stage' approach category were operating as WOFEs in China. Nine out of this 14 (a majority) had international experience with other countries before entering China, and China was seen as a new destination to expand to. Five of the SMEs in WOFE category however had no prior internationalisation exposure and China was the first country they had internationalised their businesses to. The owners/managers of three of these five SMEs were well familiar with overseas business operations in their previous jobs, and used their knowledge and experience of international businesses to influence the internationalisation of these SMEs to China. One of these five SMEs, Vehicle Warranty Co had actually run a different business in China previously and as a result had considerable knowledge and experience of China's market prior to establishing their business. Another SME, which was an architecture firm, entered the Chinese market using a joint venture type arrangement with a Chinese company, with an already existing job in hand, and then had established WOFEs after spending some time in the market after they had gathered some knowledge and experience about doing businesses in China with their partner. As the following quotation indicates:

15 years ago . . . To create new business, so that comes about as a result of a client in China coming here, we look at something for them, we work on it from here and so that creates an opportunity for us to open an operation in China and that's pretty well the kind of way that kind of connection works.

(Case 34: Architect Co)

There were another two SMEs that had entered China without any prior internationalisation experience, however two of them entered China via Hong Kong and were consultancy businesses. The reasons for internationalisation to China by the

SMEs utilising WOFEs are varied from growth to survival strategies, where Case 13 had done this for growth purposes and Case 10 had done this for survival:

> The company wants to grow and evolve and the firm has been doing a fantastic job in Australia adding business units and buying others.
>
> (Case 13: Vehicle Warranty Co)

> One thing that is difficult for our business in Australia is the market is very small so it's a very saturated market, it's almost impossible to expand. So it's a case of survival for us. China is kind of unexplored territory such as computation or biotechnology and also we think to start a business earlier. We think it's better to install a company in China, although probably not as many businesses as we expected but in five years' time I'm sure there will be so it's easier.
>
> (Case 10: Medical Research Co)

The above SMEs also believe they must be present in China's market for strategic reasons as China is going to be the centre of the Asian market:

> We sell around the world. China is developing very fast and if you want to talk about the long-term future of the pharmaceutical industry . . . if you don't look into the China market I think you made a mistake.
>
> (Case 8: Biotech Co)

Some SMEs had followed their competitors and entered the Chinese market to maintain their global competitive position in respect to much larger multinational enterprises:

> Our end game was not to just move all our manufacturing from Australia to here but it was to leverage what we already have in Australia and put it on a more global basis because we do compete with global companies on what we do. We know from a price basis we cannot compete from Australia.
>
> (Case 21: Box Co)

Overall it appears that the firms who became WOFEs did in fact follow the stages approach, where they built knowledge and experience over time, and they did have the resources to internationalise. Interestingly, the firms that did have WOFEs were generally larger firms in terms of employee size as they had an average of 124 employees working for them, whilst importing firms had an average of 25 employees, exporters 73, and BIC firms had 29. This suggests that size, and hence resources, may be explanatory for why these firms internationalise with particular entry modes.

The above findings suggest that the stages model of the firm is explanatory for this type of WOFE firm's internationalisation process. As a result, we develop the following propositions:

Proposition 2.3a: Innovative SMEs that internationalise as a WOFE are more likely to use the stages model of internationalisation.

Proposition 2.3b: Innovative SMEs that internationalise as a WOFE are more likely to do so because they are larger by employee size than other entry modes and have more resources than others.

Born in China (BIC) firms and internationalisation

In this study, there were 10 firms that we classified as (BIC) firms or entrepreneurial start-ups. We believed that they demonstrated a 'rapid' approach to internationalisation to China, as they established their businesses based on the presentation or examination of the opportunities in the Chinese market. Some of these firms had entered China's market via Hong Kong to develop their regional presence in the greater Chinese market, as the following quote shows:

> We'll do business internationally through our Hong Kong Company. So to do serious business in China, you need to have a Chinese company. Internationally everything will go through Hong Kong and it's not an issue.
>
> (Case 35: Shop Co)

A majority of the BIC SMEs demonstrate similar characteristics, and in particular a number of them had significant international experience which led them to creating their own businesses. For example, seven of the owners of the BIC firms had significant exposure to the Chinese market (including Hong Kong) and some did have wider experiences in other parts of Asia too, for example Japan and Korea. As a good example of this, the owner of one of these SMEs dealt with China for close to 30 years in previous jobs (as an employee), but also had a different business in Australia for a number of years. The business in China runs with a partner who is a local Chinese, as the following quote demonstrates:

> I had my own business in Australia; I had my own factories in Australia for a number of years. Then I sold that business a few years ago, managed another shop fitting company for a while and then set up their offices up over here in China and that didn't work out for me so I decided to leave and do my own business again. So I've set up our own business over here (China).
>
> (Case 35: Shop Co)

But not all SMEs had significant experience in China, and some had come on a whim to China, and had serendipitously (Crick and Spence, 2005) set up their business. This had varied from people coming to China for a short leisure stay, others attending a business seminar in Melbourne on 'the mystique of the Chinese market', and then one being an English language training teacher, who then discovered an entrepreneurial opportunity to provide English training services to Chinese businesses. The following provides an example of this serendipity:

> I was just travelling around the world, got to China; got a job within one internet session, teaching English, which I then spent three months working in and then quit. But that got me started and the guy that knocked on

my door, the very first guy that I met, foreign face, literally knocked on my door then three months later we thought, let's set up our own business. So we did. We just happened to fall into doing it and we just happened to meet each other by accident.

(Case 11: HR Consult Co)

Another individual had a similar story: the owners of this SME had international exposure though serendipity, and were involved with advising commencing businesses in China:

Mine is a very strange story. I'd worked in industry and in academia, back and forward. I took a full-time contract with the French business school and enrolled in a PhD in Paris; on the way I stopped for six weeks to work at a university in China and that was eight or nine years ago and I'm still here so I didn't finish my PhD. When I came, I had some ideas, I'd worked in industry quite a bit, I'd worked in the region quite extensively . . . and really liked what I saw in China and so I tried to do something in China.

(Case 30: Consult Co)

It's interesting to note that international business can come about through these rather unplanned events (Crick and Spence, 2005). Another entrepreneur had stated that he spent a number of weeks/months in China looking for a business to acquire (Social Media Co). He then found a social media company based in Shanghai, and had never looked back, and was operating a successful business there, again indicating a fast internationalisation for this business owner:

The firm is here (China) to create value to the sports, entertainment and tourist industries by creating new technologies and innovations that help these international clients develop their businesses in China.

(Case 27: Social Media Co)

So overall for this section we develop the following propositions:

Proposition 2.4a: BIC firms are more likely to use a born-global or INV approach to internationalisation, and will hence rapidly internationalise to China.
Proposition 2.4b: BIC firms are more likely to be established by owners who are entrepreneurial, have a Chinese background, experience and networks in international markets.
Proposition 2.4c: BIC firms are more likely to be established through serendipity.

Discussion

This chapter examined the applicability of two main internationalisation theories, the stage theory (Johanson and Vahlne, 1977) and the INV/born-global approach (Knight and Cavusgil, 1996; Oviatt and McDougall, 1994), and it was found that both of these theoretical models had relevance for the internationalisation of these innovative SMEs, with the majority of firms (21) subscribing to the stages model, and then the remaining 14 subscribing to the INV/born-global approach. This was interesting as it demonstrated that the two different theories were relevant for internationalisation of these innovative SMEs, and that these firms displayed different characteristics. We also explored the role of different entry modes in this internationalisation process, and we found that there were distinct differences in how internationalisation occurred for these entry modes.

In particular, importing innovative SMEs were less likely to want to internationalise further using the stages model (Johanson and Vahlne, 1977), and therefore the theory that as a firm builds up experience, knowledge and time in a market will lead them to further internationalisation may not be explanatory. Rather the influence of the strategic decision of the firm, and what they want to do, is. On another note there was evidence from the exporters that they were interested in further internationalisation although they lacked the resources to do it, mainly due to their small sizes. This influence was poignant for one exporter who stated that they would like to further internationalise to China, however did not have the resources to do it, and needed a partner to do it. It was therefore apparent that these innovative exporting firms faced the LOS, and future researchers are encouraged to examine this in greater detail.

For the WOFE firms, it was apparent that most of these firms had internationalised in a step-by-step approach, as per the stages approach, with some SMEs strongly following this theory. It is also noted that these SME types seemed to have more resources in general, as measured by employee size, to devote to internationalisation and therefore did not face the LOS that the other SMEs faced. The role of experience, knowledge and time in the market was highly beneficial for these firms.

The final firms we examined are the BIC SMEs, who were entrepreneurs having established their business in China, and they had no parent company firms in Australia, but were run by Australians, with some having a Chinese background. These innovative SMEs were more likely to start quickly, their managers were entrepreneurial, they seized opportunities quickly and luck and serendipity played a role. In addition, a lot of these individuals had previous Chinese experience, knowledge and contacts in a previous organisation or career, which they had used to establish their new BIC SME.

We present these findings in a two-by-two typology, with internationalisation theories on one continuum, and then experience/knowledge/contacts on another continuum (see Figure 2.1).

Conclusion

Overall in this chapter, we have examined the internationalisation process for these innovative SMEs, and we found that it varied by either the stages model or the born-global/INV approach. A further examination of this revealed that entry mode had some influence on the internationalisation of the firm, and on

	Time, experience, knowledge and contact	

Born-global/INV	Importing
	Not interested in further
	    internationalisation
	Strategic decision to stay as
	    an importer
		BIC
		Entrepreneurial
		Lots of contacts/networks
		Knowledge
		Experience
		Chinese Background
		Rapidly Established
		Serendipity

Stages Approach	Exporting
	Firms develop experience/
	    knowledge
	Firms wishing to expand to
	    the next stage
	Liabilities of smallness as a
	    barrier
		WOFE
		Step-by-step approach most
		    evident by these firms
		Knowledge, experience and
		    contacts are important
		Abundance of resources

Figure 2.1 Typology of innovative SME internationalisation

the behaviours and the characteristics of the firms. The main findings were that WOFEs did display the characteristics of the stages model, importers were not interested in further internationalisation, exporters faced the LOS as a barrier and the BIC firms internationalised via a born-global/INV approach. Future research may test the propositions that we developed in this chapter, to examine whether they stand true for much larger populations of firms. In addition, the chapter has practical relevance for SMEs wishing to move from one entry mode to another, or to know how to quickly establish a business in China, and utilise their entrepreneurial skills, knowledge, experience and contacts to do that. The role of serendipitous opportunity should also be examined.

References

Andersen, O. (1993). On the internationalisation process of firms: A critical analysis. *Journal of International Business Studies*, 24:2, 209–231.

Andersson, S., Gabrielsson, J., and Wictor, I. (2004). International activities in small firms: Examining factors influencing the internationalisation and export growth of small firms. *Canadian Journal of Administrative Sciences*, 21:1, 22–34.

Autio, E., Sapienza, H., and Almeida, J. (2000). Effect of age at entry, knowledge intensity, and imitability on international growth. *Academy of Management Journal*, 43:5, 909–924.

Barney, J. B. (1991). Firm resources and sustained competitive advantage. *Journal of Management*, 17:1, 99–120.

Bilkey, W. J., and Tesar, G. (1977). The export behavior of smaller Wisconsin manufacturing firms. *Journal of International Business Studies*, 9, 93–98.

Coviello, N. E., and McAuley, A. (1999). Internationalisation and the small firm: A review of contemporary empirical research. *Management International Review*, 39:3, 223–237.

Coviello, N. E., and Munro, H. J. (1997). Network relationships and the internationalisation process of smaller software firms. *International Business Review*, 6:4, 361–384.

Crick, D. (2009). The internationalisation of born global and international new venture SMEs. *International Marketing Review*, 26:4/5, 453–476.

Crick, D., and Spence, M. (2005). The internationalisation of 'high performing' UK high-tech SMEs: A study of planned and unplanned strategies. *International Business Review*, 14:2, 167–185.

Dimitratos, P., Johnson, J. E., Plakoyiannaki, E., and Young, S. (2016). SME internationalization: How does the opportunity-based international entrepreneurial culture matter? *International Business Review*, 25:6, 1211–1222.

Fan, T., and Phan, P. (2007). International new ventures: Revisiting the influences behind the 'born-global' firm. *Journal of International Business Studies*, 38:7, 1113–1131.

Freeman, S. (2000). SMEs and the Dynamics of the Internationalisation involvement process. *ANZMAC 2000 Visionary Marketing for the 21st Century: Facing the Challenge*. Conference publication.

Gomes-Casseres, B. (1997). Alliance strategies of small firms. *Small Business Economics*, 9:1, 33–44.

Hannan, M. T., and Freeman, J. (1984). Structural inertia and organizational change. *American Sociological Review*, 49, 149–164.

Harveston, P. D., Kedia, B., and Davis, P. (2000). Internationalisation of born global and gradual globalizing firms: The impact of the manager. *Advances in Competitiveness Research*, 8:1, 92–99.

Ibeh, K. (2003). On the internal drivers of export performance among Nigerian firms: Empirical findings and implications. *Management Decision*, 41:3, 217–225.

Johanson, J., and Mattson, L. G. (1993). Internationalisation in industrial systems – a network approach. In Hood, N., and Vahlne, J. E. (Eds.), *Strategies in Global Competition*. New York: Croom Helm, 287–314.

Johanson, J., and Vahlne, J. E. (1977). The internationalisation process of the firm: A model of knowledge development and increasing foreign market commitments. *Journal of International Business Studies*, Spring/Summer, 23–32.

Johanson, J., and Vahlne, J. E. (1990). The mechanism of internationalisation. *International Marketing Review*, 7:4, 11–24.

Johanson, J., and Vahlne, J. E. (2009). The Uppsala internationalisation process model revisited: From liability of foreignness to liability of outsidership. *Journal of International Business Studies*, 40, 1411–1431.

Johanson, J., and Wiedersheim-Paul, F. (1975). The internationalisation of the firm – four Swedish cases. *Journal of Management Studies*, 12:3, 305–322.

Knight, G. A. (2001). Entrepreneurship and strategy in the international SME. *Journal of International Management*, 7:1, 155–171.

Knight, G. A., and Cavusgil, S. T. (2004). Innovation, organizational capabilities and the born- global firm. *Journal of International Business Studies*, 35:2, 124–138.

Knight, G. A., and Cavusgil, S. T. (1996). The born global firm: A challenge to international theory. *Advances in International Marketing*, 8, 11–26.

Kuivalainen, O. (2003). *Knowledge Based View of Internationalisation – Studies on Small and Medium Sized Information and Communication Technology Firms.* Doctoral thesis, Lappeenranta University of Technology, Finland.

Lopez, L. E., Kundu, S. K., and Ciravegna, L. (2009). Born global or born regional&quest: Evidence from an exploratory study in the Costa Rican software industry. *Journal of International Business Studies*, 40:7, 1228–1238.

Love, J. H., and Roper, S. (2015). SME innovation, exporting and growth: A review of existing Evidence. *International Small Business Journal*, 33:1, 28–48.

McDougall, P. P., and Oviatt, B. M. (2000). International entrepreneurship: The intersection of two research paths. *Academy of Management Journal*, 43, 902–908.

McDougall, P. P., Oviatt, B. M., and Shrader, R. C. (2003). A comparison of international and domestic new ventures. *Journal of International Entrepreneurship*, 1:1, 59–82.

McDougall, P. P., Shane, S., and Oviatt, B. M. (1994). Explaining the formation of international joint ventures: The limits of theories from international business research. *Journal of Business Venturing*, 9, 469–487.

McGaughey, S. L., Welch, D. L., Liesch, P. W., Petersen, B., and Lamb, P. (2002). Evolving strands of research on firm Internationalisation: An Australian-Nordic perspective. *International Studies of Management and Organization*, 32:1, 16–35.

McKinsey & Company. (1993). *Emerging Exporters: Australia's High Value-Added Manufacturing Exporters.* Melbourne: Australian Export Council.

Moen, Ø. (2002). The born globals. *International Marketing Review*, 19:2, 156–175.

O'Cass, A., and Weerawardena, J. (2009). Examining the role of international entrepreneurship, innovation and international market performance in SME internationalisation. *European Journal of Marketing*, 43:11/12, 1325–1348.

Oviatt, B. M., and McDougall, P. P. (1994). Toward a theory of international new ventures. *Journal of International Business Studies*, 25:1, 45–64.

Oviatt, B. M., and McDougall, P. P. (2005). Defining international entrepreneurship and modelling the speed of internationalization. *Entrepreneurship: Theory & Practice*, 29:5, 537–553.

Peng, M. W. (2001). The resource based view and international business. *Journal of Management*, 27:6, 803–829.

Rammer, C., and Schmiele, A. (2008). Drivers and effects of internationalising innovation by SMEs. ZEW Discussion Papers, No. 08–035 [rev.]. Leibniz Information Centre for Economics. Centre for European Economic Research.

Rialp, A., Rialp, J., and Knight, G. A. (2005). The phenomenon of early internationalizing firms: What do we know after a decade (1993–2003) of scientific inquiry? *International Business Review*, 14:2, 147–166.

Rodrigues, J. (2007). The internationalisation of the small and medium-sized firms. *Prometheus*, 25:3, 305–317.

Sapienza, H. J., Autio, E., George, G., and Zahra, S. A. (2006). A capabilities perspective on the effects of early internationalisation on firm survival and growth. *Academy of Management Review*, 31:4, 914–993.

Stinchcombe, A. L. (1965). Social structure and organizations. In March, J. G. (Ed.), *Handbook of Organizations.* Chicago: Rand McNally & Firm, 142–193.

Taylor, M., and Jack, R. (2013). Understanding the pace, scale and pattern of firm internationalization: An extension of the 'Born Global' concept. *International Small Business Journal*, 31:6, 701–721.

Welch, L., and Luostarinen, R. (1988). Internationalisation – evolution of a concept. *Journal of General Management*, 14:2, 34–55.

Wicramasekera, R., and Bamberry, G. (2003). Exploration of born global/international new Ventures: Some evidence from the Australian Wine industry. *Australasian Journal of Regional Studies*, 9:2, 207–220.

Zaheer, S. (1995). Overcoming the liabilities of foreignness. *Academy of Management Journal*, 38:2, 341–363.

3 Making innovation work in China for foreign SMEs

Introduction

The extant literature on small and medium-sized enterprises (SMEs) and innovation has had a strong focus on exporting as an important part of the internationalisation process of SMEs (Love and Roper, 2015), with less focus on other entry modes such as wholly owned foreign entities (WOFEs) or born-global firms such as those born in China (BIC), which are the focus of this current chapter. This chapter also focuses on addressing the key research question such as: "how is innovation used for the SME internationalisation?". Several related questions remain to be addressed, such as, "what types of innovation do SMEs use in the Chinese market?"; "does it help the SMEs with their competitive advantage and how?"; "are these innovations incremental or radical?" and "are these innovations accepted by the Chinese market?" We summarise the findings in relation to how they may provide insights for innovative SMEs who wish to do business in the Chinese market. To start addressing these questions, the current chapter examines the contexts of both Australia and China in regards to innovation, as this context may influence the way in which SMEs can internationalise using different types of innovation.

Australian context for innovation

An examination of the Australian context reveals that Australia is a reasonably innovative country, however it is often critiqued for not doing the best it can, i.e. Australia could be more innovative by spending more money on research and development (R&D) activities, and SME internationalisation, which may lead to more product/service innovation. According to the Australian Government (2016), innovation is about doing something differently, and creating value out of doing it, and is an important element of developing productivity and economic growth for a country. Innovation allows for an accelerated pace of technological change, which causes structural changes and opportunities in countries, industries and employment (Australian Government, 2016), and therefore the Australian government, businesses and individuals see it as important to engage in innovative activities. Innovation also creates advantages and distinction for firms in markets, and thus is helpful in international markets. The total R&D fund in Australia was valued at $33.3 billion, which is devoted to activities such as knowledge application, transfer and creation (Australian Government, 2016) which includes the creation of new products, ideas and processes. The Australian Government (2016) identifies that to build an innovative country, there must be a mix of the right 'culture', 'networks', 'skills', 'infrastructure', 'money' and 'policy' for promoting innovation. Despite there being a number of well-known innovations in Australia, for example the Black-Box, Pacemakers, WI-FI, the bionic ear, IVF technology and polymer bank notes to name but a few (Australian Geographic, 2017), Australian firms are generally seen to lack novelty, newness and the development of new products (Australian Government, 2016). Part of the reason for a lack of novelty has been the fact that Australian firms are less likely, in comparison to firms in other countries, to invest or spend money on innovation and R&D activities.

Nevertheless, Australia still spends a reasonable amount of Gross Domestic Product (GDP) on innovation, for instance statistics show that Australia spends 2.13 percent of GDP on R&D (Mazzarol, 2015), however this is seen as one of the lowest amounts as compared to other members of the Organisation for Economic Cooperation and Development (OECD) countries, where the average is 2.63 percent. In addition, there have been calls for Australia to increase their spending to 3 percent. A reasonable level of innovation in Australia may be due to a reasonably smart population with a relatively high proportion of people educated at the masters and PhD level (Australian Government, 2016).

Innovation is more important than ever, as Australia has moved away from being a manufacturing based economy, to one that is a smart economy, but this has had more to do with necessity rather than want. Australia no longer has a strong and vibrant manufacturing sector, so they do need to do something else. Government officials argue that Australian companies can be successful in Asian markets (Australian Government, 2012) through innovation, however whether this is actually possible is questionable, thus, it is the focus of this chapter to explore this possibility. We now turn to innovation in China as the second context of this book.

Chinese context for innovation

In recent years, China has overpassed the US economy in manufacturing and exporting, and is well-known to be the world's factory. In addition, China is also predicted to pass the American economy with its strong spending on R&D. A Boston Consulting report revealed that the US spent $500 billion on R&D in 2015; in comparison, China was predicted to spend $658 billion on R&D by 2018 (Davidson, 2017), which is much more than the American spending of $312 billion projected in 2018. In 2014, the percentage of spending on R&D of the total GDP in China was 2.04 percent, it was reported that Australia has a similar amount to China (OECD, 2017). However, because the Chinese economy is much bigger, this means that this translates into a much larger dollar amount of $376 billion, in comparison to Australia with smaller population size, which is calculated to be only spending $21.5 billion dollars (OECD, 2017). With China opening its doors, and joining the world economic stage since 1979, China's economic development has moved from being rural and agrarian to manufacturing, and to being the world's factory and largest manufacturer and exporter, to today being focused on building an innovative nation (Tian, 2007). For instance the focus of the 13th five-year plan is on innovation, internet and new media and information technology (King, Wood and Mallesons, 2016) and it is well known that the Chinese government is very focused on creating an innovation ecosystem (McKern, 2017). In the Chinese innovation ecosystem, a number of things are apparent: 1) research institutions should be developed in science and engineering; 2) funds need to be allocated to high quality research; 3) tax policies should enhance investment and venture capital, 4) incentives should be provided to commercialised ideas and 5) a culture needs to be developed that is supportive of science and entrepreneurship through education (McKern, 2017).

This is reflected in the fact that investment in innovation is extremely high in China, and as a result we see many elements of an innovation society, including approximately 150 or so high-tech business parks, the incredible increase of patent filings and publications in scientific journals, large amounts of export of high-tech manufactured products and finally the development of global innovative companies such as Huawei, Haier and Alibaba to name but a few (McKern, 2017). In addition, China now has millions of university graduates every year, with over 1000 PhD students. China has developed many innovation networks and clusters, and focused on the development of the 'new' products, processes and services (Davidson, 2017). China is now recognised to be a global innovator going into the future. Similar to Australia, and what many researchers and business commentators have said, the role of government in creating policy, and the environment for innovation is paramount. Thus, it is crucially important for the government to create innovative policy, which assists in developing an innovation ecosystem to support fundamental research and commercialise research outputs with the establishment of necessary mechanisms and incentives. China is reported to have a strong state intervention just to attempt to achieve this goal (McKern, 2017).

Literature review

There is quite a large and diverse body of literature examining the role of innovation in SME internationalisation and how this might influence performance. Innovation is first defined and the various types with their characteristics are discussed.

Defining innovation

Innovation can include the development of new products or services, systems or even new markets such as internationalisation (Schumpeter, 1962), and firms may gain an increased commercial value through the introduction of new or improved products or processes (Australian Manufacturing Council, 1995). The literature generally points to the fact that there are many types of innovation from product, process, marketing and even the business/paradigm innovation, and that firms will use different types of innovations, and this will have differing effects on their internationalisation (see Love and Roper, 2015 for a discussion of these issues). Product innovation is defined in the literature as "a good or service that is new or significantly improved. This includes significant improvements in technical specifications, components and materials, software in the product, user friendliness or other functional characteristics (OECD, 2017). Previous research (Love and Roper, 2015) indicates that product innovation is one of the most commonly used forms of innovation used by SMEs engaged in internationalisation, and results in greater performance for these SMEs. The next form of innovation is process innovation, which is defined "a new or significantly improved production or delivery method including significant changes in techniques, equipment and/or software" (OECD, 2017). Market innovation can be defined as "a new marketing method, which involves significant changes in product packaging, product placement, product promotion or pricing" (OECD, 2017). Finally business innovations, or what is sometimes referred to as "paradigm" innovation, is defined as the organisation's process for introducing new ideas, workflows, methodologies, services or products (OECD, 20177). The final type of innovation we consider is service innovation, which is a more recently examined form of innovation in the international business literature, where Kuntuu and Torkeli (2015, p. 85) define it as "a way to fulfil customer needs through an evolutionary process of dynamically combining and recombining service elements". The question emanating from these definitions of innovation is "what forms of innovation do SMEs use in their internationalisation, and how does this help with creating a competitive advantage?".

In addition to the different types of innovations, innovation can vary by how incremental it is, or how radical it is, which is further broken down into whether an innovation is architectural innovation (i.e. the whole product), or whether it is just the innovation of a component of a product (Henderson and Clark, 1994). This is conceptualised into the Henderson and Clark (1994) typology, which classifies innovation into these four different dimensions. So interestingly, those firms that are producing disruptive technologies or products are likely to be engaged in radical innovation, and those firms that are doing much smaller innovations, that are not entirely game changing are referred to as "incremental innovations". Based on the two dimensions, "incremental" and "radical", identified by Henderson and Clark (1994), we ask the question about which degrees of innovation these SMEs use in the internationalisation literature. We now move on to reviewing the literature on innovation/SME internationalisation and performance.

Innovation and SME internationalisation

Ansoff (1965) suggests that internationalisation and innovation are two forms of growth strategies that firms can use; going international opens up new markets to firms, and being innovative also does, and opens the firm up to servicing the market better. Going global is an overwhelming task for some SMEs that generally lack sufficient manpower, financial resources, language ability and international perspectives. However, innovation and internationalisation have been seen as ways for firms to gain a competitive advantage (Onetti and Zuchella, 2008). Scholars do argue, and find that innovation and internationalisation are inter-related (Onetti et al., 2012; Cassiman and Golovoko, 2011; Golovoko and Valenittin, 2011; Ganotakis and Love, 2011). Researchers also suggest that innovation can help with export initiation to begin with (Rees and Edwards, 2010; Higón and Driffield, 2010; Nguyen et al., 2008). Other researchers have also found reverse effects, that when a firm becomes international, it is required to innovate, especially when operating in very different market places (Golovko and Valentini, 2011; Kafouros et al., 2008). Therefore, there is an overlapping relationship between innovation and internationalisation.

O'Cass and Weerawardena (2009) found that international entrepreneurial SMEs pursued organisational innovation to a larger degree than non-exporters. Huber (1991) found that the use of certain entry modes into a foreign market will influence the SMEs' future product innovation. In particular, licensing and alliances are positively associated with product innovation, consistent with prior research on licensing and alliances (Huber, 1991). These modes of entry usually provide access to a wider pool of knowledge and create avenues for knowledge sharing.

Crick and Spence (2005) argue that rapid expansion might be more appropriate for innovative SMEs, rather than step-by-step expansion as explained by the *U and I stages models* (presented in Chapter 2). Crick and Spence (2005) find that entrepreneurial culture, opportunistic strategies and short-term goals were found to be important for the internationalisation of innovative firms. Denicolai, Hagen and Pisoni (2015) investigate the effect of an entrepreneur's background on their strategic choices around innovation and internationalisation. In particular they find that family firms are less likely to be international and innovative and that team based organisations tend to be more innovative and international than a solitary one-man-controlled firm, which may display product and process innovation, but limited scope of internationalisation. Denicolai (2015) finds that internationalisation tends to be related to the type of innovation, rather than R&D intensity or novelty.

Innovation, internationalisation and firm performance

Innovations may be used as a strategy for survival, growth and overall performance. Porter (1990) provides a good argument for why there might be a relationship between firm performance and innovation. He states that "companies achieve competitive advantage through acts of innovation" (Porter, 1990: p.75). So to beat one's competition, a firm needs to engage in ongoing innovation at multiple levels. Growth may be achieved if innovation enables the expansion of existing markets or entry into new markets (Porter, 1990). On the other hand, firms may be forced to match the innovation of rivals to maintain market share.

Recent internationalisation literature investigates the effect of internationalisation on innovation (Boermans and Roelfsema, 2016), and finds that internationalisation positively impacts on performance. In particular, internationalisation increases firm performance directly and indirectly, whilst the indirect impact of innovation on firm performance is significant (Boermans and Roelfsema, 2016). The results suggest that there needs to be internationalisation for innovation to have an effect. There is some debate about whether a firm is first innovative, which leads them to internationalisation, or whether a firm being international makes them innovative because they are exposed to ideas in the foreign market, which they absorb and use to develop new ideas (Boermans and Roelfsema, 2016; Hagemejer and Kolasa, 2011). Boermans and Roelfsema (2016) find that for those firms that are more active internationally, they will have a greater amount of innovation, and perform better. Interestingly, recent research on service innovation tells a different picture. In particular, Kunttu and Torkeli (2015) find that service innovation (SI) has a positive relationship with firm performance, but not with the degree of internationalisation. There is also a debate in the literature about whether an SME can manage or handle both internationalisation and innovation at the same time, but given that these two factors are self-reinforcing, and require similar skills and resources, this may be possible (Kuntuu and Torkeli, 2015), or pose a difficulty as one function may drain the resources off the other function. Interestingly Kuntuu and Torkeli (2015) find that innovative service activities explained higher performance, whereas it did not explain higher growth, or higher degrees of innovation.

The association between innovation and firm performance depends on the performance measurement and the characteristics of a given organisation. That is, the utilisation of objective or subjective performance indicators such as sales or self-reported performance may lead to different research results and different combinations of innovation, such as a combination of technological and marketing innovations, may also result in divergent organisational performance. Previous studies of the relationship between innovation and performance provide mixed results, some positive, some negative, and some showed no relationship at all (Capon, Farley, and Hoenig, 1990; Li and Atuagene-Gima, 2001). According to Pratali (2003), incremental technological innovations help improve company competitiveness with the ultimate aim of increasing company value. In addition, researchers reported that innovative marketing aims at increasing product consumption and has a positive influence on firm sales. Furthermore, continuous work process innovation was regarded as the most important action for improving short-term profitability (Soderquist, 1996). Many small companies also succeeded in introducing more radical innovations because of their genetic makeup (Stringer, 2000), which may include agility and creativity among other factors. However, some argue that the linkage of radical innovation and performance is an S-curve shape because of diminishing research effort and resource inefficiencies (Foster, 1986). According to Varadarajan and Jayachandran (1999) the role of innovation is critical in delivering higher firm performance for SMEs in foreign markets.

The Innovation Cycle Report (Australian Manufacturing Council, 1995: 5–6) states that innovative firms are much more likely to export, and they are more competitive against other firms. This result indicates that SMEs experience more barriers to innovation than larger firms. The main barriers identified by the ABS survey (2010–2011) were a lack of skilled persons within the business or within the labour market, a lack of access to additional funds, cost of development, government regulation or compliance, uncertain demands for new goods and services, adherence to standards and lack of access to knowledge and technology (Commonwealth of Australia, 2011). The above literature suggests that there is an innovation-performance relationship. The next section presents the data analysis methods for this chapter.

Data analysis methods

In this chapter, the data was analysed in the following ways. Firstly, the search term "innovation" and similar words such as "innovative" were searched for in the interviewee text. As innovation was defined as consisting of different types of innovation, namely product, service, service/product, process, marketing or paradigm innovation, we read word-for-word the interview transcripts and classified the firms into the most appropriate innovation types. We also looked at whether this created a competitive advantage for the SME, as reported by the respondent, and the entry modes they were using. We then analysed whether the innovations were considered to be incremental/radical, and whether there were any issues around this innovation in the Chinese market. Table 3.1 presents the overall coding of key themes drawn from the data analysis.

Findings

We organise the findings into two sections. The first part is related to the forms of innovation that the participating SMEs used, and the second part analyses how

Table 3.1 Overall coding of innovation terms in the interviews

Name	Sources
Innovation/Innovative	35
Product innovation	7
Service innovation	7
Product/Service innovation	5
Process innovation	8
Marketing innovation	3
Business/Paradigm innovation	5
Degree of Innovation	
Incremental innovation	29
Radical innovation	6
Acceptance or values of innovation in the Chinese market	27

their choice of a different type of innovation created a competitive advantage for SMEs.

Types of innovation used by the SMEs

Most of the SMEs had utilised more than one type of innovation, however, it was apparent that one innovation type always dominated the other, and the innovations were categorised into their most dominant.

Product innovation

In the study, there were seven SMEs who were utilising product innovation as their main innovation (Table 3.2). Product innovators were using either the importing or WOFE modes. All of the importing firms in the sample had taken the approach of looking for innovative and new products to import, rather than producing themselves, as Furniture Co had highlighted:

> We are not self-innovative; innovative from the point of view that we're actively looking for innovation around the world from our suppliers. We need to work in conjunction with our suppliers to be innovative; also be quite aware of the price of innovation we bring to the table.
>
> (Case 1: Furniture Supplier)

Similarly, Rubber Co, an importer, did not innovate themselves, rather they were always looking to develop and source new products based on client demands, as they made components to large auto manufacturers. So whilst innovation is their focus, they did not use the Chinese market as a place to sell their innovation, rather a place to save on costs. Interestingly, the importers had engaged in product innovation to sell to the Australian domestic market, but were seeking to do this at a cheaper cost by sourcing supplies from China, and thus gaining a competitive advantage. We also provide an example of a firm utilising a WOFE, and innovating the products that they offer. A representative from Box Co (Case 21), a metal box manufacturer had stated:

> Innovation, a lot of our stuff changes, particularly direct segment products. We've recently partnered with a company based here to make what we call smart power rail solution, we've designed to go into racks, the thing is networked into your network and can actually look and monitor. This is a new product for Australia and new market segments.
>
> (Case 21: Box Co)

In this example, the firm was innovative, developing new products, and was trying to achieve a competitive advantage in the global market place, and was using China as a location to produce these innovations at lower costs. One interesting aspect of this SME was that most of the innovation based activities, including

Table 3.2 Product innovation

Pseudonym	Why it is one?	Entry mode	How does the innovation help them with being successful?
Case 1, Furniture Co	Increased product range	Importing	Assisted in having a great product range for customers in Australia.
Case 2, Rubber Co	Develop new moulded products	Importing	Accessed new products in the Chinese market.
Case 3, Chemical Co	Improved new products for the dry-cleaning industry	Importing	Was able to access new products in the Chinese market.
Case 17, Metal Frame Co	Structural steel solutions; Design and erect space frame systems	WOFE	Steel solutions for framing that Chinese builders wanted.
Case 21, Box Co	Segmentation and new products creating metal boxes	WOFE	Able to use China as a low cost location for production, to compete globally and to be able to transfer their innovations to China.
Case 22, Medical Equip Co	Develop new medical instruments and technologies	WOFE	Gains advantages by developing new technologies/ products, commercialising them and bringing them to market, which is not so prevalent in the Chinese market.
Case 23, Print Co	Service range and new products: Offering printing solutions for different products range (clothes, surf boards)	WOFE	Utilised technology that no other Chinese firm was using, making them more efficient.

R&D, occurred in Australia, where the company deliberately employed highly educated individuals. Apart from their internationalisation to Suzhou, China, the company was trying to train up and transfer this innovation based mentality to their Chinese staff, which at the start was lacking skills and knowledge for innovation. However, the company's goal was to transfer their innovative practices to the Chinese subsidiary so that they could not only manufacture innovations but also develop them. They had also utilised the Chinese market to be a global and low-cost supplier to the world.

Metal Frame Co was innovative in the sense that they developed new designs as per their client's requirements, and they also incorporated local opinion when developing their designs, which provided better outcomes in terms of client satisfaction. For example:

> When we first came to China, steel structure was an innovation, to come here and do steel structure we were like a market leader. I think you've got to discuss a lot of stuff with the Chinese guys because like even though they're not necessarily making the decisions, a lot of things they know better than you. You don't always have to take their opinion but there's a lot of the time you should.
>
> (Case 17: Metal Frame Co)

In addition, this SME had used advanced software design when developing and presenting designs, which was not commonly used in the Chinese market, which had given them an added advantage against the competition and made them more successful. Interestingly, their product was not seen as an innovation in their home country, Australia, but was in China, because no one else was supplying it. Therefore, Metal Frame Co had first mover advantages.

Print Co targeted differences in customer needs and were innovative with customising products accordingly, and per their view, many Chinese factories had difficulty with customising, but they were able to. They were also innovative from the perspective of buying new capital equipment that other competitors did not have, which had advanced technologies, setting themselves apart from the competition, as the following quote suggests:

> Innovation or our main advantages would be able to customise what people want. I know a lot of Chinese factories have difficulty with that. So with our digital printing we're able to offer the customised prints in the highest quality on to textile and that's a real major advantage because with that we're able to develop new things. We're even doing surfboards with digital prints in them that have never been seen before – we're playing with different products that have never been made before.
>
> (Case 23: Print Co)

As a result, this SME was able to offer services to clients that other competitors were not able to offer which gave them an advantage. The firm also had an innovative approach towards marketing, and customers can make their orders online so they can deliver quickly as per their customer requirements.

This suggests that when a firm is innovative from one perspective, that they may also be innovative on other fronts, leading to a multitude of benefits and success. In summary, WOFE product innovative firms demonstrated similar characteristics; some were servicing the Chinese market, some were using China as a base to produce cheaper products or gain Chinese know how, and some were offering products/services that might not necessarily be an innovation in the Australian market, but were innovations in the Chinese market. Therefore, the SMEs saw themselves as market leaders/pioneers in the Chinese market.

Service innovation

There were seven firms that were classified as using service innovations, as demonstrated in Table 3.3. The service innovation firms were using exporting, WOFEs

Table 3.3 Service innovation

Pseudonym	Why it is one?	Entry mode	How does the innovation help them with being successful or gaining a competitive advantage?
Case 7, Biotech Co 3	Runs clinical trials for firms wishing to develop new drugs, with clients in China	Export	Incremental improvements assist them with being successful.
Case 12, Accounting Co	Developed a new virtual Chief Financial Officer (CFO) for businesses in China	WOFE	Other local accounting businesses not offering this service, and there is a high demand for this.
Case 13, Vehicle Co	Offered a vehicle warranty service for Chinese second-hand car owners	WOFE	No other businesses providing this service in China. Whilst the service is not particularly innovative in developed markets, it was seen as an innovation in the Chinese market.
Case 14, Office Co	Service office, and service innovation	WOFE	Offers innovative office space and services that go past the offering of most competitors.
Case 19, Architect Co 1	Multiple innovative architectural services under one roof	BIC	Able to use a variety of talented staff to deliver innovative architecture to the Chinese market.

Pseudonym	Why it is one?	Entry mode	How does the innovation help them with being successful or gaining a competitive advantage?
Case 20, Architect Co 2	Using their design philosophy to bring to the market an architectural/town planning service that no other architectural firms are providing. Very artistically orientated design firm.	WOFE	Allows them to be busy, and very much in demand by local clients.
Case 34, Architect Co 3	Innovative because they have a range of different professionals on board.	BIC	Diversity, flexibility and reputation that other architect firms can't offer.

or BICs as entry modes. Accounting Co gave a good example of a service innovation; as they were an accounting firm, and offered a "virtual CFO" service, which allowed companies to outsource their CFO function to them without having to pay a full-time salary for an employee, and only pay for the services they required, as the following suggests:

> We do have a service called the Virtual CFO which we introduced as a very new concept to the local accounting service industry which is like a part-time based CFO for a company, like appointing a part-time or casual based, even project based, CFO for maybe a foreign company here who needs that kind of support or to a local company here to support their business.
>
> (Case 12: Accounting Co)

This service was an advantage for them, as it was to many clients, especially foreign SMEs based in China needing this service, especially when they were cash strapped and trying to develop a foothold in the Chinese market. The other firms in the service innovation category were Vehicle Co, Office Co and then three architectural firms. These businesses were all service companies, offering unique and differentiated services in the Chinese market. Interestingly, some of the architectural firms had talked about their unique designs:

> The things we can do best compared to lots of overseas offices in China from America, Japan or from Europe is that we use it as a contemporary design

to interpret traditional Oriental culture. That is our strength by complying heritage design and laws, and then implementing more modern designs.

(Case 34: Architecture Co 3)

In this situation, this firm used their own innovative design in developing customised solutions for the Chinese market. Similarly, Architecture Co's innovation was based on their design philosophy: "I think it probably is the design philosophy" (Case 20). Another architectural firm stated that their innovation had stemmed from the mix of people that they had on board:

Planners, urban designers, landscape architects, architects actually working on a job as opposed to just having landscape guys or a planning guy or whatever.

(Case 34: Architect Co 3)

This example demonstrates that having a mixture of staffing is important for developing the innovative capacity of the firm, so that they can offer their clients a range of innovative services. Interestingly, the firms in the service innovation category were either utilising the WOFE or BIC entry mode, suggesting that to offer their innovative services, the SME's business had to be located in the market, which is similar to the findings from the international service based research, that argue that for hard services, the firms need to be located within the market (Erramilli and Rao, 1990).

Product/service innovation

There were also five SMEs that were providing both products and services at the same time that were considered innovative (see Table 3.4). Firms in this category were either in exporting or using WOFEs. The firms in this category provided a service alongside products, or vice-versa. Security Co, was a good example of a firm in this category. Security Co was a security perimeter fencing company, where their products and services were innovative in the sense that they were using latest technology fibre optics. This product/service was provided in product in conjunction with other systems integrators. The systems integrators included large multinationals, who they would partner with to provide products/services to Chinese clients:

We took some innovative approaches to fibre sensing including early patents on some areas that were well known that's in the pre-optical fibre days and also in the optical fibre era and developed those techniques and patented them to come up with a sort of unique algorithm to that because we were the first company in the world that could take a cable that was fibre. We not only developed algorithms to detect intrusions and bit by bit improve them but we were able to make very, very innovative use of two way lasers.

(Case 4: Security System)

Table 3.4 Product and service innovation

Pseudonym	Why it is one?	Entry mode	How did it help with gaining a competitive advantage
Case 4, Security Co	Patent for optical fiber: Design and install security systems using fiber optical cables	Exporting	Innovation products and services that Chinese customers wanted.
Case 5, Man Control Co	Leading edge manufacturing control equipment: Supply and service purpose built equipment	Exporting	New manufacturing machine controls not offered in the Chinese market.
Case 6, Pneumatic Co	System integration using electronics: Offering integrated solutions and hardware products	Exporting	Not yet, as business still developing at the time of interview.
Case 8, Biotech Co 1	Developer of diagnostic medicines/tools/run health programs and research services	WOFE	Constantly researching, and developing new drugs, ideas, health programs and diagnostics.
Case 10, Biotech Co 4	Drug discovery service, and also developing their own IP/products.	WOFE	Chinese Government is trying to invest in innovation, so makes it a very welcoming place for this SME.

An exporter SME subcontracting to China on a project basis that provided computer controlled plant and equipment solutions for manufacturing industries (pharmaceutical and food and beverages), stated that the product and service they provided was innovative, because each job is customised. They originally provided services to large multinationals, and some Chinese firms, but realised that they needed to develop their own status in China (Case 5, Man Control Co). As the products they offered in China were for automation, they were finding it difficult to sell their products because most factories in China rely on labour, not automation. In this instance, innovation may not always be beneficial for success, and the demand for their service was reasonably low:

> Because of the work involved, it has to be innovative because the firm provides services to manufacturing areas predominantly. Most of our customers

are top tier MNEs and if we are not ahead of the rest of the clan then the firm does not have any business.

(Case 5: Equipment Service)

This is interesting as it suggests that innovations and improvements can only be successful when the context permits them to be successful, suggesting a contingency approach to the internationalisation of these innovations. The firm adapted its service and products in Chinese markets to suit customer/client requirements, for example it was difficult for them to address the issue of different expectations for price and quality level in the Chinese market environment as compared with Western expectations, which was critical for their success in the Chinese market.

Process innovation

There were seven SMEs in the study which utilised process innovation (see Table 3.5), and these SMEs were engaged in exporting, WOFEs and a BIC. Some examples had included Resources Co, Processing Co, Meat Co and Milk Co. Most of the SMEs in this category were seeking to reduce the costs of production in China. Milk Co considered themselves to be innovative in the sense that they were not constrained by company bureaucratic policies and principles, which meant they could innovate their distribution processes in China in a way that suited the firm and the Chinese environment, which assisted in being successful:

We've got this growing organisation where people within it aren't constrained by rules. As an example this is the distribution model, and we don't have to follow how it was done previously, because we are a flexible organisation. We can make our own way, and do something new.

(Case 24: Milk Co)

Similar to Milk Co, Meat Co had set up a WOFE in Hong Kong to assist with exporting organic beef. The main innovation that this individual firm was engaged in was the development of their supply chain, which ensured quality throughout to provide the firm with a competitive advantage, as no other firms were doing this:

The firm was very innovative perhaps 20 years ago in regard to establishing a vertically integrated supply chain. So while we don't own the properties, we don't own the abattoir, we've developed a supply chain to assure the quality control and safety all the way through the chain and while we can say now everyone does that, well they didn't do those 20 years ago.

(Case 25: Meat Co)

As another example, Resources Co was able to improve the processing of their raw materials using the China operation. The SME had found immense cost

Table 3.5 Process innovation

Pseudonym	Why it is one?	Entry mode	How did it help with gaining a competitive advantage
Case 6, Pneumatic Co	System integration using electronics: Offering integrated solutions and hardware products	Exporting	Not yet.
Case 16, Processing Co	Improvement of business systems	WOFE	Can only innovate incrementally to improve product offerings as the Chinese market is price sensitive.
Case 24, Milk Co	Flexible supply chains, processes and think outside the box ideas	WOFE	Allowed them to quickly grab opportunities in the Chinese market.
Case 25, Meat Co	Innovative supply chain	WOFE	Other firms don't use such an innovative approach.
Case 26, HR Consulting Co	Innovative provision of HRM services and training	BIC	Offered a highly innovative and professional approach, that other firms don't provide.
Case 29, Consulting Co 2	Innovate around process, using technology	BIC	Streamlines business, makes it more efficient that other competitors are not using.
Case 30, Finance Co	Innovative processes around client care	BIC	The innovative client solutions that this firm provided assisted them with developing good relationships with their clients.

saving as a result of shipping raw materials to China and bagging them there, where labour costs were much cheaper, rather than in Australia:

We were planning our innovation strategy for our whole company from a 'how do we become more innovative?' perspective rather than 'here's a particular product or technology that we want to develop'. Bagging in China is an innovation over the last 10 years or so, rather than in the past we would bag products in Australia and the bagging costs and then container shipping from Australia all up were say $140 a tonne whereas we can ship it bulk from Australia for $40 a tonne and then bag it in China for $20. So it's a labour offshoring but also not just that; we're more efficient with our shipping in as much as you can ship in bulk by conveyors rather than containers.

(Case 15: Resources Co)

As a result, it is evident that firms can use process innovation in China to more efficiently do business in the Chinese market or globally. In summary, these SMEs used new or significantly improved delivery methods to be competitive in their market sectors in the Chinese market by delivering better quality goods/services for competitive prices. It appears that SMEs in this category believed that process innovation not only provided efficient solutions for their businesses but also gave them cost advantages to keep them competitive in China and across the world. It was interesting to note that only the firms engaging in process innovations included one exporter, a WOFE and BIC, whereas the importers/exporters were not, so the location benefits of China had given added advantages to these SMEs locating there.

Market innovation

An analysis of the case studies revealed that there were three SMEs who had utilised market innovations (See Table 3.6). These firms were located in China as WOFEs or BIC firms suggesting that those firms located in China can probably design and develop more appropriate marketing strategies for the market, because they know the market better. The following quote from Recruitment Co highlights how they focused on a particular market segment to be innovative:

We're a service provider; we have to be innovative on a day-to-day basis if we're doing headhunting. We are innovative in the sense of our how we identify our candidates. We have to use technology and it's available and so on but everyone else is doing that as well. I wouldn't say if innovation makes me a leader in that respect, I'm not. Where I was innovative was taking an opportunity in that mining space and taking that as my market. That was innovative and no-one else had done that.

(Case 11: Recruitment Co)

So whilst overall, Recruitment Co was not innovative in the provision of their services, they were innovative in terms of the way they marketed themselves. In addition, the Managing Director of Recruitment Co had developed an association, which he had used in a "cunning" way (as described by himself), to market himself and his SME to potential clients, which assisted in developing reputation, which he believes gave him immense advantages in the market. Build

Table 3.6 Marketing innovation

Pseudonym	Why it is one?	Entry mode	How did it help with gaining a competitive advantage?
Case 11, Recruitment Co	Differentiated themselves through marketing and being a niche player. Also used innovative ways to market using network memberships	WOFE	New manufacturing machine controls not offered in the Chinese market.
Case 18, Build Co	Innovative in adapting and advertising in the market	WOFE	Good budget for marketing, and use of new social media tools.
Case 32, Marketing Co	Marketing innovation and creatively doing it	BIC	Being creative, not doing what everyone else is doing and the use of social media/ technology to help out.

Co's innovation was also a marketing one, by offering different elements in their services, which included safety management, quality management and environmental management. Similarly, Marketing Co was also classified as a marketing innovation because they were marketing themselves, and used their creative flair and relationship based approach at the local Chamber of Commerce events to draw in potential customers. These relationships had provided many benefits to this SME, such as word of mouth referrals.

Business innovation

In this analysis, business innovation is defined as the introduction of new ideas/ business models. In the sample we classified five SMEs into this category. Interestingly, all of these firms were BIC firms. The most interesting example of business innovation in the sample was that of Social Media Co, who had sought to bring together the divided world of different social media platforms in the west, versus what is in existence in China. Social Media Co did this by translating the social media accounts of foreign owned firms that wanted this translated into Chinese social media platforms:

> Let's say you're the Melbourne Demons football team and you want to talk in Chinese to Chinese people and Chinese social media: instead of hiring an

agency, PR firm or a local team, you can pay as little as $200 a month. Our firm can do your Facebook page with this technology and actually grab it all, package it to China and then publish it into your brand in Chinese social media accounts and then you have access to see everything in English. So that's obviously an innovation that we've introduced.

(Case 27: Social Media Co)

The firm had also developed a number of unique celebrity events etc., that were high impact and unique. The manager of Arbitration Co discussed how he found his niche in the market, from an innovative perspective:

The unique thing about this is that because so many of the Chinese lawyers have very limited experience in international arbitration they tend to lose and they tend to think that they're losing because the foreign parties are biased or the arbitrators are biased because they're Chinese which is not really true. They lose because they just don't have adequate experience.

(Case 31: Arbitration Chamber)

The SME firms focusing on business innovation understood that Chinese law firms were expensive, with some of the top ones more expensive than the biggest US and UK firms. The key gap this firm found in the market was that Chinese firms are expensive though, and many are inexperienced in arbitration practice; firms cannot afford international firms in addition to Chinese lawyers as Chinese law firms' charges are high:

The idea behind this business was that it's a one stop shop then for a whole lot of international law, different languages, different legal skills and you don't always have to employ a whole law firm; you can employ an individual to assist you because mostly you don't need a whole law firm to assist you. Eventually, one person can review your documents or your strategy. So they can keep their costs down by just hiring an individual and having them assist the Chinese team. I say that we are sort of a bridge, tailored service.

(Case 31: Arbitration Co)

In summary, it had appeared that Australian SMEs used innovation in their internationalisation process (to China) and adopted different types of innovation. Researchers (Siedschlag and Zhang, 2010; Doloreux and Laperrie're, 2014; Ripolles Melia, Blesa, and Roig, 2010; Harris and Li, 2008) have argued that firms with international activities were more likely to invest in innovation relative to firms that served only the domestic market and were more likely to be successful in terms of innovation output. The results indicate that not only Australian SMEs utilised innovation entering the Chinese market. The results of the study by Doloreux and Laperrie're (2014) support the view that SMEs used a different type of innovation in the internationalisation process and the results of the current study demonstrate this feature as well. According to Doloreux and Laperrie're (2014) product and process innovations are the dominant types of innovations, most

Table 3.7 Business innovation

Pseudonym	Why it is one?	Entry mode	How did it help with gaining a competitive advantage?
Case 27, Social Media Co	Overall business model innovative, with the provision of social media translation for foreign firms and events into Chinese social media.	BIC	No other firms provide this service.
Case 28, Consulting Co	Innovated around their business model, trying to consult, and bringing innovative Australian businesses with venture capital in Australia.	BIC	Seen as a way to help firms imagine what their business might be like in a few years.
Case 31, Arbitration Co	Developed a new Arbitration Chamber that was not in operation in China.	BIC	No other business in the Chinese market was providing the service, although there was a great need for this product.
Case 33, Investment Co	Saw innovation as being agile, creative, how they connect with clients and relationships/ having street smarts.	BIC	Crafting solutions for clients which made them feel good.
Case 35, Shop Co	Innovation as always updating the business/ideas/ thinking.	BIC	Meant that they didn't get left behind.

likely due to the fact that the firms must adapt themselves to new markets. A significant number of SMEs (19 out of 35 firms) used product, service or product/ service innovation, with seven using process innovation and the remainder using marketing/business/paradigm innovation, and the other 16 as secondary innovation, supporting the view of Doloreux and Laperrie're (2014). Therefore, product or service innovations help businesses sell their interesting and new products in international markets, which assists with a range of things such as

Table 3.8 Innovation and entry mode

Innovation type	Entry mode
Product	Importing, WOFE
Service	Exporting, WOFEs and BICs
Product/Service	Exporting/WOFEs
Process	Exporting/WOFEs/BICs
Marketing	WOFEs/BICs
Business/Paradigm	BICs

profitability, increased sales and economies of scale etc. According to Siedschlag and Zhang (2010), the strongest innovation-productivity link appears to be for firms with process innovation; process innovative SMEs in the study also confirm these previous results that process innovations make efficiency and productivity improvements. So overall it appears that innovation does matter for firms operating in international markets.

Although there were only small numbers for each innovation type, we did find that there were some patterns in regards to the entry modes that these firms were using, which are summarised in Table 3.8.

Radical or incremental innovation

The research literature and topical news points to the question as to whether firms use radical innovation or more incremental innovation. Recently a news article stated that it is difficult for firms to develop the next "hot shot, ground breaking" innovation due to the fact that it is expensive for these firms to invest in this R&D (Deeb, 2014). Innovation is also a very risky business, because organisations and venture capitalists may invest significant sums of money into projects, which do not eventuate with outcomes (Deeb, 2014). Therefore, firms have less of an appetite to invest in R&D, and as a result, innovation is stifled, and this becomes even more pronounced for SMEs that face the 'liability of smallness'. However, as the above literature and cases highlighted, there are pay offs from innovation, and innovation doesn't always mean investing huge amounts of money into new products, or processes, but can also be about innovating the everyday things, for example as Milk Co had stated that "we are always open to trying new things".

The results indicated that 29 out of the 35 SMEs studied demonstrated that they adopted 'incremental' innovation, where they kept changing existing business activities progressively, irrespective of the type (product, service, product/service process, market or business) of innovation they did adopt, for example:

> From an innovative perspective we run clinical trials at an early stage for commercial sponsors. Also from that perspective there's a level of innovation but it's probably incremental.
>
> (Case 10: Biotech Co 4)

From a resourcing perspective, it may be more manageable for SMEs to conduct incremental innovations, as they are not so timely or costly to implement. The rest of the SMEs (6) were categorised into 'radical' innovation, as they adopted innovation in more disruptive ways:

> We've always changed steps. You do it for a while and then you start to work out where you want to be and it's quite a big change so we've evolved our business model in a big step where we moved away from being a provider of services to others to closing the doors and now licensing in technology and raising our own capital and doing it for ourselves. So that was a big change.
>
> (Case 22: Medical Equip Co)

The above findings are interesting, as it concurs with the topical news (Deeb, 2014; Charam and Lafley, 2008). For the SMEs who adopted 'radical' innovation they in general focused on business model innovation and new technology or processes innovation with unprecedented performance features and created a dramatic change that transformed existing markets, or created a new business model. They did explore new technology although uncertainty was high for them. For the SMEs who were classified as using 'radical' innovation they had used a new business concept in the market and applied these new business concepts or models to the Chinese market which helped them with establishing a successful business.

In summary, the SMEs investigated in this study utilised mostly 'incremental' approaches to innovation, as opposed to radical approaches (Henderson and Clark, 1994) in their internationalisation to the Chinese market. As previous research indicates, firms, and more specifically SMEs, are less likely to engage in radical innovation because it is costly and requires a lot of resources. However, what is probably more manageable for SMEs is engaging in 'incremental' innovations so as to improve products, services and processes, as what a number of participants have suggested: any innovation is a good innovation. Research indicates that these progressive changes can significantly increase business performance (Sundbo, 1998). It can be considered as a series of improvements introduced which help maintain or improve competitive position overtime. On the contrary, a radical or disruptive innovation is one that has a significant impact on economic activity of firms in the market where the firm is located and it concerns complete disruptions to the existing operations and requires a change in the business model (Gadrey, Gallouj and Weinstein, 1995). Radical innovation entails the introduction of radical new products, but also high uncertainty with high risks.

However, even though the study's results do not confirm this observation, it demonstrates that radical innovation is being adopted by SMEs who are offering innovative services to the Chinese market. The incremental innovation approach was being adopted by SMEs who adopted all innovation types, products, process, marketing and business, however notably and interestingly 'radical' innovation was adopted mainly by SMEs who did business service type of innovations.

The value of innovation in the Chinese market: standardisation or adaptation

A standout theme that emanated from the interviews was that these SMEs innovations were not necessarily accepted by the Chinese market for a range of reasons, and therefore it either made it difficult for the firm to offer the innovation to the Chinese market, which meant that firms were unsuccessful with that innovation, or required them to be adapted.

Two of the exporters (Security Co and Medical Equip Co) had difficulties with selling their innovations to the Chinese market due to differences in the Chinese context and the fact that Chinese technologies did not meet the standards that the products offered by Security Co needed to operate effectively, as the following quotation indicates:

> So we do see more stated technical performances claimed in China that aren't backed up by practical reality that you probably don't see elsewhere. That might happen elsewhere but probably not some of the markets we've seen and we've seen a lot.
>
> (Case 5: Security Co)

Medical Equip Co SME was of the opinion that innovation in China was risky as local firms/people/consumers, in general, are not willing to go out of their comfort zones to be innovative or purchase innovative products or use innovative services, which is indicated in the following quote:

> Innovation can be seen as risky in China if it has not been done before here. I think it really comes down to the people seeing innovation as risky and if it is more expensive I think it really challenges some people to push for it because they probably don't want to go out of their comfort zone and take that risk.
>
> (Case 4: Medical Equip Co)

As the quotation suggests, SMEs take risks in introducing innovative products or services as customers are not willing to accept such products or services immediately. In addition, the quote suggests that the Chinese consumer is risk averse, which is supported by the Hofstede concept that Asian cultures score on high on uncertainty avoidance (Itim International 2017). A similar view was expressed by a Biotech Co 2, who believed that China had not matured yet compared with the rest of the developed world in the pharmaceutical industry, which posed a challenge:

> In the pharmaceutical industry, especially in China, there is still a serious lack of real innovation in terms of technical knowledge.
>
> (Case 9: Biotech Co 2)

According to the firm, a lack of innovation in the market provided them an opportunity to introduce innovative processes to the market without significant competition from the local market. This difference in perceptions around innovation had also caused problems for a firm charging a higher price:

> The typical wash plant in China, it's a lot larger footprint, it probably uses different equipment which is seen as probably not high tech or what is available on the market but it is very common in China. It's looking at different areas of the wash plant.
>
> (Case 16: Resources Co)

A few SMEs, in particular a design consultancy firm, found that it was almost impossible to be innovative with their products/services as a majority of their Chinese clients/customers did not appreciate innovation but they did appreciate lower prices and shorter delivery times. Incorporating environmentally friendly and sustainable solutions to their products/services that provide long term benefits were not acceptable in general terms by the Chinese clients and customers:

> So (design) innovation is very hard to actually get in China because they work on the theory that if I change how I build something then it's going to take me longer to build and it will cost me more money at the beginning so they've been rabbiting on about being a dream, great buildings and that is all rubbish. They're not interested in spending money because they know they can sell it anyway so introducing innovation into design is actually quite hard because they don't really see the value in it.
>
> (Case 19: Architect Co 1)

The firm operating in China with this understanding hence designed mainly with a focus on cost and time effectiveness. It was interesting that innovations may not always make a firm successful in the Chinese market, i.e. it would be expected that innovation would make the SME more successful in the market, but this did not appear to be the case. It was found in this instance that innovative products/services were not always welcomed or accepted by the Chinese market, or that cultural/institutional context effects influenced the ability to provide these innovative services/products in the Chinese market. Future researchers are encouraged to investigate these issues to determine whether this is relevant for other contexts, or whether this issue is specific to China.

Conclusion

The results demonstrate that all Australian SMEs investigated used innovation in their internationalisation process to the Chinese market, and as the literature indicates there are a number of advantages that come to firms when they offer various types of innovation. The findings also demonstrate that taking an innovative approach in the things that firms do will help them, whether it be their approach, their products, processes or others. These results suggest that there is an important role played by innovation for these firms in their internationalisation. The results also provide evidence that innovation and internationalisation are closely linked and depended on each other. SMEs' internationalisation to China significantly relied on innovation they offered to the Chinese market, but the implementation of innovation in the Chinese market could be problematic, because of the non-acceptance of new ideas/products, or new features of products that the Chinese did not want to pay for. It suggests that whilst innovation can provide advantages to firms, in foreign markets, these innovations may be seen as a liability of foreignness (LOF), which causes difficulties for the firms to try and sell their products to local markets. Therefore, it is important for firms to do appropriate research on the foreign market conditions to determine whether the innovation will in fact be accepted by the foreign market, given different cultural and institutional conditions. Firms should hence take a contingency approach when internationalising their innovations to the Chinese market.

References

Acs, Z. J., and Audretsch, D. B. (1990). *Innovation and Small Firms.* Cambridge, MA: MIT Press.

Australian Bureau of Statistics. (2012). Barriers to innovation, www.abs.gov.au/aus stats/abs@.nsf/Products/8167.0~201011~Main+Features~Barriers+to+Innovati on+and+General+Business+Activities+or+Performance?OpenDocument, retrieved on 14 August 2013.

Australian Geographic. (2017). 20 Australian inventions that changed the world, www.australiangeographic.com.au/topics/history-culture/2010/06/australian-inventions-that-changed-the-world/, retrieved on 9 July 2017.

Australian Government. (2012). Australia in the Asian century white paper, http://asiancentury.dpmc.gov.au/white-paper, retrieved 16 November 2014.

Australian Government. (2016). Global innovation strategy. https://industry.gov.au/innovation/GlobalInnovationStrategy/index.html, retrieved on 19 July 2017.

Australian Manufacturing Council. (1995). *The Innovation Cycle: Practical Tips From Innovative Firms.* Melbourne: Australian Manufacturing Council.

Boermans, M., and Roelfsema, H. (2016). Small firm internationalization, innovation and growth. *International Economic Policy*, 13, 283–296.

Boso, N., and Cadogan, J. W. (2012). Entrepreneurial orientation and market orientation as drivers of product innovation success: A study of exporters from a developing economy. *International Small Business Journal*, 31:1, 57–81.

Capon, N., Farley, J. U., and Hoenig, S. (1990). Determinants of financial performance: A meta analysis. *Management Science*, 36:10, 1143–1159.

Commonwealth of Australia. (2011). *Key Statistics Australian Small Business.* Australian Government, Department of Innovation, Industry, Science, and Research.

Crick, D., and Spence, M. (2005). The internationalisation of 'high performing' UK high-tech SMEs: A study of planned and unplanned strategies. *International Business Review*, 14:2, 167–185.

Davidson. (2017). Why is China beating the US at innovation, www.usatoday.com/story/money/2017/04/17/why-china-beating-us-innovation/100016138/, retrieved on 18 June 2017.

Deeb, G. (2014). The 5 reasons that big companies struggle with innovation, www.forbes.com/sites/georgedeeb/2014/01/08/the-five-reasons-big-companies-struggle-with-innovation/#1125615a2958, retrieved on 17 July 2017.

Doloreux, D., and Laperrie're, A. (2014). Internationalisation and innovation in the knowledge-intensive business services. Service Business, 8, 635–657. doi:10.1007/s11628-013-0211-0.

Drucker, P. F. (1998). The discipline of innovation. *Harvard Business Review*, November–December.

Erramilli, M. K., and Rao, C. P. (1990). Choice of foreign market entry modes by service firms: role of market knowledge. *Management International Review*, 30:2, 135–150.

Foster, R. N. (1986). *Innovation, the Attacker's Advantage*. New York: Summit.

Gadrey, J., Gallouj, F., and Weinstein, O. (1995). New modes of innovation. How service benefits industry. *International Journal of Service Industry Management*, 3:4, 16.

Harris, R., and Li, Q. C. (2008). Evaluating the contribution of exporting to UK productivity growth: Some microeconomic evidence. *World Economy*, 31:2, 212–235.

Higón, D. A., and Driffield, N. (2010). Exporting and innovation performance: Analysis of the annual Small Business Survey in the UK. *International Small Business Journal*, 29:1. 4–24.

Huber, G. (1991). Organizational learning: The contributing processes and the literature. *Organization Science*, 2, 88–115.

Itim International. (2017). Geert Hofstede – China, https://geert-hofstede.com/china.html, retrieved on 10 July 2017.

Kafouros, M. I., Buckley, P. J., Sharp, J. A., and Wang, C. (2008). The role of internationalization in explaining innovation performance. *Technovation*, 28:1/2, 63–74.

King, Wood & Mallesons. (2016). China's 13th five year plan: Innovation, internet plus, new media and information technology, www.kwm.com/en/au/knowledge/insights/china-13th-5-year-plan-innovation-technology-media-internet-plus-20160414.

Kunntu, A., and Torkeli, L. (2015). Service innovation and internationalisation in SMEs: Implications for growth and performance. *Management Revue*, 26:2, 83–100.

Kylläheiko, K., Jantunen, A., Puumalainen, K., Saarenketo, S., and Tuppura, A. (2011). Innovation and internationalization as growth strategies: The role of technological capabilities and appropriability. *International Business Review*, 20:5, 508–520.

Lafley, A. G., and Charam, R. (2008). *The Game Changer: How You Can Drive Revenue and Profit Growth With Innovation*. New York: Crown Business.

Li, H., and Atuagene-Gima, K. (2001). Product innovation strategy and the performance of new technology ventures in China. *Academy of Management Journal*, 44:6, 1123–1134.

Lin, Y-Y. C., and Chen, Y-C. M. (2007). Does innovation lead to performance? An empirical study of SMEs in Taiwan. *Management Research News*, 30:2, 115–132.

Love, J. H., and Roper, S. (2015). SME innovation, exporting and growth: A review of existing evidence. *International Small Business Journal*, 33:1, 28–48.

Mazzarol, T. (2015). Will the National innovation and science agenda deliver Australia a world class national innovation system? System deliver a https://theconversation.com/will-the-national-innovation-and-science-agenda-deliver-australia-a-world-class-national-innovation-system-52081.

McKern. (2017). Disruptive Asia, innovative China and what it means for Australia, www.afr.com/leadership/innovation/disruptive-asia-innovative-china-and-what-it-means-for-australia-20170608-gwn8ks.

Murray, R., and Edwards, R. (2010). Innovation roles in SME internationalisation. International *Conference on Management Science & Engineering* (17th) November, pp. 24–26, Melbourne, Australia.

O'Cass, A., and Weerawardena, J. (2009). Examining the role of international entrepreneurship, innovation and international market performance in SME internationalisation. *European Journal of Marketing*, 43:11/12, 1325–1348.

OECD. (2017). Gross domestic spending on R&D, https://data.oecd.org/rd/gross-domestic-spending-on-r-d.htm, retrieved on 10 July 2017.

Organisation for Economic Cooperation and Development (OECD). (1997). *The Measurement of Scientific and Technological Activities: Proposed Guidelines for Collecting and Interpreting Technological Innovation Data*. Brussel: European Commission.

Porter, M. E. (1990). The competitive advantage of nation. *Harvard Business Review*, March-April, 73–93.

Pratali, P. (2003). Strategic management of technological innovations in the small to medium enterprise. *European Journal of Innovation Management*, 6:1, 18–31.

Rammer, C., and Schmiele, A. (2008). *Drivers and Effects of Internationalising Innovation by SMEs*. Leibniz Information Centre for Economics. Centre for European Economic Research.

Ripollés Meliá, M., Blesa Pérez, A., and Roig Dobón, S. (2010). The influence of innovation orientation on the internationalisation of SMEs in the service sector. *The Service Industrial Journal*, 30:5, 777–791.

Schumpeter, J. A. (1934). *The Theory of Economic Development*. Cambridge, MA: Harvard Economic Studies.

Siedschlag, I., and Zhang, X. (2010). Internationalisation of firms and their innovation and productivity. *Economics of Innovation and New Technology*, 24:3, 183–203.

Soderquist, K. (1996). Managing innovation in SMES: A comparison of companies in the UK, France and Portugal. *International Journal of Technology Management*, 12:3, 291–305.

Stringer, R. (2000). How to manage radical innovation. *California Management Review*, 42:4, 70–88.

Sundbo, J. (1998). *The Theory of Innovation: Entrepreneurs, Technology and Strategy*. Cheltenhman, UK: Edward Elgar.

Tian, G. (2007). *Managing International Business in China*. Cambridge: Cambridge University Press.

Varadarajan, P. R., and Jayachandran, S. (1999). Marketing strategy: An assessment of the state of the field and outlook. *Academy of Marketing Science Journal*, 27:2, 120–144.

Weerawardena, J. (2003). The role of marketing capability in innovation-based competitive strategy. *Journal of Strategic Marketing*, 11:1, 15–35.

4 Building networks in a foreign environment

Introduction

As small and medium-sized enterprises (SMEs) face barriers in internationalisation, and a lack of resources, one way to overcome these barriers is through the utilisation of networks, contacts and social capital. This begs the question 'what networks and social capital do SMEs utilise to assist with internationalisation?', and 'how does this assist in overcoming liabilities of foreignness (LOFs) and creating advantage in the foreign environment?' In this chapter, how networks assist in overcoming the LOFs will be described, first by a review of the literature and then by an analysis of the participants' responses. The chapter will then consider how these networks created competitive advantage for these SMEs in the foreign market.

Literature review

The review of the literature is divided into four sections: networks and LOF, network process, social networks, networks and innovation and government support networks. Each of these sections will examine the literature from a different perspective to identify various roles of networks in internationalisation.

Networks and liability of foreignness

The extant literature confirms the importance of international networks in providing information about international business practices and institutional knowledge; helping stimulate awareness of foreign market opportunities and identifying foreign exchange partners; providing legitimacy and attractiveness of the internationalising firm and promoting moral obligation within the network of partners (Boehe, 2011; Elodie and Caroline, 2012; Schweizer, 2013; Musteen, Datta and Butts, 2014). The use of networks by small enterprises has received much attention in the literature (Coviello, 2006).

Firms use their social networks to achieve their strategic objectives (Nahapiet and Ghoshal, 1998). SMEs link internal and external resources in networks to pursue strategic objectives such as entering a new market (Blomstermo, 42004;

Coviello and Munro, 1997; Moen, 2002; Sharma and Blomstermo, 2003). Networks provide SMEs access to resources in the international market, which enables them to overcome their isolation in the globalised market (Musteen, Francis and Datta, 2010; Hashim and Hassan, 2008; Rutashobya and Jaensson, 2004). Networks help SMEs to identify opportunities and support them with their internationalisation. The value of foreign country networks is determined by that country's specific advantages, where firms will leverage their internal and external resources to pursue strategic objectives (Rugman, Oh, and Lim, 2012). Consequently, the use of networks to support internationalisation may greatly differ by country.

A key point of interest has been the relational social capital that firms build as a way of creating opportunities and capabilities to grow beyond their home market (Prashantham and Dhanaraj, 2010). Internationalisation networks may be inherited or actively constructed by entrepreneurs. Ciravegna, Majano and Zhan (2014) argued that the analysis of network building mechanisms, however, is limited and more empirical research in this area is required. Hohenthal, Johanson, and Johanson (2014) confirm this by noting that there are many qualitative case studies describing the process but few articles that have analysed the process and treated the network as a dynamic phenomenon (Fletcher, 2011; Guercini and Runfola, 2010; Sharma and Blomstermo, 2003).

Network strategy is the deliberate set of objectives and activities undertaken to build various types of relationships and capabilities, in order to enter foreign markets (Hohenthal et al., 2014). Qualitative studies from Coviello (2006) and Coviello and Munro (1997) have identified the importance of building the relationship first in the foreign market. Relationships are important as they bring knowledge and opportunity (Chetty, Ojala, and Leppäaho, 2015; Meyar and Skak, 2002). An international network strategy for an SME will have the goal of supporting and accelerating its internationalisation and success. It will lead to increased resource commitments in foreign markets. From a resource perspective, international networks provide SMEs with access to critical resources.

If a foreign SME does not have the support of a local network in the foreign country network, they will find it more difficult to internationalise than an SME located within a network (Johanson and Vahlne, 2009). The lack of network support creates a LOF (cost of foreignness in the country, also considered in Chapter 7). Networks help eliminate their LOF or reduce the risks and liabilities that international businesses face when they internationalise (Falize and Coeurderoy, 2012). Lu and Beamish (2001) suggest that forming alliances with local partners who can overcome a deficiency in host country knowledge is an effective strategy for managing internationalisation. For example, Handfield et al. (1999) determined that SMEs with technologically advanced suppliers have higher innovation potential.

Network building can commence with encounters with business partners, clients and suppliers. This simple form of interaction allows an internationalising SME to understand the market, gain insight into that industry's standard business practices and build trust (Wilson and Mummalaneni, 1990). Trade associations and government bodies can also form useful network members and assist internationalising SMEs through joint activities and knowledge development (Spence, 2000).

Falize and Coeurderoy (2012) argue that networks reduce the risks and liabilities that international businesses face when they internationalise. According to Zizah et al. (2010) networking or relationships influence the awareness of international opportunities, which they suggested is the most influential factor for internationalisation. Mohammad and Filho (2009) similarly found that network relationships will determine the pattern of internationalisation for the SME and the success will reflect the ability to maintain international networks.

Network process

Network processes are a key contributor to the building of resources, knowledge and opportunity identification in a foreign market (Meyar and Skak, 2002). Mohammad, Hossein and Staffan (2012) found that foreign market networking processes play a crucial role in developing competitive advantage. They allow foreign organisations to test ideas, develop trust, collect information, identify new opportunities and specialise in specific opportunities (Coviello and Munro, 1997). The capability to develop and exploit networks is one of the strongest predictors of internationalisation success for SMEs (Chetty and Campbell-Hunt, 2004; Etemad, 2004; Harris and Wheeler, 2005). Gesmer et al. (2012) suggested that innovative SMEs should use cooperation with partners to reduce resource based constraints, either by joint ventures where equity is shared, or through a contractual arrangement without equity, such as licensing or management contracts, to obtain the resources that may be required.

Meyer and Skak (2002) suggested that the international SME network process can be described from three perspectives: the dynamics of entry, events in and expansion of the network and motivations that increase commitment. Audrey et al. (2006) found, however, that SME owner-managers in Australia and Northern Ireland face similar challenges in developing, passing on and encouraging the networking activities within their organisation. The issues included transference of trust, lack of networking competence among staff, hesitancy of owner-managers to let go, the need to develop commercial skills of employees, a reluctance of staff to assume networking responsibilities and the need to match staff to clients/customers (Audrey et al., 2006).

Social networks

Networking – social, internal or external – is a more valuable resource for competitiveness in the Chinese market than managerial skills and/or technological resources (Xia, Qiu and Zafar, 2007; Al-Laham and Souitaris, 2008). Zhou, Wu and Luo (2007) suggested that social networks will help internationally oriented SMEs to internationalise more rapidly and successfully. The social dynamics standpoint of the internationalisation process also confirms this observation

(Ellis, 2000; Harris and Wheeler, 2005). Lianxi, Wei-ping and Xueming (2007) determined that home-based social networks also assist with internationalisation by providing knowledge of foreign market opportunities, advice and experiential learning and referral trust and solidarity. International entrepreneurs would need interpersonal ties and social interactions to obtain information, such as knowledge of potential market opportunities, personal advice and experiential learning and referral trust and solidarity, in order for them to lead a successful internationalisation.

SMEs that operate within social networks experienced a more rapid and experiential learning advantage. SMEs that are born-global through network resources demonstrate the importance of the speed and scope of informal social networks (Chetty and Campbell-Hunt, 2004; Etemad, 2004; Harris and Wheeler, 2005). Examination of the effect of networks on the internationalisation of born-global SMEs will provide a better understanding of how this process occurs (Oviatt and McDougall, 1994) and will inform the literature on network capitalism across different countries (Redding, 1990; Boisot and Child, 1996; Oleinik, 2004).

Networks and innovation

According to Chetty et al. (2010) networks vary depending upon the level of internationalisation and the type of innovation that the SME is utilising. SMEs with limited network relationships will internationalise and innovate incrementally, but those with diverse network relationships will adopt radical internationalisation and innovation. SMEs tend to compensate for fewer internal resources available for innovation and for internationalisation (by acquiring external resources and complementary assets Chetty and Wilson, 2003; Teece, 1996) through their network relationships. These network relationships include the firm's customers, suppliers, competitors, government and educational institutions (Johanson and Mattsson, 1988). Network relationships also provide the SME with diversity of knowledge, a key ingredient for recognizing potential new innovations (Möller et al., 2005), and opportunities in international markets (Johanson and Vahlne, 2009). According to Håkansson and Snehota (2006) all business takes place in a network context and so there is an inter-dependency amongst members of this network, which was also stated by Johanson and Mattsson (1988).

Partanen, Chetty and Rajala (2014) identified the brokerage role of agents who help link up the firm to unconnected networks. This brokerage role provides insight on how agents are used to find new customer leads for SMEs adopting radical innovation and to find new distributor and distributor partner leads in incremental innovations. Gellynck, Vermeire and Viaene (2007) determined that international businesses can gain innovation competencies from searching for networks in small regions of the host country, as well as across the whole host country. When the host country is large, as in the case of China, different regions are likely to offer different networks.

Johanson and Vahlne's (2009) argument that an organisation's internationalisation is influenced by its networks suggests that internationalising SMEs will be more successful with their internationalisation when their partners are committed to assisting the business to develop through internationalisation. For example, SMEs are likely to internationalise by following customers or suppliers to the foreign market (Child and Rodrigues, 2008; Harris and Wheeler, 2005; Crick and Spence, 2005). Other networks that can provide formal support for internationalisation include government trade and investment bodies, chambers of commerce and industry associations. Internationalising through membership of the supply-chains of large organisations can provide another form of network which influences the internationalisation mode of the SME. Whilst this approach to internationalisation would reduce the risks and costs, it would also lead to a high level of future dependency on the supply chain (Al-Laham and Souitaris, 2008).

Government support networks

Governmental support is important for internationalising SMEs (Mort and Weerawardena, 2006). Success with internationalisation for SMEs has been found to be the result of engagement with public institutions to fostering international competitiveness of the companies (Guillermo et al., 2014). It normally forms a central component of their knowledge development and international expansion (Meyar and Skak, 2002). Yu-Ching, Kuo-Pin and Chwo-Ming (2006) found that host country governments can influence firms' FDI decisions and the more incentives a host country offers the more inward investment it will receive. O'Gorman et al. (2011) found that export promotion organisations (EPOs) played an important role in identifying foreign opportunities and customers, facilitating introductions to international customers, providing foreign market knowledge and as a resource provider. Despite this, they determined that only 7 percent of internationalised SMEs used available support mechanisms (Falize and Coeurderoy, 2012).

Analysis results

The role of networks was described extensively by the participants. An analysis of the number of responses and number of participants making that reference is shown in Table 4.1. Interestingly, the participants representing importing and exporting companies contributed 10 percent or less of the responses to any of the terms (with the exception of government support – 18 percent). The 10 percent or less response rate for most of the network terms was disproportionate to the number of companies involved as 21 percent of the companies represented by the participants had entered the market as importers or exporters. This suggests that, possibly with the exception of government support, these network factors were predominantly of interest to the WOFE and BIC entry mode participants. As Table 4.1 also shows, government support and the relationship between LOF and networks appeared to be of interest to both WOFE and BIC market entrants. Association networks and networks in general were of particular interest to WOFEs and social capital was of particular interest to BICs.

Table 4.1 Number of references and number of participants identifying network terms

Network term	References	Sources	Case no	No from import/ export
Government support	311	34	8, 10, 17, 20, 21, 28, 29, 30, 33, 34,	56–18%
Association networks	198	33	8, 10, 12, 14, 24, 28, 32,	19–10%
Networks	159	32	8, 10, 12, 14, 24, 28, 32	13–8%
Social capital	131	27	27, 28, 29, 30, 34	9–7%
Networks and liabilities of foreignness	314	33	8, 10, 12, 14, 16, 21, 26, 27, 28, 29, 30, 32, 34	19–6%

Network term	References	Sources
Government support	311	34
BICs	132	10
WOFES	117	13
Exporters	46	4
Association networks	198	33
WOFEs	164	15
Networks	159	32
WOFEs	126	14
Social capital	131	27
BICs	111	8
Networks and liabilities of foreignness	314	33
WOFEs	137	12
BICs	158	10

Entry Mode	References	Sources
BICs	401	10
Government support	132	10
Social capital	111	8
Networks and liabilities of foreignness	158	10
WOFEs	544	17
Government support	117	13
Association networks	164	15
Networks	126	14
Networks and liabilities of foreignness	137	12
Exporters	60	4
Government support	46	4

The large number of responses from the participants confirmed that networks factors were critical to the participant's internationalisation. The interviews indicated that these SMEs utilised networks or connections (including guanxi) not only entering for China, but also maintaining their operations. A participant from the construction management industry summarised this point succinctly:

> I think in China currently networks and guanxi is definitely priority. Maybe it's the culture.
>
> (Case 18: Build Co)

The participants indicated that networks have significant influence in their internationalisation process. The dyadic relationship between parties is influenced by the partners' other relationships as they provide opportunities as well as constraints (Anderson et al., 1994). These networks help them to enter China and find opportunities in the market to survive. As what Mainela and Puhakka (2011) state, networks provide information on business opportunities and business partners in international markets and transfer general market knowledge. Networks provide introduction and access to far located or to unknown possible business partners. Networks create access to international marketing networks, such as distribution networks and legitimate the firm in the market. Networks provide a basis for interacting with others, thus making it possible for a firm to learn and develop skills needed in internationalisation. Finally, networks may also inhibit the international growth possibilities for the firm.

The SMEs used different types of networks, formal to informal, government agencies to make personal contacts. The literature suggests that SMEs engage in several types of networks, each with different degrees of involvement (Seifert, Child and Rodrigues, 2011). Lechner and Dowling (2003) identify five different types of networks that firms use at different development stages: social networks; reputational networks; "coopetition" (cooperating with competitors); marketing networks and knowledge, innovation and technology. Varamaki and Vesalainen (2003) provide five different types of networks that differ in their degree of cooperation; ranging in order from loosest to tightest cooperation, these are development circle, loose cooperative circle, project group, joint venture and a joint unit. As per the analysis of results, not only formal business relations but personal or social relations play a key role in the internationalisation process. Some researchers (Chetty and Wilson, 2003; Lechner and Dowling, 2003) have highlighted the importance of social relationships in SME networks. These social relationships provide the SMEs with information, finance, access to other networks and reputation.

SMEs rely routinely on network relationships to help them overcome the obstacles associated with entering new markets. It can offer some degree of protection against the risks associated with foreignness, newness and smallness. These new insights have stimulated enquiry into social capital, which may be defined as social relationships that confer an actual or potential benefit (Naphiet and Ghoshal, 1994). The theory of social capital suggests that firms create, and are embedded in, a web of relationships which may offer access to resources and opportunities of different natures. Different meanings have been attached to social capital. Some researchers view it in terms of resources which may be available to the firm through participation in networks (Coleman, 1988; Nahapiet and Ghoshal, 1998), while others conceive it in terms of the unique characteristics that define loosely connected social structures (Bourdieu, 1980; Coleman, 1988; Putnam, 1993). There are several sources indicating how social capital can trigger and foster internationalisation (Johanson and Mattsson, 1988). The role of networks in the internationalisation of SMEs focused on the benefits of such networks, with only a few (e.g., Chetty and Agndal, 2007; Coviello and Munro, 1997) addressing the potential downside of networks in the context of SME internationalisation. Contrary to the earlier quotation, however, another participant expressed the opinion that guanxi (i.e. networks or connections) is not that important in China today:

> That networking side of things five to 10 years ago was extremely important in China though networks are probably not as important as they used to be now.
>
> (Case 1: Furniture Co)

Most SMEs are able to reach international markets only through the help of third parties, which vary from individual agents to institutions that provide formal support for export activities. These involve the governmental Trade and Investment bodies, Chamber of Commerce and industry associations. One common way in which SMEs may access foreign markets is through piggy-backing on MNCs (Child and Rodrigues, 2008). On this basis, certain roles for networks in the internationalisation of firms can be suggested (see also Harris and Wheeler, 2005).

On the other hand, an important role in entrepreneurial networks is played by brokers linking the members of different networks (cf. Granovetter, 1973). The brokers facilitate actions of entrepreneurs by increasing the reachability and connectedness of people with complementary interests. Aldrich and Zimmer (1986) suggest venture capitalists, for example, to act as brokers since they are able to connect entrepreneurs to supporters like technical experts, management consultants or financial planners. Government advisers, in turn, although noted as promising, have in practice been seen in only minor roles (e.g., Crick and Jones, 2000). A network with many weak ties facilitates the capitalising on opportunities because through weak ties the entrepreneur is likely to receive more diverse information. Information about new products or services will spread more widely through strong ties (Mainela and Puhakka, 2011).

The traditional view of entry that is overcoming various barriers is becoming less important than internationalising undertaken to strengthen a firm's position in the network (Johanson and Vahlne, 2009). It is argued that existing business relationships make it possible to identify and exploit opportunities and have a considerable impact on the particular geographical market a firm will decide to enter and on which mode to use.

The analysis of the survey responses shown in Table 4.1 suggests that the internationalisation entry mode will influence the type of network that the SME develops. To examine this theme in detail, the interview results are presented in the section below according to the entry mode structures identified in this research, importation, exportation, WOFEs and BICs.

Networks used by importer SMEs

All three SMEs involved with importing goods and services from China stated that networking and connections were a vital element in their businesses. A chemical products importer suggested physical visits are vital in their networking.

> Talking physical networks, it is important finding contacts. For instance, visit factories physically to meet those who can either work with us, either to supply or to distribute.
>
> (Case 3: Chemical Co)

The importing SMEs were also able to use social capital to develop their relationships. A number of them found that their Australian cultural background provided them with initial social capital, on which they could build business networks. An importing furniture SME explained this as follows:

> Certainly within China relationships are a very big part of business. They like Australians, they like the way we do business and a lot of the priorities you get within a company in China are through the relationship that you have with them.
>
> (Case 1: Furniture Co)

Another of the participants representing an importer SME suggested that state agencies provide networking opportunities for new firms entering China. Two out of three importer SMEs used state based government support to help in finding connections when they made their first entry to China. One used a government trade organisation (Australia) and another importing SME received support from a government trade mission. The remaining importer SME used trade shows and exhibitions in facilitating first entry to China market. Two of these importers use agents in China for their business activities, as shown in Table 4.2.

Networks used by exporting SMEs

All four SMEs who were involved with exporting activities argued that networks or 'connections' were important in doing business in China. They were also extensively involved in making contacts to establish networks. The exporter SME

Table 4.2 Network adoption by importer SMEs

Case number	Pseudonym	Business type	Network in entry	Network in operation	Role of networks
1	Furniture Co.	Manufacturer/Distributor	Initial contacts via Austrade, State council	Use local agents	Facilitate entry, connect with local manufacturers
2	Rubber Co.	Manufacturer/Distributor	Initial contacts via trade shows and exhibitions	Link with the innovative networks	Connect with local manufacturers
3	Chemical Co.	Manufacturer/Distributor	Initial contacts via super trade mission of Victorian government	Use local agents	Facilitate entry, connect with local manufacturers

below used trade shows, trade missions and exhibitions in establishing initial contacts in the market.

> Our initial contacts were through trade shows, exhibitions, occasionally through internet. No local partners or representative.
>
> (Case 6: Pneumatic Co)

This firm used innovative networks such as professional groups and high-tech parks in building relationships with local businesses and they suggested that relationships with local authorities was helping to establish their business, however, when interviewed this firm was still experiencing a lack of success, possibly due to the limited network development as described below:

> We sought to link in or build into any relationships with Chinese innovative networks; we just [got] involved with a lot of high tech parks and things like that throughout China – what I've also done is being involved in a couple of professional groups, network groups with the concept of forming clusters and getting involved in local organisations that way but that hasn't gained any traction either.
>
> (Case 6: Pneumatic Co)

One of the exporting SMEs had entered China via a 'connection' they had (customer driven) and another entered the Chinese market using a network or connection with one of their MNE clients:

> We've looked at innovation networks in China, but we've never really seriously thought to go that way. We were approached by some of our client (MNE), we've done work there (China) for them (client).
>
> (Case 4: Security Co)

This participant explained that they built strong relationships in the early stage of sales. They suggested that developing relationships in China was far more complicated than in western countries. An Equipment Service firm confirmed this by suggesting that there is no straight way of entering the Chinese market without connections:

> You don't get anything done in China unless you involve yourself with other people within China because the whole market is really developed around relationships with people. There is no straight way of jumping into the market. It's not what you know it's who you know.
>
> (Case 5: Equipment Co)

The participant further stated that their business relied upon relationships or partnerships. This SME attended trade missions with the Australian Government and used Chinese based Association consultants. Another exporter reported on attending trade shows held as Australia-China cooperation to develop networks, but found it was a very slow process:

> We've done a trade mission and Austrade. I think maybe there's always been a big promise of a lot of relationships developing from China but it's been very slow so it's not a market that we see is going to be a big game changer for us in the immediate term.
>
> (Case 7: BioTech Co 3)

Table 4.3 summarises the use of networks/connections by exporting SMEs in entering and operating businesses in the Chinese market.

Networks used by WOFEs

All 18 SMEs in the WOFE category stated that networks were crucial and used networks and/or connections to enter China. According to a medical research and biotechnology WOFE, relationships were important and without good relationships it was difficult to survive:

> One of the very strong differences in a business sense is that people in Australia will happily do business with people they don't get along with but that just doesn't happen in China. It's all built on having a good relationship and then you may or may not do business. It's a matter of making sure that those relationships are good or else there is no future.
>
> (Case 8: Biotech Co 1)

This participant also suggested that appreciating Chinese culture is a good way of building strong relationships; trust was another factor in building strong business relationships:

> It's important to understand the value of relationships and relationship building and the importance of sitting down over a meal and showing appreciation for Chinese culture.
>
> (Case 8: Biotech Co 1)

Networks based on contacts from prior work was another important form. One participant indicated that the network that they had made of local contacts through a previous job assisted them to enter the Chinese market:

> So that comes about as a result of a client in China coming here, we look at something for them, we work on it from here and so that creates an opportunity for us to open an operation in China and that's pretty well the kind of way that kind of connection works.
>
> (Case 19: Architect Co 1)

Table 4.3 Network adoption by exporter SMEs

Case number	Pseudonym	Business type	Network in entry	Network in operation	Role of networks
4	Security Co	Supply and Installation service	Entered via network opportunity (relationship with MNE)	Built strong relationships and trust at the early stage of their business to promote sales.	Facilitate entry, marketing (sales promotion) support
5	Man Control Co.	Supply and maintenance service	Trade missions and VECCI consultants in China.	Use network groups to get contacts to get involved	Support service for entry and looking for marketing support with network groups (not success though)
6	Pneumatic Co.	Supply/install Hydraulic systems	Entry via (customer) connection	Use innovative networks such as High tech parks, professional groups	Facilitate entry, marketing (sales promotion) support
7	BioTech Co. 3	Clinical trials (service)	Initial contacts via Trade mission and Austrade	Word of mouth, attending trade shows by Australia-China bodies or government authorities and personnel level networks.	Support service for entry and looking for works via networks (recommendations)

Interestingly, however, some participants expressed the view that networks are not required for dealing with the Chinese government as the process is formalised. China offers a large range of opportunities for developing business networks and many of the participants were of the opinion that the networking opportunities available to them in China were better than those available in Australia, as the following quote indicates:

> Hong Kong is the largest community of expat Australians outside London and the network as well; networking opportunities are extraordinary in Hong Kong so in compared with Australia's head office in Brisbane.
>
> (Case 25: Meat Co)

Generating business opportunities was an important function for the networks of this group of participants. The more sophisticated organisations represented in the study developed network strategies and divided their networks into channels:

> We generate our business referrals and network. We are going to the networks and we are using different strategies.
>
> (Case 12: Accounting Co)

Indications of credibility and strength are also important in developing business networks in China. Many of the participants followed the Chinese practice of establishing impressive premises in order to support the development of their networks. This was summarised by one of the WOFE SMEs:

> The way to build credibility in China is to show your cash, to show that you are something of substance rather than just a maybe pretend.
>
> (Case 13: Vehicle Warranty Co)

Expertise and location choices, such as setting up in innovation hubs, are also factors which can influence the development of networks, according to the participants. One participant found that their expertise was a key factor in developing their business networks, as the following quote indicates:

> Architecture, it's usually a contact is made where somebody perceives you have an expertise. They approach you over that expertise and then we grab a hold of that opportunity and work on it. Some people develop things by being social with people and they make friends and those friends employ them. That's not really how we've done it.
>
> (Case 19: Architect Co 1)

Government support was also utilised by the WOFE SMEs in this study as contact information and to provide some social capital (due to the status of government connections in China) with which these organisations could build their business networks. A medical research and biotechnology WOFE SME in the study providing medical research services developed both personal and institutional type networks in China through a government trade agency (Austrade):

> Not only personal networks but institutional and corporate recognition are important. The Ministry of Health and people like that know us well enough and so when we talk to people, if they talk to people further up the food chain, they get positive reinforcement of working with us.
>
> (Case 8: Biotech Co 1)

Government and Association support was sufficient to enable some of these SMEs to connect with Chinese State Owned Enterprises (SOEs), although reputation as an international business was also a contributor. This was very important for some of the SMEs, for whom SOEs were their major customer group:

> A lot of our customers or clients in China would be SOEs. Essentially being an international company, all the major SOEs are willing to meet us and form a relationship with us. I suppose, you have the relationship building events and so forth and the presentations.
>
> (Case 16: Processing Co)

Participation in conferences and on industry boards was another approach taken by some of these SMEs to connect with appropriate customer groups. In addition to developing business networks, however, the participants also indicated that social relationships (guanxi) were essential for a continual flow of jobs:

> There are still areas where you need some guanxi. We got a contract; it was because we knew someone that we developed a relationship with who knew someone else who we had to trust.
>
> (Case 17: Metal Frame Co)

Developing social networks, however, seemed to be a slower process than the development of business opportunity networks, as the following quotation demonstrates:

> We want to expand our relationship in the Chinese market. I think we will spend another at least half a year or even a year to build a network here and get ourselves known to the market.
>
> (Case 12: Accounting Co)

Social networks in China can also be very complex, as a participant representing a printing company suggested:

> It's good to understand how things are running in China; even people's relationships are very complex here.
>
> (Case 23: Print Co)

Location factors can also affect the relative effect of social, compared to business networks for internationalisation success. One participant suggested that this is due to the different cultures in the different regions in China. This finding suggests that matching the selected location in China to the organisation's social and business network building skills may be an important success factor:

> So in the south east part of China it's more, the culture there is more important so where you say definitely personal relationship is the key. But like in Shanghai or the south, the network is important but the network doesn't have to be a very personal network; you don't have to build the personal relationship to do business. But if you go further inland, I agree the personal relationship is a key.
>
> (Case 9: Biotech Co 2)

To initiate the development of social networks, many of the WOFE SMEs relied on personal connections. One of the participants was able to use personal connections to rapidly establish their business in organic baby food for which there is a strong market demand in China:

> I'd actually had a friend, that we knew up here and she moved over to Pudong and she was really interested in helping us out so she kind of did a bit of legwork, went through trying to find good people to talk to there. To start with our business very much relied on distributors on local markets. We've got 22 distributors across China in different places.
>
> (Case 24: Milk Co)

Where relationships with the Chinese government are required, they can be difficult to maintain. The SMEs in the study reported that they relied on support from local companies to assist them, as the following quotation indicates:

> I think it's never possible for the individual to have a good governmental relationship. It's a different language, it is a different business culture here.
>
> (Case 14: Office Co)

Networks used by BICs

The BICs rated networks as being very important to the establishment of their business:

> Without feeling confident that I had the right networks, or at least a good network, I would not have gone out on my own. So, yes, I think networks in Asia are fundamental to anybody's business.
>
> (Case 32: Marketing Co)

The BICs in the study were substantial users of government, agency and personal contacts in the development of their networks. Some of these networks were extensions of their original networks in Australia, as the following quote indicates:

> I've got a network back in Australia, I've got a small network over here in China too – we can help clients here and we have a pretty good network here.
>
> (Case 30: Arbitration Co)

The BICs were more particular about the organisations which they allowed into their networks and how they were introduced. They used background checks and were also careful to use network building approaches with which they were familiar. Some of these SMEs preferred not to develop their networks using guanxi as they did not feel that they had sufficient control to produce the correct outcomes, as the following quotation indicates:

> In our business we've tried to avoid guanxi because I think most foreigners don't have it here. The nature of relationships vary from place to place even within China and I think it's not to say we don't have relationships but that kind of notion of Chinese guanxi.
>
> (Case 30: Arbitration Co)

The value of relationships as part of business networks was also considered to vary according to the industry and business structure by the BICs participating in the study. They all concurred, however, that relationships with government bodies, local associations and participating in conferences were important for the establishment of business networks. Despite the BIC's formal approach to the establishment of business networks, the networks themselves did not need to be formal as the following quotation indicates:

> I think informal networks are probably stronger and more relevant, more to the point.
>
> (Case 26: HR Consult Co)

Other sources of network building used by the BICs included entrepreneur organisations, engagement with the boards and meetings of local and global groups, sponsoring conferences and events, informal community relationships, home country associations and commercial events, as the following quotations indicate:

> I'm a member of the EO, Entrepreneurs Organisation globally, and there are about 50 members in Shanghai, 8000 in the world. EO has been very helpful because that's a very exclusive network of people to join, so it's quite expensive to join, you've got a requirement to join, it's not easy to fulfil but once you're in it's an awesome network globally. I'm part of Aust-Cham too.
>
> (Case 27: Social Media Co)

So not only was I a member of the Chamber but I was a founding chairperson of their media and marketing committee and so it's the networks that an organisation helps you create – as an organisation that is interested in helping you create networks. I mean the Chamber is a good starting point for anybody who's coming into Hong Kong and needs to connect with other organisations because they will facilitate introductions.

(Case 32: Marketing Co)

Interestingly, this group of SMEs did not choose to locate themselves in innovative zones, such as innovation hubs or science parks and did not rely on the proximity of other innovative organisations to build their business networks. Some of these SMEs even entered the market without prior networks or connections and built these during their start-up phase. The networks established in this way were created over long timeframes, as the following quotation indicates:

Network is very important, built up over 30 years. Also referral, networking here, word of mouth makes a difference. What we don't have the time or the resources at the moment to do is to really exploit social media.

(Case 28: Consult Co 1)

Supply chain relationships proved to be important for the BIC SMEs in the study, in many cases proving to be key network relationships for their organisation:

We've got good relationships with the logistics companies so they help us do it. But initially when you start the ball rolling it's we don't want to deal with those people, but once you start breaking the walls down and work together and they're happy with what you deliver, the relationships get easier but initially it's a nightmare.

(Case 35: Shop Co)

Social capital was again important for the development of these SMEs' networks. In many cases, the social capital that they developed provided them with unique opportunities, as the following quotation indicates:

There are jobs simply because of the relationship I've got with particularly one company in Shanghai. A lot of the jobs that I go to them with, if I was just anybody they'd say sorry we're not interested. But because we've got that connection that goes back such a long time and we've got a very close family connection with the owners of the factory and they just tell their staff that whatever 'G' wants just do it.

(Case 35: Shop Co)

Other members of the BIC segment of the sample held different views about the value of networks for this type of organisation. They offered a pragmatic perspective in which a business network was primarily based on mutual benefit, rather than trust, knowledge and cooperation as the motivations. This critical perspective offered in this quotation reflects a more clinical perspective about networks and network reliance.

> I'm going to have lower fees and I'm going to develop relationships with developers and stuff and then when I have a relationship I'll increase my fee, it doesn't happen. They're not interested in a relationship unless it benefits themselves. If it benefits you they'll think they're paying too much so your relationship is naff. It all comes down to money.
>
> (Case 34: Architect Co 3)

Discussion

The findings above confirmed the central role of networks in the internationalisation of the SMEs included in the study. These findings are now considered in relation to the literature. This discussion uses the structure adopted for the findings section and considers the findings above in relation to each of the organisational structures, WOFEs and BICs.

Importing SMEs

All importers entered the Chinese market using contacts via Australian authorities or contacts made via attending trade exhibitions. Their networks in the Chinese market were mainly local agents or links with local network services. The agents provided initial support by providing essential information about potential Chinese business partners and opportunities available in the Chinese market – otherwise unknown to them. This finding is consistent with the literature which has also determined that most SMEs are able to reach international markets only through the help of third parties (Rodrigues et al., 2012). These third parties include individual agents and institutions that provide formal support for international activities. Importing SMEs may belong to several networks which are more or less independent or which could also overlap in their specialties. These findings also extended Rodrigues et al. (2012), Agndal et al. (2008), Ellis (2000) and Raugh's (2001) findings that relevant networks for internationalising SMEs include agents, distributors, suppliers, professional and industry associations, customers, government trade and investment bodies, Chambers of Commerce and industry associations by confirming that these supply to importing international SMEs. These findings also confirmed that the importing SME's motivations were research access to information and market knowledge as suggested by the above research for internationalisation in general.

Most of the SMEs suggested that relationships with key actors, such as agents, customers and institutions at home and abroad helped to reduce costs. Since most of the importing SMEs knew little about China and its business environment, finding the appropriate partners, agents or representatives was crucial. Building trust with them became essential to reduce institutional, financial and agency risk (Child and Rodrigues, 2004). Some of these SMEs relied on their partners and agents to assist them to understand the Chinese legislation and tax systems and to deal with ethical situations.

The finding that these SMEs used trade exhibitions to find potential network partners in China was supported by Kontinen et al. (2011) who suggested that limited international ties will cause an SME to search for relevant contacts at international trade exhibitions or trade fairs. These SMEs found some support from home country government agencies in building their networks, but they were not sufficient for their needs, forcing them to participate in the other network building activities listed above.

Exporting SMEs

Exporter SMEs suggested that there is no straight way of entering the market without networks. All four exporter SMEs in this study stated that networks or 'connections' were key to their internationalisation. Exporting SMEs use exiting connections and/or trade mission support to initially establish their business and then formal and informal connections to build their business in China. This finding was consistent with Rodrigues and Child's (2012) finding that internationalising the SME's partners in their domestic environment can include export promotion agencies and other members of export clubs and in the foreign environment they can include agents, distributors and local equity-sharing partners.

These SMEs developed their local social capital and institutional support to help reduce the liability of newness they experienced as being relatively new market entrants. Local institutional support also provides valuable information regarding factors such as informal norms dealing with economic transactions and short-cuts to bureaucratic problems.

There was some diversity on the approaches taken by the four exporter SMEs in the sample. Two of the SMEs used trade shows, trade missions and exhibitions to build business networks and access resources such as information, whilst the other two focused on existing business relationships to build the networks. Developing business networks from existing relationships, such as customer relationships, has been previously identified in the literature (Child and Rodrigues, 2008). As with the importing SMEs, making connections through formal activities such as trade missions or existing business relationships reduced the liability of newness that these SMEs faced.

These SMEs invested more effort and resources in understanding their market. Network connections would have enabled them to access more market information and make a more accurate assessment of the risks they faced. This is consistent with Johanson and Vahlne's (2009) finding that internationalisation success depends on a firm's relationships and networks. They also noted that internationalising firms are likely to follow a partner abroad if that partner firm has a valuable network position in one or more foreign countries. The findings extend the literature by identifying its application to the case of SMEs and confirms the value of using existing business relationships to develop business networks in the combined context of the psychic distance and liabilities of smallness and newness that these SMEs faced.

Home country government departments were valuable in facilitating the development of networks for these SMEs, but although they transferred social capital, they included limited information. Thus, whilst the relationships were facilitated, the correct relationships are not necessarily developed. This finding qualifies O'Gorman and Evers's (2011) finding that export promotion organisations play an important role in information mediation for internationalisation as well as facilitating introductions to international customers and providing foreign market knowledge, by questioning the ability of these organisations to introduce the exported to the correct network partners.

The findings confirmed that networks comprising the correct connections were required for the exporter SMEs to be successful in China. This finding is consistent with Burt's (1992) structural hole theory that opinion and behaviour are more homogeneous within than between groups, so people connected across groups are more familiar with alternative ways of thinking and behaving which gives them more options to select from and synthesise and new ideas. Galkina and Chetty (2015) identified this potential problem by determining that internationalising entrepreneurs may network with interested partners, instead of selecting international partners according to predefined network goals.

WOFEs

The SMEs in WOFE category stated that networks were crucial irrespective of their industry (which was different to the response of the BIC SMEs). They used home country government support for their internationalisation, particularly for the identification of networks and the social capital required to facilitate network entry. These SMEs also indicated that social capital was important for assuring the flow of work and expanding business networks. This finding is consistent with that of Xia, Qiu and Zafar (2007) who determined that networks contain valuable resources which improve the performance of foreign firms in the Chinese market. It was also consistent with Spence's (2000) finding that trade associations and government bodies can assist SMEs in internationalisation and Mort and Weerawardena's (2006) finding that government and business association networks help SMEs to take advantage of opportunities. This finding also suggests that the WOFEs were the form of internationalised SME in China which gained the broadest benefit from business networks.

These SMEs also took an active role in government and professional associations to increase the level of benefit that they gained as well as the number of organisations with which they came into contact. This approach was quite different to the lower investment form SMEs (importer and exporter SMEs) which were passive consumers of government support and the BIC SMEs which were more selective in their involvement with institutional forms of support. These SMEs also extended their network engagement activities to involvements in conferences, as well as the development of informal relationships, particularly guanxi.

This group identified guanxi as a different form of networking to the approaches that they were familiar with in their home country (Australia).

These SMEs also indicated that understanding local culture and building trust were key factors in maintaining their network relationships. This finding would reflect the fact that these SMEs operated as subsidiaries of companies located in a psychically distant culture. These conditions would lead to a constant tension within the organisation between the culture in the host country and the home country culture, requiring an effort to maintain an understanding of the local culture in order to maintain credibility and eligibility for local networks. These SMEs placed less value on low investment sources of network contacts, such as exhibitions and tradeshows, but indicated that professional institution (and higher commitment) events were effective in supporting their network development. A number of these SMEs suggested that Hong Kong provided a concentration of high level network development opportunities, including strong support from Australia and China government institutions. These SMEs were particularly concerned with accessing resources through their networks to assist them with their interaction with the Chinese government.

These SMEs also identified the importance of understanding how the role of social capital varied across China, reflecting the different cultural conditions of different locations. This finding suggests that the balance between formal business networks and social capital based resource access will vary according to the location of the SME.

BICS

The BIC SMEs used different relationships or connections for their internationalisation including home country government services, connections with professional and industry associations, entrepreneur organisations, local and global groups and personnel connections. The BIC SMEs had more relationships with their home country government institutes and were routinely members of home country business associations in China. Some of the BIC SME participants noted experiencing a high level of support from senior home country government officials for the initial development of their networks and also chose to take senior management roles in business associations located in China.

The finding that the BIC SMEs also used informal networks and found them effective in supporting their business performance was an important finding for SME internationalisation into China. Although these informal networks were not true social capital sources, this finding has some consistency with Zhou, Wu and Luo's (2007) suggestion that international business managers should consider social networks as an efficient means of helping internationally oriented SMEs to internationalise. The social dynamics perspective of internationalisation (Ellis, 2000; Harris and Wheeler, 2005; Zhou Wu, and Luo, 2007) argues that internationalisation orientations require informal network ties. In addition, Zhou, Wu and Luo (2007) found that social networks provide a mediating role, similar to that of guanxi in China. This mediating mechanism is attributed to three information benefits of social networks: knowledge of foreign market opportunities; advice and experiential learning and referral trust and solidarity. These networks are important because the investment intensity and complexity of a foreign SME operation established in China may mean that an internationalisation orientation may not provide sufficient information and knowledge for the internationalising SME to capture the opportunities available in China. This will be even more important for the BIC's born-global internationalisation process.

In addition, the network resources that the BIC SMEs would require for their establishment and development may not be located in traditional business networks. The speed and scope of informal social networks developed by entrepreneurs may mean that social capital relationships may be a more appropriate vehicle for these types of resources (Chetty and Campbell-Hunt, 2004; Etemad, 2004; Harris and Wheeler, 2005). Some of the BIC SMEs in the study were found to have been established through serendipity and unexpected connections made by the owners. This finding was consistent with Rodrigues and Child's (2012) finding that approximately one-third of born-global companies were established through serendipity. These events generated new social capital and often created the basis for trust-based personal relationship that supported the new business development.

Not all of the SMEs in the study supported the use of guanxi in internationalising to China, claiming that its value was dependent on the industry type, marketing strategies and business structure of the internationalising SME. Some of the participants suggested that the difference between guanxi and international approaches to establishing business relationships was not great and that network relationships could be built using the same approaches as an international business would take in other countries. The BICs were particularly critical about selecting the organisations they would allow to be part of their business networks. The participants representing BIC companies were also of the opinion that it was impossible to establish the business networks necessary for this type of SME until the SME was established in China. This finding is consistent with that of Kenny et al. (2011) who also found that networks have had different levels of impact and that the resources that they can provide have a significant impact on internationalisation performance. This finding suggests that internationalisation network value evaluation should consider the value of the resources available in the network for the SME, as well as constructs for the resource utilisation, such as market conditions.

Conclusion

The findings identified the importance of building networks for the success of each of the four identified forms of internationalised SMEs in China. They also identified a variation in approaches for development and the purpose of networks for each group. The analysis also determined that the high investment SMEs (wholly owned foreign entities (WOFEs) and BIC) provided more frequent responses to questions about networks (providing over 90 percent of the responses), despite representing less than 80 percent of the participants. This suggests that these SMEs were more informed and concerned about network development and operation. Whilst some evidence of attention to network development for the importer and exporter SMEs was identified in the responses, the findings indicated that the WOFE and BIC SMEs had a more complex, critical and extensive approach to network building. The BIC SMEs were particularly cautious about selecting the organisations they allowed into their networks and were the only SMEs in the sample that specifically mentioned conducting background checks of potential partners.

Interestingly, the importer and exporter SMEs appeared to have fewer options for identifying potential network members available to them, but were also more heavily reliant on the information that their network provided. This may have partly reflected their limited physical investment and engagement in China relative to the other two forms of SME. The greater attention and diversity of approaches taken for developing networks by the WOFE and BIC SMEs may also have reflected the longer-term nature of their network relationships (some of the participants referred to networks lasting 30 years) as well as the greater level of investment in their Chinese operations. The use of home country government support to identify potential network members was a feature of the approaches taken by all four types of SMEs. The findings indicated that, whilst home country government support introduced a high level of social capital into the network partner search process, the ability of home country government agencies to target and provide information about the most appropriate network members in China was limited. This would have been due to the large psychic distance between the two countries in the study.

Social capital was also an important feature of the network relations developed by the participants. Social capital functioned independently of business networks and provided the most benefit in the start-up stages of internationalisation, especially for the WOFE and BIC SMEs. The greater benefit from social capital for the high investment SMEs may have reflected their greater investment presence in the Chinese market, which would include the demonstrations of investment and permanency that organisations display in China to gain credibility. The greater investment and demonstration of permanency by the WOFE and BIC SMEs, as well as the greater complexity and intensity of these high investment entry modes, would have increased the effectiveness of their social capital in supporting their internationalisation. Social capital appeared to include a higher commitment form of relationship than business networks for the SMEs and possibly allowed more flexibility, which would have been important in assisting the SMEs in their start-up phase.

References

Al-Laham, A., and Souitaris, V. (2008). Network embeddedness and new venture internationalisation. Analysing international linkages in the German Biotech industry. *Journal of Business Venturing*, 22:4, 566–591.

Audrey, G., David, C., Ken, G., Aodheen, O., Richard, L., and Bill, P. (2006). Networking in SMEs: Findings from Australia and Ireland. *Irish Marketing Review*, 18:1, 21–28.

Boehe, D. M. (2011). Exploiting the liability of foreignness: Why do service firms exploit foreign affiliate networks at home? *Journal of International Management*, 17, 15–29.

Boisot, M., and Child, J. (1996). From Fiefs to Clans and network capitalism: Explaining China's emerging economic order. *Administrative Science Quarterly*, 4, 600.

Chetty, S. K., Ojala, A., and Leppäaho, T. (2015). Effectuation and foreign market entry of entrepreneurial firms. *European Journal of Marketing*, 49:9/10, 1436.

Chetty, S. K., and Wilson, H. I. (2003). Collaborating with competitors to acquire resources. *International Business Review*, 4, 1261–1281.

Ciravegna, L., Majano, S. B., and Zhan, G. (2014). The inception of internationalization of small and medium enterprises: The role of activeness and networks. *Journal of Business Research*, 67, 1081–1089.

Coviello, N. E., and Munro, H. J. (1997). Network relationships and the internationalisation process of smaller software firms. *International Business Review*, 6:4, 361–384.

Crick, D., and Spence, M. (2005). The internationalisation of 'high performing' UK high-tech SMEs: A study of planned and unplanned strategies. *International Business Review*, 14:2,167–185.

Ellis, P. (2000). Social ties and foreign market entry. *Journal of International Business Studies*, 31:3, 443.

Elodie, G., and Caroline, M. (2012). SME dependence and coordination in innovation networks. *Journal of Small Business and Enterprise Development*, 2, 263.

Etemad, H. (2004). Internationalisation of small and medium-sized enterprises: A grounded theoretical framework and an overview. *Canadian Journal of Administrative Sciences*, 21:1, 1–4.

Falize, M., and Coeurderoy, R. (2012). The Network Approach to Rapid Internationalisation among Born-Global and Born-Again Global Firms: The Case of the Global Innovation Network. Louvain School of Management. *Working Paper Series Louvain School of Management*.

Fletcher, R. (2011). Internationalisation strategies for SMEs in the decade ahead: are our theories relevant? *International Journal of Entrepreneurship and Innovation Management*, 13, 246–262.

Gellynck, X., Vermeire, B., and Viaene, J. (2007). Innovation in food firms: contribution of regional networks within the international business context. *Entrepreneurship & Regional Development*, 19:3, 209.

Guercini, S., and Runfola, A. (2010). Business networks and retail internationalization: A case analysis in the fashion industry. *Industrial Marketing Management*, 6, 908.

HA[yen]kansson, H., and Snehota, I. (2006). No business is an island: The network concept of business strategy. *Scandinavian Journal of Management*, 3, 256.

Handfield, R. B., Ragatz, G. L., Petersen, K. J., and Monczka, R. M. (1999). Involving suppliers in new product development. *California Management Review*, 42:1, 59–82.

Harris, S., and Wheeler, C. (2005). Entrepreneurs' relationships for internationalisation: Functions, origins and strategies. *International Business Review*, 14:2, 187–207.

Hashim, M. K., and Hassan, R. (2008). Internationalisation of SMEs: Options, incentives, problems and business strategy. *Malaysian Management Review*, 43:1, 63–76.

Johanson, J., and Mattson, L. G. (1988). Internationalisation in industrial systems – a network approach. In Hood, N., and Vahlne, J. E. (Eds.), *Strategies in Global Competition*. New York: Croom Helm, 287–314.

Johanson, J., and Vahlne, J. E. (2009). The Uppsala internationalization process model revisited: From liability of foreignness to liability of outsidership. *Journal of International Business Studies*, 40:9, 1411–1431.

Lianxi, Z., Wei-ping, W., and Xueming, L. (2007). Internationalisation and the performance of born-global SMEs: The mediating role of social networks. *Journal of International Business Studies*, 38, 673–690.

Lu, J. W., and Beamish, P. W. (2001). The internationalisation and performance of SMEs. *Strategic Management Journal*, 22:6/7, 565–586.

Meyar, K. E., and Skak, A. (2002). Networks, serendipity and SME entry into Eastern Europe. *European Management Journal*, 20:2, 179–188.

Mohammad, A. R., and Filho, F. (2009). Internationalisation of SMEs: A multi case study. *European Business Review*, 22:6, 608–623.

Mohammad, R. S., Hossein, D., and Staffan, B. (2012). Rapid Internationalisation of SMEs From Resource Based View: A longitudinal Study of a Pharmaceutical Company in Iran. Unpublished.

Moller, K., Partanen, J., Rajala, R., and Westerlund, M. (2007). Exploiting the b2b knowledge network: New perspectives and core concepts. In Naude, P., Zolkiewski, J., and Henneberg, S. (Ed.), *The SME Context: A Network Perspective*. Manchester: Manchester Business School.

Mort, S. G., and Weerawardena, J. (2006). Networking capability and international entrepreneurship: How networks function in Australian born global firms. *International Marketing Review*, 23, 549–572.

Musteen, M., Datta, D. K., and Butts, M. M. (2014). Do international networks and foreign market knowledge facilitate SME internationalization? Evidence from the Czech Republic. *Entrepreneurship: Theory and Practice*, 4, 749.

Musteen, M., Francis, J., and Datta, K. (2010). Corrigendum to 'The influence of international networks on internationalisation speed and performance: A study of Czech SMEs'. *Journal of World Business*, 45, 197–205.

Nahapiet, J., and Ghoshal, S. (1998). Social capital, intellectual capital, and the organizational advantage. *Academy of Management Review*, 23, 242–266.

O'Gorman, C., and Evers, N. (2011). Network intermediaries in the internationalisation of new firms in peripheral regions. *International Marketing Review*, 28:4, 340–364.

Oleinik, A. (2004). A model of network capitalism: Basic ideas and post-Soviet evidence. *Journal of Economic Issues*, 38:1, 85–111.

Oviatt, B. M., and McDougall, P. P. (1994). Toward a theory of international new ventures. *Journal of International Business Studies*, 25:1, 45–64.

Partanen, J., Chetty, S. K., and Rajala, A. (2014). Innovation Types and Network Relationships. *Entrepreneurship: Theory & Practice*, 38:5, 1027.

Prashantham, S., and Dhanaraj, C. (2010). The dynamic influence of social capital on the international growth of new ventures. *Journal of Management Studies* 47, 967–994.

Rugman, A. M., Oh, C. H., and Lim, D. S. (2012). The regional and global competitiveness of multinational firms. *Journal of The Academy of Marketing Science*, 2, 218.

Rutashobya, L., and Jaensson, J. E. (2004). Small firms' internationalisation for development in Tanzania: Exploring the network phenomenon. *International Journal of Social Economics*, 31:1/2, 159–172.

Saeedi, M. R., Dadfar, H., and Brege, S. (2011). *Rapid Internationalisation of SMEs From Resource Based View: A Longitudinal Study of a Pharmaceutical Company in Iran*. Sweden: Department of Industrial Marketing, Linkoping University.

Schweizer, R. (2013). SMEs and networks: Overcoming the liability of outsidership. *Journal of International Entrepreneurship*, 11:1, 80–103.

Sensis Business Network. (2012). Small and medium enterprises, September, http://about.sensis.com.au/IgnitionSuite/uploads/docs/September%202012%20Sensis%20Business%20Index%20FINAL.pdf.

Sharma, D. D., and Blomstermo, A. (2003). The internationalization process of born globals: A network view. *International Business Review*, 12:6, 739–753.

Spence, M. (2000). Overseas trade missions as an export development tool. *Journal of EuroMarketing*, 9:2, 113–126.

Teece, D. J. (1996). Firm organization, industrial structure, and technological innovation. *Journal of Economic Behavior & Organization*, 31, 193–122.

Wilson, D. T., and Mummalaneni, V. (1990). Buyer-seller relationships as a bonding process: A preliminary conceptualization. Working draft, Pennsylvania State University, University Park, PA.

Xia, Y., Qiu, Y., and Zafar, A. (2007). The impact of firm resources on subsidiary's competitiveness in emerging markets: an empirical study of Singaporean SMEs' performance in China. *Multinational Business Review*, 15:2, 13–40.

Yu-Ching, C., Kuo-Pin, Y., and Chwo-Ming, J. Y. (2006). Performance, internationalisation, and firm-specific advantages of SMEs in a newly-industrialized economy. *Small Business Economics*, 26, 475–492.

Zhou, L. X., Wu, W. P., and Luo, X. M. (2007). Internationalization and the performance of born-global SMEs: The mediating role of social networks. *Journal of International Business Studies*, 38:4, 673–690.

Zizah, C. S., Rosman, M. I., Brenda, S., and Lanny, E. (2010). Influential factors for SME internationalisation: Evidence from Malaysia. *International Journal of Economics and Management*, 4:2, 285–304.

5 Being a foreign entrepreneur in China

Introduction

Small and medium-sized enterprises (SMEs) are one of the most entrepreneurial forms of business in most industries and international SMEs are even more entrepreneurial in behaviour because of their decision to operate in a foreign environment. The entrepreneurial behaviours displayed by the participant SMEs included adopting novel processes and management techniques, applying innovations differently to the competition, developing new markets, influencing market development and introducing new business structures not present in the market (such as the combination of importing from the home country operations, combined with local processing, which was adopted by the participants from the agricultural industry). In order to adopt these entrepreneurial behaviours with the limited resources available to them, SMEs have been found to utilise their networks to support their implementation (Elodie and Caroline, 2012; Nordman and Tolstoy, 2016). Commercialisation of product innovations is one of the big challenges for SMEs due to the barriers that limited organisational resources create (Do et al, 2014). Large organisations are able to devote substantial internal resources to these endeavours, however, limited resources can require SMEs to enter partnerships in order to bring innovative products to the market (Braga, Gualandri and Venturelli, 2008; Chye, 2011; Nordman and Tolstoy, 2016). In an international context, this can often result in a partnership providing both market knowledge and assistance with commercialisation. This type of partnership, when operating a foreign market can create more complexity for the SME, which brings its own challenges.

Chapter 3 considers the innovation process in particular. This chapter considers the entrepreneurial behaviours of the SMEs that create the business development, partnerships and opportunities for commercialising innovations and utilising the innovative capabilities of the organisation. The behavioural dimensions of entrepreneurship that are considered in this chapter include autonomous behaviours, risk-taking, competitor orientation and proactiveness (Lumpkin and Dess, 2001). Innovation was considered separately in Chapter 3 and will be considered as a natural output of the entrepreneurship process in this chapter. Entrepreneurial motivation will also be considered as it is an important feature of the entrepreneurship process (Garcia-Cabrera, Garcia-Soto and Duran-Herrera, 2016; Hui-Chen, Kuen-Hung and Chen-Yi, 2014; Mani, 2013).

This chapter commences with a review of the extent SME entrepreneurship literature, examining each of Lumpkin and Dess's (2001) behavioural dimensions of entrepreneurship (autonomous behaviours, risk-taking, competitor orientation and proactiveness) within the structural framework of identity, motivation and performance. The constructs from this literature are then compared with the experiences of the SMEs interviewed for this book. The chapter concludes with a consideration of how these findings extend the extant literature and suggestions for future research. Please see the introduction chapter for a detailed description of the participants, how the data was collected and analysed and the objectives of the study. Chapter 3 provides a detailed examination of the innovation process and Chapter 4 considers the networks that these entrepreneurs formed.

Literature review

This literature review considers Lumpkin and Dess's (2001) dimensions of entrepreneurial behaviour of autonomous behaviours, risk-taking, competitor orientation and proactiveness, which are referred to as entrepreneurial orientation or EO. They are considered within the internationalisation framework of the factors which create identity as an entrepreneur, motivate the establishment of a business and affect performance. The literature reviewed in this chapter addresses both the general entrepreneurship literature as well as the international entrepreneur literature. The international entrepreneur literature is relatively new and lacks the development of constructs evident in the more developed entrepreneurship literature (Hilmersson and Papaioannou, 2015; Kauppinen and Juho, 2012; Kungwansupaphan and Siengthai, 2014; Turcan and Juho, 2014). This chapter will introduce some new constructs to the international entrepreneurship literature. The literature review concludes with an integration of the different perspectives of entrepreneurial behaviour identified in the literature, against which the findings from the interviews with the participants as they internationalised to China are compared.

Entrepreneurial orientation and identity

Entrepreneurial identity is the perception of the entrepreneur that some of their behaviours are entrepreneurial, rather than (for example) professional or managerial (Lheureux and Auzoult, 2017). Entrepreneurial identity has received some attention in the literature, however, entrepreneurial orientation (entrepreneurial values and attitudes) has been the subject of extensive research (Covin and Miller, 2014). This is probably due to the fact that entrepreneurial identity is more strongly associated with the antecedents that create it (Farmer, Yao and Kung-Mcintyre, 2011; Karhunen, Olimpieva and Hytti, 2017; Lheureux and Auzoult, 2017; Navis and Glynn, 2011; Obschonka 42015), whilst entrepreneurial orientation is more strongly associated with entrepreneurial behaviours

(Anderson, Covin and Slevin, 2009; Chen, Chang and Chang, 2015; Covin and Miller, 2014; Gathungu, Aiko and Machuki, 2014; Manoochehr and Mohammad Hasan, 2016). Entrepreneurial orientation is a willingness to innovate and rejuvenate market offerings, take risks with creating new products, services and markets, and take an aggressive stance in regard to competition (Knight, 2000; Miller, 1983). Entrepreneurial orientation in internationalised companies results in greater innovativeness, pro-activeness and risk-taking (O'Cass and Weerawardena, 2009) and accelerates the internationalisation process (Mohammedi and Schnepper, 2015). It can be observed at both the organisational and the individual level, particularly where the CEO is an entrepreneur (Covin and Slevin, 1991; Glavas and Mathews, 2014; Knight, 2000). Entrepreneurial orientation is central to the exploitation of international entrepreneurial opportunities (Mostafa, Wheeler, and Jones, 2006; Slevin and Terjesen, 2011) and accepting the risks associated with international environments (Jantunen, Puumalainen, Saarenketo and Kyläheiko, 2005; Wang, 2008). As will be discussed in the following sections, it is also positively associated with SME performance (Kusumawardhani, McCarthy and Perera, 2009).

Not surprisingly, entrepreneurial orientation has been found to significantly influence the level of entrepreneurial identity (Lheureux and Auzoult, 2017; Manoochehr and Mohammad Hasan, 2016). Farmer, Yao and Kung-Mcintyre (2011) found that entrepreneurial self-identity was a strong predictor of the ability to discover new opportunities, but more so for new entrepreneurs than for experienced entrepreneurs. Counter to this, entrepreneurial self-identity has been found to increase with entrepreneurial experience (Obschonka et al., 2015). Professional scientific entrepreneurs more often self-identify with their professional role than their entrepreneurial role and view the two roles as separate activities (Karhunen, Olimpieva and Hytti, 2017; York, O'Neil and Sarasvathy, 2016). High-tech entrepreneurs, however, are the exception and have been found to associate strongly with their entrepreneurial identity (Yitshaki and Kropp, 2016). The conditions in the location in which the business is located can also influence the propensity of the entrepreneur to identify with their entrepreneurial or professional role (Gill and Larson, 2014; Navis and Glynn, 2011). Interestingly, ties with entrepreneurial communities were found to significantly influence entrepreneurial intentions (Lheureux and Auzoult, 2017), but not entrepreneurial self-identity.

Motivating factors for entrepreneurship

Values, personal attitude (including self-identification as an entrepreneur) and the perception that there is an opportunity to behave as entrepreneurs are key motivators for entrepreneurial behaviour (Hui-Chen, Kuen-Hung and Chen-Yi, 2014; Jayawarna, Rouse and Kitching, 2013; Obschonka et al., 2015; Uy, 2011; Yitshaki and Kropp, 2016). The motivating effect of the opportunity perception includes awareness of institutional barriers for SME internationalisation (Garcia-Cabrera, Garcia-Soto and Duran-Herrera, 2016). Culture also plays a key role in entrepreneurial motivation; Indian, Chinese and Vietnamese entrepreneurs are motivated by the opportunity for personal control and financial rewards (Mani, 2013; Perri and Chu, 2012). Interestingly, entrepreneurial motivation amongst young people in the Middle East and North Africa has been found to be relatively uncommon (Centre, 2013). Bacq, Hartog and Hoogendoorn (2016) and Farmer, Yao and Kung-Mcintyre (2011) suggest that entrepreneurs are motivated by the knowledge that their creativity can lead to an advantage in the market, which may explain these findings. This idea was also supported by Hayter's (2015) finding that academic entrepreneurs are motivated by opportunities for research profile development, such as the opportunity to relocate to a foreign country. Cultural factors may also affect sources of entrepreneurial motivation, for example, Chinese foreign entrepreneurs have demonstrated an increasing likelihood to relocate to Canada as the local Chinese community there develops (Wong and Ng, 2002).

Entrepreneurial performance

As noted earlier, entrepreneurial orientation is positively associated with performance (Rauch 42009; Shepherd and Wiklund, 2005). Performance is also positively moderated by the ability to link to external opportunities (Gathungu, Aiko and Machuki, 2014; Jayawarna, Rouse and Kitching, 2013; Rodríguez-Gutiérrez, Moreno and Tejada, 2015). The effect of the skills that this orientation provides on performance, however, varies as the organisation develops. The effect of these skills on performance is greater in low technology industries than in high technology industries (Covin and Covin, 1990). Product innovation skills have the greatest effect in the early stages of the organisation's developmental performance (Song, Di Benedetto and Song, 2010). Competitive aggressiveness is part of entrepreneurial orientation and has also been found to directly affect performance (Becherer and Maurer, 1997; Lumpkin and Dess, 2001). The performance of international entrepreneurs is also, unsurprisingly, positively affected by foreign market knowledge (Mariola, 2016; Musteen, Datta and Butts, 2014).

Performance is also influenced by the entrepreneur's social capital and is moderated by the competitive intensity of the industry in which they are operating, for both domestic and international entrepreneurs (Becherer and Maurer, 1997; Hernandez-Carrion, Camarero-Izquierdo and Gutierrez-Cillan, 2017; Hmieleski and Baron, 2009; Lu and Beamish, 2001; Ngoma, 2016). Home country based social capital has even been found to improve the performance of international entrepreneurs (Zhou, Wu and Luo, 2007). Similar to motivation, innovation performance is influenced by the entrepreneur's perception that they have the opportunity to function as an entrepreneur and their tolerance for risk (Jiarong and Shouming, 2016; Manoochehr and Mohammad Hasan, 2016). Innovation performance in large business is also influenced by internal networks (Chen, Chang and Chang, 2015). Internationalisation performance is affected by entrepreneurial orientation which affects the perceived opportunities for internationalisation (Vasilchenko and Morrish, 2011). Interestingly, the agreeableness of the entrepreneur was found to have the greatest positive effect on the performance of social enterprises, although higher levels of openness were found to have a negative effect (Liang 42015).

Putting it all together

The literature indicates that entrepreneurial orientation is a key feature of entrepreneurial behaviour from the perspective of identity, motivation and performance. Entrepreneurial identity can be influenced by the values and attitudes of the individual, and this can affect the ability of new entrepreneurs to identify new opportunities. Entrepreneurial identity also increases with experience and as a result of local conditions, such as operating within an entrepreneurial community. Entrepreneurial orientation and the perception that the entrepreneurial behaviours will result in a competitive advantage are key motivators for entrepreneurial behaviours, however, there is some evidence that they may be affected by the entrepreneur's culture and other factors, such as industry, financial rewards or community norms. Entrepreneurial orientation influences the entrepreneur's performance and determines which entrepreneurial behaviours are applied as the business develops. This has a subsequent effect on performance. Social capital is also a significant contributor to several aspects of entrepreneurial performance, including innovation and financial performance.

These findings suggest that we should expect the responses from the participants to reflect the entrepreneur's self-identity, motivation, performance, values and attitudes to form explanations for their entrepreneurial orientation, behaviour and success.

Interview findings and analysis

This section presents the findings and analysis of the interviews with the participants representing 35 SMEs operating in China. It identifies the primary themes and considers the factors that the interview participants identified and which made their entrepreneurial ventures successful. It also explores the motivation that encouraged them to initiate the venture in China and the management style and focus that they adopted in their Chinese operations. This section concludes with a summary of the principal approaches taken by the participants for each of five first order constructs of entrepreneurial behaviour identified as themes in the data.

The relationship between the findings and the literature will not be discussed in detail in the interview findings and analysis section. The discussion section considers the identified first order constructs in relation to the literature. The discussion section compares the findings to the literature based framework of entrepreneurial identity, motivation and performance and to the entrepreneurial orientation of autonomous behaviours, risk-taking, competitor orientation and proactiveness. The discussion section also explains how the identified behaviours and decisions extend our current understanding of SME entrepreneurship and the literature.

Overview: identification of constructs

To commence the analysis, the themes (first order constructs) that emerged from the data will be presented. The discussion of the constructs in this section includes a consideration of the number of responses from the participants for each of the constructs, as well as a description of how the responses are distributed across the industry sectors in the sample and a consideration of whether the constructs were more relevant to particular industries. The industry distribution for the constructs with small numbers of responses has not been included as these constructs were not considered to be representative of the entire sample, but were included because the participants provided strong evidence for the existence of that construct.

The three higher-order constructs identified in the responses were business success factors, management style and focus and the motivation to establish the entrepreneurial venture. The first order constructs on which the higher-order constructs were based were creating differences, planning, motivation, management style and a focus on opportunity effects. Interestingly, although the interview protocol incorporated elements from all of the entrepreneurship constructs identified in the literature, the participants' descriptions of their behaviours in response were very generalised. Frequently, the entrepreneurial activity was explained using an example, or was embedded in a detailed description of the outcome of the entrepreneurial activity. For example, one participant described their entrepreneurial orientation as:

> You've got to be self driven. I know people can work in lots of different areas, I suppose part of my business is that I can work anywhere, I can be on a beach and doing my work, I can be in a different country and do my work, as long as I've got a Wi-Fi connection.

This was quite different to the participant's responses to, for example, the barriers to internationalisation, which were much more factual and concise (see Chapter 7). The participants may have been less conscious of being an entrepreneur and were more conscious of being a manager who needed to deal with the liabilities of operating a foreign SME in China.

The form of entrepreneurial orientation represented by the first order constructs identified has the greatest commonality with the scientific form of entrepreneurial orientation identified in the literature. In this entrepreneurial orientation, the entrepreneurs had a stronger association with their scientific professional management role, than with their entrepreneurship role (Karhunen, Olimpieva and Hytti, 2017; York, O'Neil and Sarasvathy, 2016). This is a valuable finding as well, as the literature has just begun to empirically examine the impact of entrepreneurial self-identity on the behaviours that they display (Farmer, Yao and Kung-Mcintyre, 2011; Karhunen, Olimpieva and Hytti, 2017; Lheureux and Auzoult, 2017). The literature considering the roles of entrepreneurs has until recently overlooked the issue of self-identify as an explanatory factor for the behaviours

(Corbett and Hmieleski, 2007). The participants in this study displayed entrepreneurial behaviours, but did not identify the activities that they undertook as being entrepreneur's activities. They described their behaviours in terms such as responding to local competition or managing human resources, even though the approach they took to these activities was very entrepreneurial, such as creating and taking responsibility for the industry networks that supported their customers. This finding suggests that these participants did not require self-identity as an entrepreneur in order to adopt entrepreneurial behaviours. It also suggests that the participants' entrepreneurialism must be identified through their actions, rather than through their self-identification.

The first order constructs of self-identity and motivation were individually identified in the literature, however, they were co-jointly identified by the participants. Factors which influence performance attracted extensive attention in the literature and were thematically represented by the participants as three first order constructs that lead to the higher order construct of success factors. The literature also examined the factors which influence the way in which entrepreneurs establish their businesses. This was partially represented by the identified management style and focus construct, although this construct considered the ongoing operations of the business and not just its establishment.

The first and higher-order constructs identified in the data were categorised into the structure shown in Figure 5.1. This figure indicates that the higher order construct of success factors had the largest number of first order constructs, ranging from the impact of the opportunities that they experienced, through to planning how they would differentiate themselves and the actions that they took to achieve this. By comparison, the range of comments relating to the two constructs of management style and focus and the construct of motivation were much broader, did not relate to the other constructs and so each constituted a higher-order construct. The identification of three higher order constructs (success factors, management style focus and motivation) from the interviews was also consistent with the literature reviewed earlier in this chapter. It was interesting that knowledge was not identified as a first or higher order construct, as literature would suggest, but was found to form part of the first order constructs of opportunity effects and planning. The literature identifies the importance of knowledge for the internationalisation of SMEs (Child and Hsieh, 2014; Costa, Soares and de Sousa, 2016; Mariola, 2016; Musteen, Datta and Butts, 2014), however, if knowledge forms part of a larger construct, it may be methodologically more appropriate to examine the impact of that construct on the internationalisation of SMEs.

A particularly interesting finding was the large proportion of comments identified relating to the construct of management style and focus, relative to the number of comments identified for the theme of motivation. The comments for each of the three different success factor constructs were also similarly greater in number than the comments regarding motivation. This finding may reflect the participant's focus on being an entrepreneur, rather than identifying as an entrepreneur. The number of responses for each of the constructs is shown in Figure 5.2.

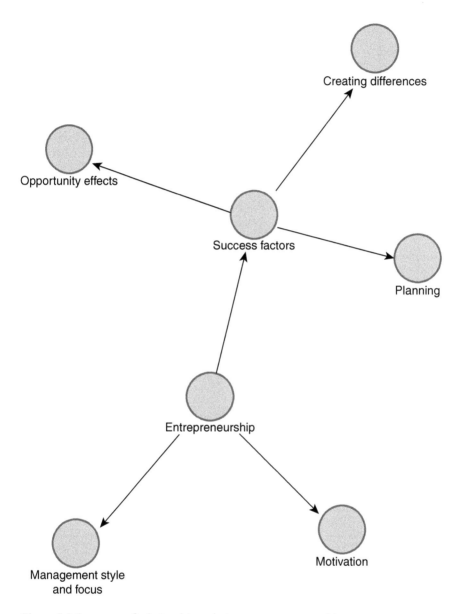

Figure 5.1 Structure of relationships relating to entrepreneurship

The total number of responses identified which related to entrepreneurial activities in the participant's activities in China was 83. Table 5.1 shows the number of participants and the number of responses received for each of the constructs. The highlighted constructs have been included for the purpose of structure. The

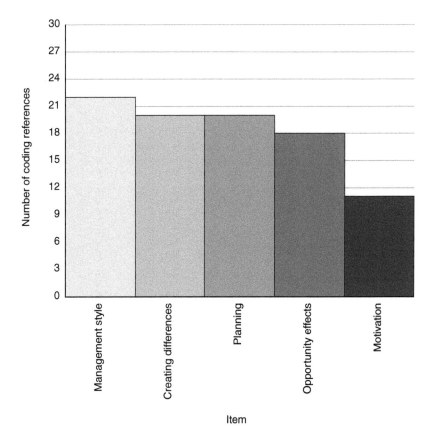

Figure 5.2 Frequency of responses to each of the identified constructs

Table 5.1 Number of participants and number of responses for each construct

Name	Participants	References
Entrepreneurship	23	83
Success factors	19	52
Planning	11	18
Creating differences	12	18
Opportunity effects	9	16
Management style and focus	16	21
Motivation	6	10

number of participants and references for each of the higher order constructs represents the total number of comments in its first order constructs.

All of the constructs received a good number of responses from a range of different participants. No responses were received that didn't fit into one of the constructs and five responses were jointly coded to two constructs. No responses were coded to more than two constructs. The responses that were coded to two constructs were detailed and example based and, for practical purposes, could not be divided into single responses, although they contained information pertaining to both constructs.

Details of the findings

This section describes the findings relating to each of the constructs and presents examples from the interviews.

Planning

As shown in Table 5.1, the construct of planning received 18 comments from 11 different participants. Responses were received from four service, four manufacturing, two finance and one technology participant. Interestingly, no responses were received from agribusiness industry participants. This is an interesting finding because both of the agribusiness participants had established WOFE investments in China and it would have been logical to have engaged in planning as part of this entrepreneurial business development. The limited focus on planning for the subsidiary may reflect the very high demand for their agricultural products (because of their green and safe image) and the fact that the operations in China were just one part of a larger international supply chain.

One of the main themes in the planning construct comments related to the importance of possessing knowledge of the market, specifically what competitors were doing and what customers wanted. When describing the entrepreneurial organisational activity of establishing operations in China, one participant pointed out that "you have to know your market, you have to be very focused on your market and you can't be distracted" and another commented that "I've spent more than 10 years here learning how the Chinese do business" (Case 11: Recruitment Co). Other planning issues connected to the entrepreneurial organisational activity of establishing operations in China related to identify the most suitable market segments and the best locations. For example, one participant noted a "very conscious decision to be here in the industrial park" and another noted "for me with the long tail concept and chasing the smaller customers that's certainly what we're doing here in China". The process of selecting entry structures is discussed in detail in chapter 2.

The remaining comments regarding entrepreneurial planning related to operationalising a novel business concept or practice, for example one participant stated "we had a brainstorm and we said who do we offer the most value to and we decided we offered the most value to Australian companies". Other comments supported these findings, but demonstrated through example, that flexibility and adaptability was also an important component of the entrepreneurial process of establishing operations in China and that plans often needed to be changed significantly; "it's never in concrete so it seems to morph and change and evolve over time and I think part of that is to recognise that". For the 28 participants that established either a BIC or WOFE in China these capabilities (or the version necessary for operations in China in the case of the WOFEs) did not exist prior to the establishment of the operation and so developing them was part of the entrepreneurial activity.

Creating differences

This construct attracted 18 comments as well, but this time from 12 participants. Responses were received from seven service companies, three manufacturing, one agribusiness and one finance company, suggesting that the service companies had thought more extensively about creating differences in the market. The comments described the range of different mechanisms through which the organisation could differentiate themselves. They predominantly focused on areas where competition was low or separating out the existing competition. For example, one respondent noted that:

> They want to deal with us so we just play off that but for us we're in a really unique spot because we are driven by innovation, we are driven by entrepreneurship, delivering more in that category than industry but you've got to be so delicate about how you do it and how you communicate that because you know there's 10 Chinese looking and going I can do that far cheaper than he's doing.
> (Case 22: Medical Equip Co)

The participants also commented that they focused on ensuring that they maintained this point of difference. For example, one participant commented that "we constantly make sure that we're staying ahead of anyone who tries to, not copy us, but introduce new products and the second part of that is to make sure that we're seen" and another participant commented that "I've got an understanding of what's happening in China in terms of how it's unfolding". The remaining comments referred to the entrepreneurial commitment required to maintain this differentiation. One of the most entrepreneurial features of these organisations was their ongoing commitment to being different and at the front of their central technologies or processes. For example one participant noted that "it has to be innovative because we provide services to manufacturing areas and predominantly if we're not ahead of the rest of the clan then we don't have any business" and another commented that "I think early days would have just been persistence".

Opportunity effects

The participants identified many opportunities that the Chinese business environment presented which enabled them to engage in entrepreneurial behaviour. The combination of their entrepreneurial orientation and these opportunities resulted in creative and unique business development responses which provided the SME with a competitive advantage or outcome such as a strengthened market position or business growth. This first order construct received 19 comments from nine participants; this was the least number of comments received in the three constructs in this group and involved significantly fewer participants. The greater number of responses received were from the service companies (five), followed by the manufacturing companies (three) and responses from one of the agribusinesses. These findings again suggest that the service companies were the most aware of the effect of this aspect of success factors on their entrepreneurial operations.

One of the most significant opportunities identified was the value of being a foreigner. For example, one participant noted that "there is an interest in what foreigners might have to offer and not only for Chinese companies, but also for other foreign companies that are coming into China and who are struggling with it" and another participant noted that "I think in many ways just being an Australian company helps". These opportunities allowed the entrepreneurs to enter into deals that they otherwise would have been unable to make, however, this also required them to be creative in both their approach and the way in which they presented themselves in order to capitalise upon the opportunity. For example, one of the agribusiness participants reported that:

> We had emails, some weeks we had 100 enquiries a week, it was huge and of course in all of that was who do we actually deal with here. There was just this plethora of people who just seemed to wake up one morning and go, I know, I'm going to sell organic baby food in China and you'd get this phone call, they go hello I've got an engineering company but I've decided we're going to do baby formula.
>
> (Case 23: Milk Co)

The Australian brand could also be considered to be a resource, and this is considered in Chapter 6 – The Role of Resources and Capabilities. This also contrasts interestingly with the participants' comments regarding the liability of foreignness (LOF) discussed in Chapter 7 – Barriers, Liabilities and Costs. This opportunity was not a permanent feature of the environment, however, and other participants commented that the value of being an Australian in China had diminished. For example, one participant noted that "people used to say it's lucky you're Australian and I hear it less and less". This suggests that the SMEs had to recognise the opportunities and move quickly when they are presented. The opportunity based on being an Australia in China appears to have diminished because the Chinese markets and their local suppliers were becoming more sophisticated, reducing the context for the appearance of opportunities based on differences.

In many cases, the opportunities appeared to these SMEs as a result of a random series of events. The participants attributed these to luck, and demonstrated that they were well prepared to take advantage of any unexpected opportunities that came their way. For example, one respondent noted that "You need a bit of luck as well" and another explained:

> Another state owned enterprise company came to look at the project and said this is good and then we got a chance to bid on that and it just kind of rolled a little bit.
>
> (Case 17: Metal Frame Co)

Another entrepreneurial feature of the SMEs was the extent to which they would pursue the opportunities available to them. The SMEs experienced a range of challenges inherent in the Chinese marketplace, which they had to overcome in order to be able to take advantage of the opportunities available there as well. One of these was the power asymmetry between large State Owned Enterprises and small to medium suppliers in China: "small to medium enterprises, we don't get that much attention". These SMEs generally responded to these power symmetries (and other challenges) by exercising a high level of flexibility which allowed them to pursue other potential opportunities. This flexibility could lead to changes in the direction of the business, as this participant noted:

> we've had to take a change in the business because of circumstance and our future is in specialisation. Everything I know as a businessperson, everything I know as an academic says not many competitors, emerging market, government green light and I've got a history in it.
>
> (Case 28: Consult Co)

Management style and focus

This construct attracted 21 responses from 16 participants, which was the largest number of responses for any of the constructs. The SMEs that provided these comments included eight service companies, four manufacturing companies, two agribusiness companies, one technology company and one finance company. The service companies provided 14 comments regarding entrepreneurial behaviours, which was a disproportionately large number of responses, relative to their proportion of the total number of participants. This construct identified a number of quite specific, but related themes. The themes focused on business design issues that facilitated the entrepreneurial orientation of the business. For example, one participant noted that:

> we are a very practical company in that when we do something we take it from a creative step into an innovative step and we fail and we fail fast. I think that's an important factor of business that you need to identify the problems early and then you need to break them and then you need to improve it. So innovative, we have a philosophy of start, do, notice, think, sort of company.
>
> (Case 26: HR Consult Co)

Although their entrepreneurial orientation could be quite aggressive, the participants also demonstrated thoughtful and cooperative perspectives. A number of the participants offered comments that indicated that they were concerned about their impact and about their position in China. For example, one participant noted that "we always had a mindset that we are in someone else's back garden" and another participant noted that they were "not only connected to the business world, but also connected to the community". In addition to the thoughtful perspectives, the participants also provided evidence that entrepreneurial orientation in China requires independence and self-confidence. For example, one partici-pant noted that:

> I guess potentially as the industry grows and evolves maybe there could be some experience or advice that we could work with in terms of how do you categorise this industry, how does that work. We'd have to be very proactive there but I think it's probably fairly limited. I don't think we need to rely too much on anyone else. Our business model is good in that it's a great cash flow business so it doesn't take a lot to have a profitable enterprise and then it's not relying too much on anybody really, it can pay its own way.
>
> (Case 13: Vehicle Co)

Some of the management approaches the participants described were very crea-tive. For example, one participant set up web cams in Australia so that the Chi-nese staff could see how the operations were performed there, whilst one of the agribusiness participants reported supporting a very large number of distributors in China that would not normally have been possible for an organisation of that size. The participants also frequently indicated that they were not directly focused on being innovative, but were focused on being different and reactive. For exam-ple, one participant noted that:

> the local companies that have a similar position as myself, I find aren't that innovative. They're doing things as the textbook says. What I try to do is I try to discuss a lot of things that the company could possibly do.
>
> (Case 18: Build Co)

The participants also provided many comments which described their individual entrepreneurial identities. For example, one participant noted that "you have got to be self-driven"; another participant noted that "China is not an easy place to make a dollar, it takes years", whilst a third participant noted that "it's got to be a complete disruption to the way that it was being consumed and done". Some of the participants included observation and collaboration in the development of their entrepreneurial identity. For example, one participant made use of the SME series of events run by the Australian Chamber of Commerce and another was an active member of the global Entrepreneurs Organisation.

Motivation

This construct attracted only ten comments, from six SMEs. This was the small-est number of responses and respondents of any of the constructs. The responses came from four service, one agribusiness and one technology participant. The responses indicated that these entrepreneurs were personally motivated to estab-lish operations in China because of the intellectual and personal benefits. For example, one participant noted that "Hong Kong in itself is a dynamic and inno-vative city full of interesting entrepreneurs" and another commented that "China has an enormous amount of opportunity for foreigners coming in because you're exposed to stuff you wouldn't be exposed to otherwise". These motivations sometimes resulted from an aggregation of events over the participant's career. For example, one participant noted that:

> I've lived in different countries in Asia over that period of time. I've taken advantage of the opportunity that's been presented to me which I think, including Australia, was the best thing we ever did, not because we weren't happy with what we were doing but what it did it broadened, it broadened everything. It broadened our work experiences, it broadened our perspective, it broadened our understanding of different cultures, of Asia as not just one big amorphous thing above Australia.
>
> (Case 32: Marketing Co)

Other forms of motivation, such as financial benefits, the opportunity to do something different, or the need for self-control were identified by the participants (except for one participant). This is an interesting finding as these were identified in the literature review as motivations for entrepreneurial orientation.

Risk and proactiveness

Constructs did not emerge from the data for either risk or proactiveness. Although risk was identified 21 times across all the participant's responses, only three of these referred to risk taking. The remainder of the responses referred to risk as a barrier which stopped entrepreneurial behaviour. Proactiveness, however, was much more evident, but did not emerge as a separate construct, appearing instead as a feature of the identified constructs above, such as management style and focus.

Summary of findings

The findings provide examples of each of the dimensions of entrepreneurship identified in the literature review. They suggest that the behaviours of the internationalising entrepreneurial SMEs in the study were broadly consistent with the characteristics of entrepreneurial orientation identified in the literature. Some dimensions of their entrepreneurial orientation, however, were not present in the literature. The finding that the participants focused extensively on management behaviours and displayed creative management and business differentiating approaches, but infrequently and superficially identified motivations for establishing an international entrepreneurial SME or self-identified as an entrepreneur was an important finding. This finding indicates that the entrepreneurial nature of the business, rather than the self-identification as an entrepreneur, was the motivation for the behaviours identified. It provides a valuable extension for the literature by indicating the basis upon which international entrepreneurial SMEs should be both identified and measured and will be considered in more detail in

Table 5.2 Liabilities represented by the different identified constructs

Construct	Entrepreneurship form	No. of comments	Focus
Planning	Detailed	18	Market knowledge and operationalisation of concept
Creating differences	Creative	18	Structurally separating the organisation from the existing competition
Opportunity effects	Reactive	16	Structural opportunities and flexibility
Management style and focus	Detailed	21	Strongly deterministic behaviours, externally and outcome focused
Motivation	Opportunistic	10	Previous experiences and intellectual and personal benefits

the discussion section. Hui-Chen, Kuen-Hung and Chen-Yi (2014) identified the direct effect that personal attitude and opportunity have upon the intention to become an entrepreneur which was consistent with the personal development and opportunity behaviours identified in the participants.

Table 5.2 summarises these results. It shows that creative behaviours were only identified in relation to structurally separating the organisation from the existing competition, whilst attention to detail was identified in relation to planning and management style, demonstrating informed, deterministic and output focused behaviours. By comparison, the effect of opportunity and motivation for the business were strongly reactive and focused on utilising the chance to compete, but not on using existing resources or capabilities. Resources and capabilities were primarily considered in relation to planning.

Comparison of the experiences and behaviours of the participants to the literature

This section considers how the experiences and behaviours of the interview participants compares to the observations in the literature and where this supports, extends or challenges current thinking. One of the most important findings from this research was that the entrepreneurial orientation of the participants was similar to that of international entrepreneurs operating in other countries described in the extent international entrepreneurship literature, except in some critical areas. This indicates that the rapidly changing environment and rapidly developing opportunities for entrepreneurial activity in the Chinese market did not completely change the nature of entrepreneurial orientation for SMEs in China.

One of these areas was the fact that they generally did not identify themselves as entrepreneurs and described their behaviours in terms of management practices. They also displayed a strong focus on planning, adaptation and management control activities and used innovation for the process of differentiation, but not for the process of business opportunity identification or motivation (beyond accepting the risk associated with establishing the business). Some of the participants were able to turn their LOF into an advantage by offering products or services in the Chinese market that were perceived to be more attractive when they came from a foreign source. One example of this was the provision of financing services, which were considered to be more reliable when a foreign entity was involved. Another example was the provision of milk and meat products which were considered to be more attractive because of the Australian origin of the raw materials. There also appeared to be a difference in the entrepreneurial approach taken by the service industry participants and the manufacturing industry participants, with the service industry entrepreneurs increasing their entrepreneurial behaviour as they increased their familiarity with the market and the manufacturing industry participants reducing their level of entrepreneurial behaviour as the market knowledge increased. The service companies increased their entrepreneurial activity by introducing innovative managerial practices. This was particularly evident in the development process of the development of an innovative and entrepreneurial business structure by Social Media Co and an innovative and entrepreneurial move to an emergent market by HR Consulting Co.

The SMEs in the studies demonstrated significant levels of planning associated with their international entrepreneurial orientation. This finding extends the limited extent international entrepreneur literature, such as Coombs, Sadrieh and Annavarjula's (2009) literature review based observation that entrepreneurial internationalisation is driven less by strategy and planning and more by the personal desire to set up a proposed business in a foreign location. The service participants provided the greatest number of responses of any of the industry constructs, suggesting that participants from this industry were more conscious of the importance of planning how the innovative SME would be established in China than the other participants. This may reflect a greater degree of flexibility of the service SMEs relative to the manufacturing, finance and technology SMEs who were constrained by the process or specific competitive advantage of that process (e.g. the finance participant provided foreign sourced finance opportunities which were considered to be more attractive than domestic Chinese finance). By comparison, the service SMEs had a lower commitment to infrastructure and capital which gave them more flexibility to behave entrepreneurially and were therefore more interested in planning entrepreneurial development.

The higher proportion of responses from the service SMEs in the study than for the other SMEs for the entrepreneurial orientation constructs of planning, creating differences and responding to opportunities provides an interesting finding. Although the business design and entrepreneurial activities of some of the nonservice organisations was very innovative (such as introducing technology new to the market and partnering to maximise the impact of initiatives), these participants appeared to change from the initial innovative and entrepreneurial approach used in the business design, to focus predominantly on transactional activities once they had entered the market. The service industry participants behaved differently, however. They generally entered the market with a lower level of innovation and became more entrepreneurial in their behaviours as their market knowledge increased (building a service providing valuable features not available elsewhere in the market, or taking control of their customer's industry support networks to weaken their competition). This behaviour was partially predicted by the literature which has determined that the establishment of service SMEs is strongly influenced by macro-economic and social factors (Rodríguez-Gutiérrez, Moreno and Tejada, 2015), however, the literature has little to say about the evolution in entrepreneurial orientation of internationalising SMEs. The evolution in entrepreneurial orientation for foreign SMEs over time is an important new construct for the international entrepreneur literature. This finding also provides further explanation to the literature classifying service industry entrepreneurs as introducing significant change to the industry and being influenced by the home country culture (Berglund and Tillmar, 2015; Zhao42012) by determining that the service SMEs became more entrepreneurial over time.

The findings identified the importance of environmental knowledge and focus in ensuring the success of the participant's international businesses. This provides context for Floricel's (2008) finding that entrepreneurs use planning to reduce the effect of unexpected events. It suggests that the planning may incorporate market knowledge and processes for responding to changes in the environment. The emergent nature of the markets described by the participants confirms the importance of identifying and responding to changes in the environment. It is interesting that the SMEs identified gaining market knowledge and responding as associated behaviours, which suggests that they must have adopted dynamic planning. The need to adapt and the use of dynamic planning in the emergent Chinese business environment extends Giunipero, Denslow and Melton's (2008) finding that more formal (and therefore less flexible) business plans (Klingebiel, 2012) were more likely when a domestic entrepreneur perceived a lower level of risk. The finding suggests that the same conditions apply to international entrepreneurs.

The identification of long-term planning activities, such as location selection on the basis of local supporting industries or focusing on a target market segment were behaviours that would normally be associated with domestic operations or operations in a stable environment, about which the entrepreneur had a high level of knowledge. This was an interesting finding as the participants recognised the limitations in their knowledge about their environment and its unpredictability. Dealing with regulatory approvals is a common activity for entrepreneurs and so the long-term planning activities described by the participants may have reflected the obligation for these activities in the Chinese context as well (Lougui and Nystrom, 2014; Vuong, 2016). Location in the industrial park, for example, was described by one participant as providing a simple and coordinated environment for dealing with all of the different government functions, including tax and registrations.

The participants were found to have predominantly focused on creating a difference between their organisation and the competition by inhabiting market niches where there was little competition or by staying one step ahead of the competition in terms of what they offered. This constitutes a different approach to the value creation function normally attributed to entrepreneurs in the literature, in which they compete directly with the market through differentiation or cost (Alvarez and Barney, 2005; Block, 4 2015; Davis and Olson, 2008; Wall-Mullen and Envick, 2015). It provides empirical evidence for Garud, Gehman and Giuliani's (2014) literature based argument that entrepreneurs can currently identify opportunities and contexts and Ozgen's (2011) literature based argument that entrepreneurs scanned the environment to identify these opportunities. This finding also extends Chetty, Ojala and Leppäaho's (2015) work on international entrepreneurial effectuation which found that international entrepreneurs differentiate between foreign market selection and entry using different decision-making processes, by finding that the participants actively selected atypical segments of the market in which they had chosen to internationalise, which would be one of the different decision-making processes they adopt.

The participants also utilised external foci such as networks and market information to differentiate their organisations, however, provided no evidence to suggest that they focused inwardly on making a difference by innovating within their operations. These participants took a different approach to entrepreneurs choosing to compete by internal resource driven innovation, which is an approach identified amongst domestic entrepreneurs (Block et al., 2015; Marques and Ferreira, 2009; Song, Di and Song, 2010; Wall-Mullen and Envick, 2015; Yan, 2012). It suggests that international entrepreneurs are more market focused in regards to their differentiation. This observation was further supported by the fact that the participants' references to their operations were predominantly managerial and transactional and the lack of evidence of imposing their own personal values. Their choice of entry mode added further evidence that the participants did not focus on generating a competitive advantage through the internal capabilities of their Chinese operations. These organisations predominantly entered the market by a joint venture or, where their home country capital resources allowed, via a WOFE. These entry mode selections are the same as the preferred entry approach of both SMEs and large foreign enterprises in China. This finding further extends the international entrepreneur literature strategy which calls for evidence regarding the nature of their strategic decision-making processes (Child and Hsieh, 2014; Coombs, Sadrieh and Annavarjula, 2009).

The opportunities identified by the participants as a result of their foreignness was an interesting finding. In addition to the presence of an advantage of foreignness, the participants also provided evidence to suggest that this advantage was diminishing with time as the market developed. The opportunities that foreignness represented were reducing due to increases in sophistication in China, in areas such as regulation and transparency, which reduced the positive differences between Chinese suppliers and the Australian SMEs (such as more reliable financial histories).

This finding provides an interesting extension to the LOF literature, as well as the findings in chapter 7, which identify the liabilities associated with being a foreign SME. One example is Merino and Grandval's (2012) finding that SMEs in foreign markets needed assistance with marketing and gaining market knowledge which does not consider the fact that the foreign SMEs may possess knowledge because of their foreignness that provides them with an advantage over local organisations. The associated factor, liability of outsidership (LOO) was also found to limit learning about opportunities (Fiedler, Fath and Whittaker, 2017). It can be hypothesised that the SMEs which are able to identify opportunities and acquire market knowledge may experience less LOF. This is an important finding for the LOF literature because it indicates that other factors, including having had the time to learn about the market, can reduce the LOF. It may also be argued, however, that after time companies are simply less foreign. Either way, this barrier may be more transitory for SMEs as they would be able to adapt to the local environment more quickly.

This finding also suggests that the participants gained legitimacy from their foreignness. There was some evidence in the responses to suggest that trust or novelty was increased by the foreignness of the organisation in this environment. This may reflect a lack of awareness of the foreign SME's home environment, rather than a rational basis for trust. It may also be the case that the entrepreneur is able to embody the unique business characteristics of the home country in a way that a representative of a larger organisation is not. The literature identifies the importance of a foreign SME's network connections for gaining trust, and legitimacy (Ngoma, 2016; Ratajczak-Mrozek, 2014), but does not identify the legitimacy which is gained from the SME's home country. Zhou, Wu and Luo (2007) produced some similar evidence by finding that home country social networks provided increased knowledge of opportunities and legitimacy in a foreign market, although this form of legitimacy is the result of engagement between the host country and the foreign market.

Opportunity for the SMEs also seemed to be heavily influenced by the Chinese business and socio-economic environment, suggesting some of the factors that influence opportunities for foreign SMEs there could be institutional in origin. For example government regulation, such as the decision to create special economic, trade and technology zones was a regulatory institutional force that created a significant opportunity for some of these SMEs. The literature provides some empirical evidence for the effect of institutional pressures on foreign entrepreneurs, such as the effect of changing host country regulations in their favour (Eesley, 2016) and the impact of institutional forces on large foreign enterprises is considered extensively in the literature, e.g. (Buracom, 2014; Kang and Liu, 2016; Shou, 42014). The participants also generally displayed similar responses to these opportunities, suggesting that there was an isomorphic response involved. This finding suggests that regulatory isomorphic responses affect the responses of foreign SMEs to regulation opportunities in China. The opportunities available to the participants also appeared to be significantly affected by other factors, including events and chance. The need to be flexible enough to respond to external generated opportunities when they appear probably affects the availability of foreign SMEs' limited resources for generating their own opportunities, resulting in a high dependence on the external environment. This relationship was also identified amongst internationalising Norwegian furniture manufacturing SMEs (Lindmark, 1995).

The findings indicated that the participants were very operationally and external impact focused. Kulchina (2016a) observed that we know very little about how foreign entrepreneurs manage their organisations and found that they were likely to hire more foreign employees and, in a second article, that this reduced operating costs, relative to foreign employed managers (Kulchina, 2017). The finding from this research suggests that operating cost reduction is a result of the internal focus identified in the participants, which also includes adaptation and responsiveness. The external orientation of foreign entrepreneurs, interestingly, is not identified in the literature, although evidence exists for the external orientation of entrepreneurs in general (Becherer and Maurer, 1997; Chen, Chang and Chang, 2015; Gathungu, Aiko and Machuki, 2014). The external orientation of the participants can, however, be explained by the value of the networks and market knowledge as sources of entrepreneurial opportunities (Chen, Chang and Chang, 2015; Costa, Soares and de Sousa, 2016; Gathungu, Aiko and Machuki, 2014; Musteen, Datta and Butts, 2014; Zhou, Wu and Luo, 2007).

The personal characteristics of drive and motivation and the desire to be different identified amongst the participants in relation to their management of their businesses was consistent with the behaviours of domestic foreign entrepreneurs identified in the literature (Bacq, Hartog and Hoogendoorn, 2016; Patten, 2016; Ptak-Chmielewska, 2015; Tan, Smyrnios, and Xiong, 2014). The foreign entrepreneur literature does not specifically identify the characteristics of foreign entrepreneurs and so this finding provides an important extension to this literature by identifying the key characteristics of a foreign entrepreneur's management style as having a high level of focus on disruption, responsiveness and collaboration.

The personal reward aspect of the entrepreneurial behaviour of the participants is another interesting finding which is not addressed in the foreign entrepreneur literature. The most relevant finding in the literature indicated that entrepreneurs are prepared to sacrifice some organisational performance outcomes for operating a business in a location of their choice (Kulchina, 2016b). This finding is consistent with the comments identified in the section above dealing with management style regarding the commitment required for the business and the fact that profits were not achieved quickly. Other motivations identified in the literature included improving personal wealth (Uy, 2011), which was also identified by the participants. The findings indicated that the motivation for the participants appeared to be based on opportunity, knowledge and personal development. This is consistent with the findings from the international business literature regarding the motivation-opportunity-ability theory (Kim, Werner and Pathak, 2015).

The finding that the behaviours of the participants were similar to that predicted by the domestic entrepreneur literature suggests that the current domestic entrepreneur literature can be extended to the domain of entrepreneurial internationalisation by SMEs. The important exception appeared to be in the area of self-identification as an entrepreneur. The higher level of focus on management control activities identified may be a reflection of the more complex external environment in which these entrepreneurs were operating, combined with a lower level of understanding due to the psychic distance between their culture and the culture in which they were operating. This was a particularly interesting behaviour, as the participants also identified the opportunity to work in an entrepreneurial environment as an attractive feature. It may also have been the case that the norm of entrepreneurial behaviour in China (Ngoma, 2016; Song, Di and Song, 2010; Zhao42012) caused them to identify themselves as members of the business manager/owner population, rather than business/manager owners who would consider themselves to be entrepreneurs. This finding extends Lheureux and Auzoult's (2017) research in domestic entrepreneurs in which social norms were also found to affect entrepreneurial self-identity. The effect of this norm on the motivation to internationalise is an important finding because it suggests that the opportunity to set up an international business was of greater significance to the participant than the opportunity to be an entrepreneur The personal attitude and opportunity motivations were consistent with the personal development and opportunity motivations identified in the literature (Hui-Chen, Kuen-Hung and Chen-Yi, 2014). The propensity of the participants to describe their behaviours as business management, rather than entrepreneurship, however, is different to the motivations identified for domestic entrepreneurs. This extends Farmer, Yao and Kung-Mcintyre's (2011) findings that domestic entrepreneurs identified less strongly with being entrepreneurs as their experience increased to internationalising entrepreneurs.

The finding that the participants focused on creative behaviours specifically for the purpose of differentiating themselves from the market is also inconsistent with the domestic entrepreneur literature, which suggests that entrepreneurs engage in creativity because of personal motivation and then use this to differentiate themselves in a market where they believe they can be competitive (Bacq, Hartog and Hoogendoorn, 2016; Farmer, Yao and Kung-Mcintyre, 2011; Uy, 2011). This suggests that a much more scientific approach to business development than the approach used by domestic entrepreneurs, for whom the challenges and risks are possibly lower. The finding that the differentiation process was proactive and utilised creativity, whilst the opportunity seeking process was reactive introduces a new perspective on the evolution of entrepreneurial behaviour in internationalising SMEs. It shows that international entrepreneurs do not utilise existing capabilities and, instead, stimulate the development of new capabilities and resources for the opportunity seeking process. This provides an explanation for Kemmerer's 4(2012) finding that entrepreneurs only consider rareness and inimitability to be valuable resource characteristics. It also suggests that, in the early stages, the identification of the opportunity and motivation to establish the business was a reactive, but not strongly entrepreneurial behaviour, except for the preparedness to take the risk of establishing the business. The differentiation process, by comparison, involved more innovation and creativity and was more consistent with the focus of domestic entrepreneurs choosing to enter a particular market (Block et al., 2015). This suggests a two-stage process for SME internationalisation in which entrepreneurial behaviour actually becomes stronger once the business is established and operating. This extends Obschonka et al.'s (2015) finding that domestic entrepreneurial experience increases entrepreneurial self-identity with the finding that international entrepreneurial experience increases entrepreneurial self-identity as well.

Conclusion

The entrepreneurs in this study described an overlapping set of entrepreneurial constructs to those identified in the international entrepreneurship literature, but with different content. This suggests that internationalising entrepreneurial SMEs in China possess some characteristics consistent with the literature and some characteristics reflecting the effect of the environmental conditions in China. Some of the characteristics, such as a focus on value and inimitable resource generation and the motivation of personal reward, rather than financial reward were consistent with the findings in the international entrepreneur literature. The differences, such as a higher degree of self-identity as a business manager rather than as an entrepreneur and the high level of focus on external factors, including networks distinguished the behaviour of these international entrepreneurial SMEs in China from that of international entrepreneurs described in the literature. The SMEs in this study focused on being entrepreneurial by identifying and responding to opportunities to be innovative, rather than entrepreneurship through a focus on internally driven innovation. This appeared to be a response to the rapid rate of development in China which more frequently presented opportunities than is the case in western countries, however, the availability of the opportunities to the SMEs was also much shorter than is the case in western countries.

Knowledge was found to form part of the constructs of opportunity effects and planning, rather than as a separate construct as literature would suggest. Subsequently, empirical examinations of the effect of entrepreneurial internationalisation should consider knowledge as part of a larger construct. Another interesting finding not identified in the literature was that the service industry participants demonstrated more entrepreneurial behaviours once the business was established than the non-service industry participants who actually reduced their entrepreneurial behaviour after the business was established. In both cases, however, this suggests a change in entrepreneurial behaviour as the business develops, which is consistent with findings for domestic entrepreneurs.

References

Alvarez, S. A., and Barney, J. B. (2005). How do entrepreneurs organize firms under conditions of uncertainty? *Journal of Management*, 31:5, 776–793.
Anderson, B. S., Covin, J. G., and Slevin, D. P. (2009). Understanding the relationship between entrepreneurial orientation and strategic learning capability: An empirical investigation. *Strategic Entrepreneurship Journal*, 3:3, 23.

Bacq, S., Hartog, C., and Hoogendoorn, B. (2016). Beyond the moral portrayal of social entrepreneurs: An empirical approach to who they are and what drives them. *Journal of Business Ethics*, 133:4, 703–718.

Becherer, R. C., and Maurer, J. G. (1997). The moderating effect of environmental variables on the entrepreneurial and marketing orientation of entrepreneur-led firms. *Entrepreneurship: Theory and Practice*, 1, 47.

Berglund, K., and Tillmar, M. (2015). To play or not to play: That is the question: Entrepreneuring as gendered play. *Scandinavian Journal of Management*, 31:2, 206–218.

Block, J., Kohn, K., Miller, D., and Ullrich, K. (2015). Necessity entrepreneurship and competitive strategy. *Small Business Economics*, 44:1, 37–54.

Braga, F., Gualandri, E., and Venturelli, V. (2008). *Bridging the Equity Gap for Innovative SMEs*. Basingstoke : Palgrave Macmillan, c2008.

Buracom, P. (2014). ASEAN Economic Performance, Institutional Effectiveness, and Foreign Direct Investment. *Asian Affairs: An American Review*, 41:3, 108.

Centre, O. I. D. R. (2013). *New Entrepreneurs and High Performance Enterprises in the Middle East and North Africa*. Paris: OECD [Ottawa, ON]: International Development Research Centre, c2013.

Chen, M. H., Chang, Y. Y., and Chang, Y. C. (2015). Entrepreneurial orientation, social networks, and creative performance: Middle managers as corporate entrepreneurs. *Creativity and Innovation Management*, 24:3, 493–507.

Chetty, S., Ojala, A., and Leppäaho, T. (2015). Effectuation and foreign market entry of entrepreneurial firms. *European Journal of Marketing*, 49:9/10, 1436.

Child, J., and Hsieh, L. H. Y. (2014). Decision mode, information and network attachment in the internationalization of SMEs: A configurational and contingency analysis. *Journal of World Business*, 49:4, 598–610.

Chye, E. (2011). Driving growth for SMEs through technological collaboration. *Innovation*, 10:1, 92–93.

Coombs, J. E., Sadrieh, F., and Annavarjula, M. (2009). Two decades of international entrepreneurship research: What have we learned where do we go from here? *International Journal of Entrepreneurship*, 23.

Corbett, A. C., and Hmieleski, K. M. (2007). The conflicting cognitions of corporate entrepreneurs. *Entrepreneurship Theory and Practice*, 31:1, 103–121.

Costa, E., Soares, A. L., and de Sousa, J. P. (2016). Information, knowledge and collaboration management in the internationalisation of SMEs: A systematic literature review. *International Journal of Information Management*, 36:4, 557–569.

Covin, J. G., and Covin, T. J. (1990). Competitive aggressiveness, environmental context, and small firm performance. *Entrepreneurship: Theory & Practice*, 14:4, 35–50.

Covin, J. G., and Miller, D. (2014). International entrepreneurial orientation: Conceptual considerations, research themes, measurement issues, and future research directions. *Entrepreneurship: Theory and Practice*, 1, 11.

Covin, J. G., and Slevin, D. P. (1991). A Conceptual Model of Entrepreneurship as Firm Behavior. *Entrepreneurship: Theory & Practice*, 16(1), 7–25.

Davis, A., and Olson, E. M. (2008). Critical competitive strategy issues every entrepreneur should consider before going into business. *Business Horizons*, 51:3, 211–221.

Do, T. H., Mazzarol, T., Volery, T., Reboud, S. (2014). Predicting anticipated rent from innovation commercialisation in SMEs. *European Journal of Innovation Management*, 2, 183.

Eesley, C. (2016). Institutional barriers to growth: Entrepreneurship, human capital and institutional change. *Organization Science*, 27:5, 1290–1306.

Elodie, G., and Caroline, M. (2012). SME dependence and coordination in innovation networks. *Journal of Small Business and Enterprise Development*, 2, 263.

Farmer, S. M., Yao, X., and Kung-Mcintyre, K. (2011). The behavioral impact of entrepreneur identity aspiration and prior entrepreneurial experience. *Entrepreneurship Theory and Practice*, 35:2, 245–273.

Fiedler, A., Fath, B. P., and Whittaker, D. H. (2017). Overcoming the liability of outsidership in institutional voids: Trust, emerging goals, and learning about opportunities. *International Small Business Journal*, 35:3, 262.

Floricel, S. (2008). Understanding the dynamics of strategic risks and resources in innovative ventures. *International Journal of Entrepreneurship & Innovation Management*, 8:4, 472–487.

Garcia-Cabrera, A. M., Garcia-Soto, M. G., and Duran-Herrera, J. J. (2016). Opportunity motivation and SME internationalisation in emerging countries: Evidence from entrepreneurs' perception of institutions. *The International Entrepreneurship and Management Journal*, 3, 879.

Garud, R., Gehman, J., and Giuliani, A. P. (2014). Contextualizing entrepreneurial innovation: A narrative perspective. *Research Policy*, 43:7, 1177–1188.

Gathungu, J. M., Aiko, D. M., and Machuki, V. N. (2014). Entrepreneurial orientation, networking, external environment, and firm performance: A critical literature review. *European Scientific Journal*, 7, 335.

Gill, R., and Larson, G. S. (2014). Making the ideal (local) entrepreneur: Place and the regional development of high-tech entrepreneurial identity. *Human Relations*, 67:5, 519–542.

Giunipero, L. C., Denslow, D., and Melton, H. L. (2008). Risk propensity, risk perception and business plan formalisation: A conceptual investigation. *International Journal of Entrepreneurship & Innovation Management*, 8:4, 397–416.

Glavas, C., and Mathews, S. (2014). How international entrepreneurship characteristics influence Internet capabilities for the international business processes of the firm. *International Business Review*, 23, 228–245. doi:10.1016/j.ibusrev.2013.04.001

Hayter, C. S. (2015). Public or private entrepreneurship? Revisiting motivations and definitions of success among academic entrepreneurs. *The Journal of Technology Transfer*, 6, 1003.

Hernandez-Carrion, C., Camarero-Izquierdo, C., and Gutierrez-Cillan, J. (2017). Entrepreneurs' social capital and the economic performance of small businesses: The moderating role of competitive intensity and entrepreneurs' experience. *Strategic Entrepreneurship Journal*, 1, 61.

Hilmersson, M., and Papaioannou, S. (2015). SME international opportunity scouting-empirical insights on its determinants and outcomes. *Journal of International Entrepreneurship*, 13:3, 186–211.

Hmieleski, K. M., and Baron, R. A. (2009). Entrepreneurs' optimism and new venture performance: A social cognitive perspective. *Academy of Management Journal*, 52:3, 473–488.

Hui-Chen, C., Kuen-Hung, T., and Chen-Yi, P. (2014). The entrepreneurial process: An integrated model. *International Entrepreneurship and Management Journal*, 10:4, 727–745.

Jantunen, A., Puumalainen, K., Saarenketo, S., and Kyläheiko, K. (2005). Entrepreneurial Orientation, Dynamic Capabilities and International Performance. *Journal of International Entrepreneurship*, 3(3), 223–243. doi:10.1007/s10843-005-1133-2

Jayawarna, D., Rouse, J., and Kitching, J. (2013). Entrepreneur motivations and life course. *International Small Business Journal*, 1, 34.

Jiarong, Y. U., and Shouming, C. (2016). Gender moderates firms' innovation performance and entrepreneurs' self-efficacy and risk propensity. *Social Behavior & Personality: An International Journal*, 44:4, 679–692.

Kang, Y., and Liu, Y. (2016). Natural resource-seeking intent and regulatory forces: Location choice of Chinese outward foreign direct investment in Asia. *Management Research Review*, 39:10, 1313–1335.

Karhunen, P., Olimpieva, I., and Hytti, U. (2017). Identity work of science-based entrepreneurs in Finland and in Russia. *Entrepreneurship & Regional Development*, 29:5/6, 544–566.

Kauppinen, A., and Juho, A. (2012). Internationalisation of SMEs from the perspective of social learning theory. *Journal of International Entrepreneurship*, 10:3, 200–231.

Kemmerer, B., Walter, J., Kellermanns, F. W., and Narayanan, V. K. (2012). A judgment-analysis perspective on entrepreneurs' resource evaluations. *Journal of Business Research*, 65:8, 1102–1108.

Kim, K. Y., Werner, S., and Pathak, S. (2015). When do international human capital enhancing practices benefit the bottom line? An ability, motivation, and opportunity perspective. *Journal of International Business Studies*, 46:7, 784–805.

Klingebiel, R. (2012). Options in the implementation plan of entrepreneurial initiatives: Examining firms' attainment of flexibility benefit. *Strategic Entrepreneurship Journal*, 6:4, 307–334.

Knight, G. (2000). Entrepreneurship and Marketing Strategy: The SME Under Globalization. *Journal of International Marketing*, 8(2), 12–32.

Kulchina, E. (2016a). A path to value creation for foreign entrepreneurs. *Strategic Management Journal*, 37:7, 1240–1262.

Kulchina, E. (2016b). Personal preferences, entrepreneurs' location choices, and firm performance. *Management Science*, 62:6, 1814–1829.

Kulchina, E. (2017). Do foreign entrepreneurs benefit their firms as managers? *Strategic Management Journal*.

Kungwansupaphan, C., and Siengthai, S. (2014). Exploring entrepreneurs' human capital components and effects on learning orientation in early internationalizing firms. *International Entrepreneurship & Management Journal*, 10:3, 561.

Kusumawardhani, A., McCarthy, G., and Perera, N. (2009). *Framework of entrepreneurial orientation and networking: a study of SMEs performance in a developing country*. Paper presented at the Proceedings of the Australian and New Zealand Academy of Management Conference, Adelaide, Australia.

Lheureux, F., and Auzoult, L. (2017). Me, an entrepreneur? Entrepreneurial identity, outgroup social identification, attitudes and intentions towards business creation/¿Yo, un emprendedor? Identidad emprendedora, identificación social con el exogrupo, actitudes e intenciones respecto a la creación de empresas. *Revista de Psicología Social*, 32:2, 246–275.

Liang, C.-T., Peng, L.-P., Yao, S.-N., and Liang, C. (2015). Developing a social enterprise performance scale and examining the relationship between entrepreneurs' personality traits and their perceived enterprise performance. *Journal of Entrepreneurship, Management and Innovation*, 3, 89.

Lindmark, L. (1995). Internationalization of Nordic SMEs – a study of internal and external resources to internationalization. *European Journal of Marketing*, 29:5, 86.

Lougui, M., and Nystrom, K. (2014). What obstacles do entrepreneurs encounter? *Journal of Entrepreneurship & Public Policy*, 3:2, 275.

Lu, J. W., and Beamish, P. W. (2001). The internationalization and performance of SMEs. *Strategic Management Journal*, 22:6–7, 565–586.

Lumpkin, G. T., and Dess, G. G. (2001). Linking two dimensions of entrepreneurial orientation to firm performance. The moderating role of environment and industry life cycle. *Journal of Business Venturing*, 16, 429–451.

Mani, M. (2013). Motivation, challenges and success factors of entrepreneurs: An empirical analysis. *Pertanika Journal of Social Sciences & Humanities*, 21:2, 667–675.

Manoochehr, P., and Mohammad Hasan, M. (2016). Investigating of the effect of entrepreneurial orientations on formation of entrepreneurial identity. *Management Science Letters*, 6:10, 627–634.

Mariola, C.-M. (2016). Foreign market knowledge and SME's international performance: Moderating effects of strategic intent and time-to-internationalization. *Entrepreneurial Business and Economics Review*, 4:4, 51–66.

Marques, C. S., and Ferreira, J. (2009). SME innovative capacity, competitive advantage and performance in a 'Traditional' industrial region of Portugal. *Journal of Technology Management & Innovation*, 4:4, 53–68.

Merino, P. B., and Grandval, S. (2012). Partnerships between SMEs and MNEs on foreign industrial markets: A strategy to reduce the liability of foreignness. *International Business Research*, 6, 53.

Miller, D. (1983). The Correlates of Entrepreneurship in Three Types of Firms. *Management Science*, 770.

Mohammedi, S., and Schnepper, M. (2015). The contribution of cultural diversity in the internationalisation process of an SME in Sweden : A Case Study of the IT Company CodeMill.

Mostafa, R. H. A., Wheeler, C., and Jones, M. V. (2006). Entrepreneurial orientation, commitment to the internet and export performance in small and medium sized exporting firms. *Journal of International Entrepreneurship*, 3(4), 291–302.

Musteen, M., Datta, D. K., and Butts, M. M. (2014). Do international networks and foreign market knowledge facilitate SME internationalization? Evidence from the Czech Republic. *Entrepreneurship: Theory and Practice*, 4, 749.

Navis, C., and Glynn, M. A. (2011). Legitimate distinctiveness and the entrepreneurial identity: Influence on investor judgments of new venture plausibility. *Academy of Management Review*, 36:3, 479–499.

Ngoma, T. (2016). It is not whom you know, it is how well you know them: Foreign entrepreneurs building close guanxi relationships. *Es geht nicht darum, wen du kennst, sondern wie gut du sie kennst: Wie ausländische Unternehmer enge Guanxi-Beziehungen aufbauen.*, 14:2, 239–258.

Nordman, E. R., and Tolstoy, D. (2016). The impact of opportunity connectedness on innovation in SMEs' foreign-market relationships. *Technovation*, 57/58, 47–57.

Obschonka, M., Silbereisen, R. K., Cantner, U., and Goethner, M. (2015). Entrepreneurial self-identity: Predictors and effects within the theory of planned behavior framework. *Journal of Business and Psychology*, 4, 773.

O'Cass, A., and Weerawardena, J. (2009). Examining the role of international entrepreneurship, innovation and international market performance in SME internationalisation. *European Journal of Marketing*, 43(11/12), 1325–1348. doi:10.1108/03090560910989911

Ozgen, E. (2011). Porter's Diamond Model and opportunity recognition: A cognitive perspective. *Academy of Entrepreneurship Journal*, 17:2, 61–76.

Patten, T. (2016). 'Creative?' . . . 'Entrepreneur?' – understanding the creative industries entrepreneur. *Artivate: A Journal of Entrepreneurship in the Arts*, 5:2, 23–42.

Perri, D. F., and Chu, H. M. (2012). Entrepreneurs in China and Vietnam: Motivations and problems. *International Journal of Entrepreneurship*, S1, 93.

Ptak-Chmielewska, A. (2015). Entrepreneurs – demographic profile, who has higher chances of survival? *International Journal of Management Science & Technology Information*, 16, 46–60.

Ratajczak-Mrozek, M. (2014). The importance of locally embedded personal relationships for SME internationalisation processes – from opportunity recognition to company growth. *Journal of Entrepreneurship, Management and Innovation*, 3, 89.

Rauch, A., Wiklund, J., Lumpkin, G. T., and Frese, M. (2009). Entrepreneurial orientation and business performance: An assessment of past research and suggestions for the future. *Entrepreneurship: Theory and Practice*, 3, 761.

Rodríguez-Gutiérrez, M. J., Moreno, P., and Tejada, P. (2015). Entrepreneurial orientation and performance of SMEs in the services industry. *Journal of Organizational Change Management*, 28:2, 194–212.

Shepherd, D. A., and Wiklund, J. (2005). *Entrepreneurial Small Businesses: A Resource-Based Perspective*: Cheltenham, UK; Northampton, MA: Edward Elgar, c2005.

Shou, Z., Chen, J., Zhu, W., and Yang, L. (2014). Firm capability and performance in China: The moderating role of guanxi and institutional forces in domestic and foreign contexts. *Journal of Business Research*, 2, 77.

Slevin, D. P., and Terjesen, S. A. (2011). Entrepreneurial Orientation: Reviewing Three Papers and Implications for Further Theoretical and Methodological Development. *Entrepreneurship: Theory & Practice*, 35(5), 973–987. doi:10.1111/j.1540-6520.2011.00483.x

Song, L. Z., Di Benedetto, C. A., and Song, M. (2010). Competitive advantages in the first product of new ventures. *IEEE Transactions ON Engineering Management*, 57:1, 88–102.

Tan, C. S. L., Smyrnios, K. X., and Xiong, L. (2014). What drives learning orientation in fast growth SMEs? *International Journal of Entrepreneurial Behaviour and Research*, 20:4, 324–350.

Turcan, R., and Juho, A. (2014). What happens to international new ventures beyond start-up: An exploratory study. *Journal of International Entrepreneurship*, 12:2, 129–145.

Uy, A. O. O. (2011). What motivates entrepreneurs? A study of the value systems of Filipino entrepreneur. *International Journal of Entrepreneurship*, 73.

Vasilchenko, E., and Morrish, S. (2011). The role of entrepreneurial networks in the exploration and exploitation of internationalization opportunities by information and communication technology firms. *Journal of International Marketing*, 4, 88.

Vuong, Q. H. (2016). Survey data on entrepreneurs[U+05F3] subjective plan and perceptions of the likelihood of success. *Data in Brief*, 6, 858–864.

Wall-Mullen, E., and Envick, B. R. (2015). Get a clue: How entrepreneurs can manage the service experience to differentiate themselves & provide value propositions that maximize customer satisfaction. *Entrepreneurial Executive*, 20, 1–8.

Wang, J. (2008). The Unintended Consequences of the Sarbanes-Oxley Act on Small Business. In Z. J. Acs and R. R. Stough (Eds.), *Public Policy in an Entrepreneurial*

Economy: Creating the Conditions for Business Growth (pp. 67–93): International Studies in Entrepreneurship. New York: Springer.

Wong, L. L., and Ng, M. (2002). The emergence of small transnational enterprise in Vancouver: The case of Chinese entrepreneur immigrants. *International Journal of Urban & Regional Research*, 26:3, 508–530.

Yan, H.-D. (2012). Entrepreneurship, competitive strategies, and transforming firms from OEM to OBM in Taiwan. *Journal of Asia-Pacific Business*, 13:1, 16.

Yitshaki, R., and Kropp, F. (2016). Entrepreneurial passions and identities in different contexts: A comparison between high-tech and social entrepreneurs. *Entrepreneurship & Regional Development*, 28:3/4, 206–233.

York, J. G., O'Neil, I., and Sarasvathy, S. D. (2016). Exploring environmental entrepreneurship: Identity coupling, venture goals, and stakeholder incentives. *Journal of Management Studies*, 53:5, 695–737.

Zhao, Y. L., Erekson, O. H., Wang, T., and Song, M. (2012). Pioneering advantages and entrepreneurs' first-mover decisions: An empirical investigation for the United States and China. *Journal of Product Innovation Management*, 29, 190–210.

Zhou, L. X., Wu, W. P., and Luo, X. M. (2007). Internationalization and the performance of born-global SMEs: The mediating role of social networks. *Journal of International Business Studies*, 38:4, 673–690.

6 How resources and capabilities can assist foreign SMEs in China

Introduction

It is well known that resources are helpful for small and medium-sized enterprise (SME) internationalisation. SMEs are constrained by resources due to their liability of smallness (Stinchcombe, 1986). In addition, there will be variations in resources between SMEs with some being very small, and others having up to 200 employees, and being more resource rich. Therefore, some SMEs may be very resource scarce, whilst others have sufficient organisational slack to buffer them through the tough and turbulent times, but also more resources to execute the strategies that they wish to, whereas others may not have any slack at all, and hence it is important to classify, and compare the types of resources that SMEs have, and how this assists with their internationalisation, and innovation. This chapters seeks to answer the questions "what resources do innovative SMEs use in their internationalisation?", and "are these resources helpful for innovation?"

The resource based view of the firm

The plethora of research that examines the role of resources in internationalisation generally utilises the resource based view of the firm, or what is commonly known as RBV (Barney, 1991; Penrose, 1959). The main premise of the theory is that gaining and sustaining a competitive advantage resides in the resources and capabilities of the firm and what sets it apart from the competition. Generally, it will be important for these resources and capabilities to give value to the firm, to not have substitutes, to be rare if possible and difficult to imitate (Barney, 1991). Ruzzier, Antonèiè and Koneènik (2006) suggested that the RBV provides theoretical propositions about the uniqueness of certain resources that are critical for the internationalisation process of SMEs. It has been argued that of these resource, it is most important for firms to have intangible resources that are difficult to imitate, and technological resources that assist the firm with innovating products and services, that help the firm in differentiating themselves and allow them to more successfully compete in international markets. The reason why intangible resources are so important is their lack of transparency which makes it more difficult for competitor firms to see what the competitive advantage is and copy.

According to Barney (1991) if firms have VRIN features – resources that are valuable (in the sense that they exploit opportunities and/or neutralise threats in a firm's environment), rare (among the firm's current and potential competition), imperfectly imitable and non-substitutable (cannot be strategically equivalent substitutes for this resource), they will have a competitive advantage over their competitors.

Internationalisation requires the transfer of resources abroad

On the one hand, it is important to have specific and unique resources, but managing and maintaining these resources becomes more complicated when shifting those resources from one country to another, due to the differences in the business environment (which determines their value), and the fact that competencies necessary to gain value from a resource in one country may not necessarily function in another country (Sapienza et al., 2006). This is because internationalising firms need to adapt to new routines, which allows them to react to environmental changes, and bolster their survival. Therefore, internationalisation requires not only the appropriate resources, there is also the question of whether the firm can actually transfer those resources to the foreign country, and gain an advantage from them there (Sapienza et al., 2006). Cuervo-Cazurra (2007) stated that the liabilities of foreignness (LOF) occurs when internationally transferred resources lose their innate advantage in a foreign environment. For example, when an innovation is not accepted in a foreign market, the lack of acceptance creates a LOF. A firm's ability to adapt to its new environment is reflected in its innovativeness, its ability to change, and to be flexible. The ability to innovate is a critical resource that generates value in the market place. Born-global companies require more innovation resources to create a niche market, which is less targeted by competition (Zahra, Ireland and Hitt, 2000) and more risky strategies need more resources.

Resources that are important for internationalisation and innovation

So what are some important resources for innovative and international SMEs? Innovation and internationalisation activities may require different sets of resources, or they may be complementary. For example, an internationalising firm will need human resources with international experience. This international experience maybe important for innovation as well, as it may highlight the need to know whether innovative products or services are appropriate for particular international markets. The findings in Chapter 3 confirmed this by determining that the transfer of some innovations to the Chinese market were not always successful. Or some resources that are relevant for internationalisation might not at all be needed for innovation.

Presence in international markets triggers opportunities (Sapienza et al., 2006), but also presents risks and LOF to firms, which then increases the costs of doing business – for example, insufficient market knowledge, negative country of origin image, cultural institutional differences of the home country to name a few, may cause difficulties for the firm. Presence in a foreign market may be helpful for internationalisation, but also innovation, especially where the host country, such as China, offers innovation opportunities through high tech business parks and the ability to co-locate with other technologically orientated firms, which allows SMEs to gain spillover effects.

Internationalisation requires different strategies and entry modes at different stages, which in turn, require different resources. The literature has found that the resources available to an organisation will affect the success of strategic decisions (Chang and Rhee, 2011), and influence what a firm can achieve. SMEs can only survive if they carefully weigh up the resource requirements and environmental conditions that apply to a strategic decision. This can be described as evaluating their 'resource endowment'. A firm's resources will determine if particular strategies are viable (Filatotchev and Piesse, 2009). Andrews (1971) argued that strategy "is the matching process between the resources of the organisation and opportunities in the business environment at an acceptable level of risk". This point is very apparent in the choices and strategies of the SMEs in this study. They matched their resources and capabilities with the opportunities in the external environment, but also used their capabilities to minimise risk.

The impact of organisation size is important for SME internationalisation

Firms will select an appropriate internationalisation strategy that is based on their resource endowment. Internationalisation requires a larger amount of resources than domestic operations, i.e. it increases the resource demand. It is also known that the resource base helps to reduce the effects of the LOF and improves the chances of survival. Abundant resources act as organisational slack, making international operations more feasible and less risky. Slack resources act as a buffer against bankruptcy and other downsides, risks and costs and ensures the survival of the firm (Tan and Peng, 2003). Slack resources are a firm's size (Tan and Peng, 2003) and productivity (Mishina, Pollock and Porac, 2004). It is generally important to have slack resources, as it helps the firms in turbulent environments to cope with adaptation demands or downturn risks (Sharfman, Woff and Chase, 1988). But not all SMEs will have slack resources due to their size based constraints and therefore they must get by with the resources that they have, and make do with what they don't have.

Similarly, access to more resources should also allow a firm to be more innovative, as this means that the firm has more money for resource and development (R&D) activities and may have better educated staff. SMEs specific resources representing competitive advantages allow them to successfully enter, develop and operate in international markets (Ruzzier, Antonèiè and Koneènik, 2006). The scope of internationalisation is effected by a firm's tangible and intangible resources (Tan, Plowman and Hancock, 2007). Firms with greater resource endowments have greater choices in international markets, for example they can choose more international markets and more committed resources. Slack resources of a firm are also a feature of firm survival, and are important in turbulent environments. Firm size is an indicator of slack resources. Larger firms have more managerial resources to spare. Larger firms are less affected by the LOF, as operating abroad demands significant financial resources, because they have more resources to use on these costs. It is generally predicted that if a firm gradually internationalises it will face lower uncertainty, and it will demand less resources. Gradual internationalisation will reduce the strain on the resource base and the rate with which resources have to adapt to the conditions in the foreign market. Born-globals, on the other hand require a stronger tangible resource base, due to them rapidly expanding and needing greater resources. A firm's innovation resources are an important driver for international values creations (Morck and Yeung, 1991).

Small SMEs need to do more with less. SMEs need to rely on their intangible knowledge. Knowledge assists with reducing costs and LOF. The general literature points to a range of helpful resources for internationalisation which includes intellectual, human, social and technological resources.

Types of resources used by SMEs

Resources in general can be considered stocks of available tangible or intangible factors that are controlled by a firm and converted into products or services using a variety of other resources and bonding mechanisms. Different resource classifications have been proposed, for example Amit and Schoemaker (1993) suggested seven main categories of resources: financial (size and type of capital); physical (location, plant, access to raw materials, transportation etc.); human (personnel and management); technological (product and process-related); reputation (image, brands, loyalty, trust, goodwill); organisational (management systems) and networking (firm's relationships). Wernerfelt (1995) classified resources into three groups: physical, financial and intangible resources referred to as tacit knowledge (Peng, 2001) or organisational routines and skills (Nelson and Winter, 1982). Collins (1994) proposed an alternative classification of resources which includes resources related to the firm's ability to perform basic functional activities, such as production or marketing, resources that enable the dynamic development of the firm's activities, for instance, the capabilities of product development, manufacturing flexibility or innovation management support the firm's ability to learn, adapt, change and renew over time and resources, closely related to the second, which account for the firm's ability to recognise the intrinsic value of resources. An important conceptual distinction with regard to resources is the difference between resources and capabilities. In principle, capabilities can also be viewed as resources: if resources are stocks, then capabilities are flows (Penrose, 1959) since they refer to a firm's capacity to deploy resources, using organisational processes to influence a desired end (Chandler and Hanks, 1994; Hall, 1993). Capabilities link resources in complex patterns of co-ordination between multiple agents (between people, and between people and resources) (Grant, 1991; Foss and Eriksen, 1995). Perfecting such co-ordination requires learning through repetition and this leads to organisational routines (Winter, 1995).

Based on the above definitions, the resources examined in this study have been categorised as the tangible (e.g., equipment, machinery, mail list), intangible (e.g., brand name, customer knowledge, finance) or human (skills of employees, talented managers) assets that the firm possesses and that are likely to emerge as the result of prior investments, actions or ongoing capabilities (Amit and Schoemaker, 1993). Capabilities on the other hand are what a firm does, and represent the firm's competency in deploying resources that have been purposely integrated to achieve a desired end state (Grant, 1991). We now investigate the types of resources that the SMEs used for internationalisation, and whether this was helpful for innovation.

Results of the study

The interviews provided a total of 71 references to the word "resources". The interviews were analysed to identify the tangible, intangible, human resources, organisational resources/capabilities and their sub-themes and how they the assisted the firm with internationalisation and/or innovation.

Tangible resources

Tangible resources identified in the study had included parent company support, physical presence in China, the choice of location in China and Hong Kong as a location of interest (Table 6.1).

Parent company support

Overall, there were 10 SMEs that mentioned parent company support as an important resource for their setup and ongoing operations in China, due to the resources that they provided and ongoing management and service support. This was mentioned by the importers, exporters and three WOFEs. The interview text mainly specified that parent company support helped the SMEs with the

Table 6.1 Tangible resources and mode of internationalisation

Type of resources	Number of SMEs	Importer	Exporter	WOFE	BIC
Parent company support	10	3	4	3	0
Presence in China	12		1	1	10
Location in China	13	1	1	9	2
Hong Kong as location of interest	25	1	1	13	10

day-to-day running of their businesses, and support when needed. Parent company support was seen as highly valuable by the SMEs and gave them access to more resources and financial support to effectuate strategies:

> We receive support from our head office in Australia. I think in many ways just being an Australian company can help.
>
> (Case 15: Resources Supplier)

Similarly, Vehicle Warranty Co had echoed the previous case's sentiments:

> We're just using our Australian team, our software team of maybe 60 staff. There are a lot of things they can help us with.
>
> (Case 13: Vehicle Warranty Co)

This support gave these SMEs the slack and buffer resources needed to maintain operations and ask for help when in need. Quite differently to this, all of the BIC firms did not have parent company support, as they did not originate from Australia, however, they were at times still successful, and hence parent company support was not always necessary. In relation to innovation, some SMEs had stated that their parent company had assisted with the transfer of innovative products, because in the parent company, this is where R&D took place, innovations were developed, and these were transferred to the subsidiary, as in the case of Box Co. Therefore, parent company support was important for internationalisation and innovation.

Physical presence

Physical presence in China was considered to be an important resource that provided credibility and trust to the SME in the Chinese market, but also allowed the SME to manage their operations more successfully. The importance of physical presence was identified by all BIC firms (10) and an exporter and a WOFE firm. They believed having a presence, and the firm being represented in person established the trust of their products and/or service offering to the market, and it allowed them to promote, manage and solve problems in their business, which could not be done from abroad. The following quote from Pneumatic Co indicates physical presence is essential to represent the firm in the market:

> If you don't have an on the ground presence there, it's very difficult to get consideration because they're concerned about who's here if I have a problem. Without having that on the ground there, it's proving to be, well, not impossible; it's unlikely.
>
> (Case 6: Pneumatic Co)

Having this physical presence appears to be advantageous, assisting with the management of the operations, achieving the strategy and getting known in the market and concurs with Sapienza et al.'s (2006) findings. It also allows the firm to know more about the market, and sort out problems straight away:

> If you're not in a market, you're looking at it remotely, you can make a lot of assumptions in our business which make a lot of sense from a distance but once you get up close and things become more into focus you actually realise that you are misreading it.
>
> (Case 11: Recruitment Co)

This suggests that having a presence will help the SME to internationalise and be successful and that not having a presence can have negative effects for performance in the Chinese market. According to Bausch and Van (2007) internationalising into China involves a great amount of risk that might be hard to overcome in the short run, and presence assists with overcoming the issues. This contrasts strongly with some of the literature that found that having a presence in an international market could have negative consequences (Sapienza et al., 2006), especially where the company had a negative country of origin perception. Interestingly, the analysis of the interviews revealed that presence was not mentioned alongside innovation. It is unlikely that resources were not required for innovation, however, the participant's focus on resource utilisation may have been more strongly biased toward supporting the internationalisation process.

Location in China

Concurring with Amit and Schoemaker's (1993) work, the representatives of SMEs also commented on selecting the best location in China, with 13 SMEs referring to favourable locations for their business. Office Co had commented on their strategic thought process on picking locations:

> I think the free trade area is good for us. I suppose, offer our services to those clients that have offices there for an inner-city subsidiary. . . . One of the main things is our four USPs are in a number one location so always providing an easy, accessible, great location, good IT team and flexible lease terms.

Or as one other case firm mentioned: *"Shanghai is a more convenient location for us"* (Processing Co, Case 16). Location was also mentioned in relation to innovation, with some SMEs mentioning that they choose technology parks:

> In the course of visiting lots of different technology parks in lots of different cities, this is the park where they felt that the park was the right size, the right location, had a grant scheme that they were promoting that sounded like it was a good fit for what we were doing and no real negatives.
>
> (Case 8: Biotech Co 1)

Therefore, location was considered to be an important resource that helped the firm to be efficient and assisted them to access important resources. The literature also notes that location choice is critical for the success of international SMEs (Gilbert, McDougall and Audretsch, 2008). It was also important for innovation.

Hong Kong as location of interest

Locating in Hong Kong proved to be a strong theme amongst the participants. At least 25 out of the 35 interviewees commented that aspects of Hong Kong were beneficial to their business, despite the fact that their main focus of business was in Mainland China. Some had chosen Hong Kong to register their business, although their business was predominantly Chinese based. Hong Kong was perceived to be a helpful location for internationalisation, due to the ease of setting up operations in Hong Kong, the lack of capital requirements (whereas mainland China had quite high capital requirements which was a challenge for the smaller SMEs in the study), and others were interested in overcoming the regulation controls imposed in China:

> We chose Hong Kong as it was very helpful so in a business setting up in Asia who wants to use the Hong Kong hub, Hong Kong gives people an understanding of how to go forward. I think a lot of times it's value proposition and what markets you're looking at.
>
> (Case 33: Investment Co)

Social Media Co discussed their use of Hong Kong, and how it facilitated being an entrepreneur:

> Like most younger entrepreneurs who aren't capitalised, we set up a Hong Kong company for us and as you understand there's moving capital requirements to set up a WOFE. There's no capital funds in Hong Kong which is eight days and you're done, it's wonderful. Here it takes four to six months to get a WOFE operational and registered capital has to be paid within two years.
>
> (Case 27: Social Media Co)

Social Media Co found that establishing in Hong Kong circumvented the costs associated with setting up a business in China and allowed this business to start under more supportive conditions and without extensive capital requirements. A presence in Hong Kong appeared to be less important for innovation outcomes, however some SMEs said that Hong Kong was a very entrepreneurial place, which helped them with developing their business.

Intangible resources

The intangible resources used by SMEs are listed below with the firms' mode of internationalisation (Table 6.2). Intangible resources included brand, reputation, Australian origin/brand, experience and knowledge.

Table 6.2 Intangible resources and mode of internationalisation

Type of resources	Number of SMEs	Importer	Exporter	WOFE	BIC
Brand	25	2	2	13	8
Reputation	15	1	1	7	6
Australian origin/ brand	7		4	3	
Experience	28	2	3	14	9
Knowledge	20	3		11	6

Brand

Brand names, or having a brand for the SMEs was seen as a highly significant resource for the SMEs, with around 25 of the participants suggesting that it was important to have a well-defined brand name and marketing message in the Chinese market. This was mentioned in relation to all of the entry modes (importing, exporting, WOFE and BICs). The participants indicated that this was especially important because China was so large, and had so much noise in terms of marketing communicating and it was critical for the SMEs to be known for what they do. Especially, when they were so small:

> I focus on two things. One is brand, there are the things that help our brand be seen publicly in a positive light in areas that are attractive so like we host an entrepreneurial award so it makes us look very entrepreneurial in that space.
>
> (Case 27: Social Media Co)

Biotech 1 (Case 8) summarised this succinctly in relation to the difficulty of becoming known in the Chinese market:

> The brand recognition – China is so large so if you're meeting a mid-level bureaucrat from a random second tier city government agency, there is no way that they will have ever heard of Biotech 1. Again I think people underestimate the scale of everything in China. We're a tiny little player in a very, very large pond.

Reputation

Reputation was also linked to brands. Sixteen of the SMEs indicated that they found having a reputation was significant for them in developing a presence and competitive advantage in China. This reputation had also assisted the SME with gaining initial and repeat business:

> Within the specific industry, dry cleaning industry, the company has got a fairly good reputation so it's fairly well recognised from that perspective. So

from that perspective it's probably the history as well as the recognition and reputation in the particular industry.

(Case 3: Chemical Co)

Reputation has been identified as an important resource for internationalisation (Amit and Schoemaker, 1993). Reputation did not appear to assist the firms with their innovation, however, so it contributed to success in the international market along different paths, possibly including being known for being able to provide a particular service or product. Brand experts such as Keller (1993) suggest that reputation can be leveraged by the firm for market success.

Australian origin

Linked into branding and reputation, "Australian origin" was another strong resource that the SMEs had said helped them with their Chinese business, with seven indicating that this was the case. The participants suggested that this helped them stand out from the competition, especially in relation to Chinese competitors, because the Chinese liked Australians, and trusted Australian products – especially food products in the wake of a number of Chinese food scares and poisoning. It is difficult for non-Australian firms to imitate or substitute such resources which have earned unique acceptance in the Chinese market. All four exporter SMEs and three WOFE type SMEs were of the opinion that Australian brand or Australian 'origin' has an added value in the Chinese market and had included perceptions of quality, freshness and safeness as opposed to Chinese products:

> Our Australian heritage will also help as well because maybe the other competitors entered the market and don't have the same background. Chinese people love Australia so this is huge; no doubt that is a massive advantage.

(Case 13: Vehicle Co)

This was also demonstrated in the following quote:

> And so just being from Australia, you have a certain reputation for the quality of your product and I think that helps us to set us apart from some of our competitors around the world.

(Case 25: Meat Co)

Experience

Twenty-eight participants commented on the value of their experience. International experience formed part, but mainly the SMEs had stated that they were doing what they were doing in the Chinese market due to their experience in business, either back in Australia, in other international markets or in China itself. International experience is a common factor that is explored in the literature on internationalisation (Johanson and Vahlne, 1977), which found that firms will experience better success in international markets (Johanson and Vahlne, 1990), and will more likely use higher involved modes when they have a greater amount of experience. Camisón and Villar-Lopez (2010) found that there is a close relationship between international experience of SMEs and their endowment of assets. Economic performance occurs once the SMEs utilise the knowledge they gained from international experience into an endowment of internationally exploitable, intangible assets and into a differentiation competitive strategy. The findings from this study of resources indicated that there was an important role played by experience in this study:

> This will reflect a reasonable level of international market experience, for sure. If you've been marketing into Europe for 30 or 40 years, into North America, so in a way China is more a roll out of our experience in other countries rather than a brand-new ground zero with not much relevant transferrable experience, yes, definitely a roll out of something we've done before.
>
> (Case 16: Resource Co)

Extended experience in China provides SMEs added advantages in comparison with foreign enterprises having no such experience:

> The long history of engagement in China is a very strong one and the history, and I think married to our long experience in China, is that we have a corporate mission that is aligned with what we're doing.
>
> (Case 10: Biotech Co)

It is well known that international experience is important for SME internationalisation as it reduces the LOF that SMEs face, and allows the SME to develop strategies for the market. It also allows SMEs to understand the routines that are involved with internationalisation, and applying those routines to a new situation. In summary, the findings from the analysis were supported by the literature (Camisón and Villar, 2010, Tseng, Tansuhaj and Rose, 2004) that also determined the intangible assets owned by SMEs significantly affect their internationalisation strategy and, therefore, the commitment that they take on during their international expansion process.

Knowledge

Similar to experience, knowledge was mentioned as a key resource by 20 SMEs that was used in the firm's internationalisation. Although the word "know" was highly utilised by the participants, with approximately 502 references to the word in the interview transcripts, suggesting that know and knowledge are important concepts for these firms. Meat Co had provided an example of the knowledge that was so important for them with their internationalisation to China:

> Then there's the intangible assets like our corporate knowledge and our intellectual property that you can't put a value on.

Others had suggested that the knowledge was helpful in combination with a number of other resources:

> So the best project management, the best technical knowledge, the best, the good experiences from the discovery from the Western countries are combined with the resources in China because chemistry in China is quite developed already so we combine together so basically we can get input, we can get sources from this side but sometimes we try to use their skills in chemistry to deliver.
>
> (Case 10: BioTech 3)

The below statement from a SME in the consultancy business also believes knowledge (of staff) is the key to their success.

> In our line of business having knowledge of staff is very important. We don't have a business without the knowledge. We market ourselves and pitch our business on an execution expertise, not on having 500 people who are the world's leading experts in TMT, in resources, whatever. It's not first and foremost, our industry sector knowledge; it's our expertise that's so important.
>
> (Case 30: Arbitration Co.)

The literature has identified the role of knowledge in internationalisation and that it is important for innovative SMEs to quickly learn how to adapt to new situations such as a foreign country. It also has been found that the acquired knowledge in response to new situations is more important than prior acquired knowledge (Autio, Sapienza and Almeida, 2000; McDougall, Shane and Oviatt, 1994, Weerawardena et al., 2007). The literature has also determined that internationalisation for innovative SMEs is influenced by the internal resources of the entrepreneur, such as their knowledge, skills and financial resources (O'Cass and Weerawardena, 2005). Coeurderoy et al. (2012) finds that international start-ups with high levels of knowledge, a strong commitment to the market or a strategic plan will have greater chances of survival than those that do not. Knowledge was also found to be important for innovation, as having well educated and knowledgeable staff was helpful for developing new products. In particular, the high-tech SMEs examined in this study indicated that they employed very knowledgeable staff, with some having PhDs and masters, in the R&D function of the company.

Human resources

All the SMEs in the study expressed the opinion that appropriate human resources (people with correct skills, knowledge and experiences) were their key reason for success in China, which is indicated in Table 6.3. "People" was one of the most commonly used words in the study, with more than 1000 references to the word "people" in our interview transcripts. There was a strong focus on the use of Chinese local staff, with less of a focus on the use of expatriate staff.

Table 6.3 Human resources and mode of internationalisation

Human resources	Number of SMEs	Importer	Exporter	WOFE	BIC
Western educated Chinese: Sea turtles (Haigui)	8		1	5	2
Chinese (Local) Staff	30	1	3	17	9
Owners/Managers/ Employees capabilities/ experience	28	2	3	14	9
External consultants	16	1	3	4	8
Owners/Managers' Chinese background	5	1		4	

*Western educated Chinese (*Haigui *Sea turtles)*

Western educated local staff were considered to be a valuable resource by the participants of the study, as these individuals had been exposed to both cultures and were capable of speaking Chinese language and English. The participants representing eight of the SMEs were of the opinion that Chinese staff who had studied in western parts of the world and had returned back to China (*Haigui or sea turtles*) were vital resources for their firms as they understood both 'worlds':

> We always want to have at least one Haigui in the office. . . . We would value them more, probably.
>
> (Case 28: Consultant 1)

An exporter SME below was of the opinion that this provided assistance with being familiar in this unknown territory:

> I think it will be essential to get some Western educated Chinese nationals into the business in China; they'd need to be in China.
>
> (Case 6: Pneumatic Tools)

The interview transcripts revealed that it was important for managing the interface of the international business with the Chinese context, but that Haigui's were not often utilised for innovative purposes. The research results indicate that staff have experience in both 'worlds' (Asian and Western) were popular among the SMEs (sea turtles) and considered as a key resource of the firm because of their ability of understanding both Australian cultural issues and their special ability to deal with local (China) issues. Accordingly, the SMEs in the study recruited 'sea turtles' to provide a competitive edge. According to the analysis of research results, the SMEs experienced difficulties in finding staff with correct skills (knowledge and experiences) and some SMEs blamed the Chinese education system for this issue. Some of the respondents expressed the view that locally educated staff, having experienced an authoritarian teaching system, lacked creativity. They found that local staff required a significant level of supervision and they in general do not take initiative and/or are self-driven. Hambrick and Mason (1984) supported this observation by finding that the knowledge and abilities of personnel are directly related to their education. A qualification does not automatically imply the possession of the necessary skills to work in a particular industry, nor do skilled workers necessarily have a specific qualification.

People with education in other parts of the world were limited in the Chinese market as globalisation has increased the mobility of high-skilled talent. For many countries in the developing world, the loss of such individuals represents a longstanding concern; countries such as China have now developed key policies to harness their overseas talent (Hao and Welch, 2012) and attract them back.

Chinese local staff

In a manner consistent with the findings in the literature, the SMEs focused strongly on utilising local staff. Thirty of the SMEs across all of the entry modes employed local staff and found that they were helpful for understanding the culture, building relationships in the market, and speaking the language. It appeared that being local was important for this SME:

> We're legally an Australian practice but in terms of how we actually operate we're a local business with local people doing local jobs in the local marketplace understanding local conditions and that's been very successful for us whereas there's a lot of people who've blown a lot of money by flying in and out thinking they'll get a big billion-dollar job that never got delivered.
>
> (Case 19: Architect Co)

The use of these local staff was also important for innovative activities, as the plans by Biotech 1 (Case 8), highlight:

> We would then recruit local Chinese staff and then there'll be a system of exchanges where they come here, we go there for the training and managing the R&D.

For all these reasons, it was apparent that using local staff was the most preferred method although most of the SMEs employed expatriates in key management positions. The firm below mainly employed local staff, as their involvement is vital in dealing with local factories, which is a better way for them to deal with cultural differences:

> The rest of my staff (except me) is Chinese and really the big four of our staff are Chinese Westerners who are the face for the Western customers. When we're out in the Chinese factories, there's a barrier and it doesn't matter how long I'm here because I'm not Chinese so you need your Chinese staff

that you can trust, they can get through barriers that I can't. So it's crucial to have that Chinese face to your business if you're going to do proper business here.

(Case 35: Shop Fitting Co)

The literature confirms that the level of human capital in an SME positively influences internationalisation (Ruzzier, 42007). Human capital is considered to be crucial to the recognition and exploitation of business opportunities, therefore human capital has critical importance as a resource for internationalisation (Cerrato and Piva, 2010). There has been a growing recognition that the effective management of human resources internationally is a major determinant of success or failure in international business (Scullion and Starkey, 2011).

Local staff were an essential element of the SMEs resources and expatriate staff played a vital role as well, managing, training, controlling and leading staff. SMEs also preferred recruiting expatriates with Asian experience and/or an Asian background as this experience can help the firm in many ways managing business issues in the local environment. The results demonstrate that SMEs were able to utilise their employee's local and international exposure in responding to issues associated with differences in terms of culture, ethical standards and language and communication. Cerrato and Piva (2010) argued that compared to domestic firms, international firms have to face a number of additional issues, associated with differences and variety in terms of: culture; ethical standards; behaviour of customers and suppliers; language and communication. Accordingly, the research results comply with Cerrato and Piva's (2010) findings.

According to Cerrato and Piva (2010), international activity makes it necessary for SMEs to have a greater endowment of capabilities and competencies compared to purely domestic SMEs. The SMEs in the study relied on their staff's skills and knowledge of the business, particularly the service type firms who appreciated their staff's knowledge and experience and considered them to be key resources for their business success. Cerrato and Piva (2010) stated that employees' knowledge and skills are valuable resources and are more critical to the achievement of competitive advantage than tangible or financial resources, as they are more likely to possess those characteristics (e.g. valuable, difficult to imitate or substitute) that scholars of the resource-based view have identified as sources of competitive advantage (Barney, 1991).

In internationalisation studies, the lack of qualified personnel has been found to be a relevant internal resource barrier to exporting (Leonidou, 2004; Tesfom and Luts, 2006; Pinho and Martins, 2010). SMEs also experience difficulties in hiring specialised human resources (Ortiz et al., 2009). In small firms, constraints in terms of human resources, and financial resources (to employee those human resources) make the task of identifying and operating in foreign markets more problematic.

Owner/managers' skills and capabilities

Personal skills and capabilities of owners or managers can be considered as another resource that is valuable for the firm in their internationalisation. The owner/manager of the below firm believes his education in Australia and working experiences in Asia has helped him run his business successfully in China:

> My education of business management from university in Australia is definitely a major help. I've been in Guangzhou for about eight years. I was in Taiwan for about three years.
>
> (Case 23: Print Co)

Similarly, the representative of this SME believed his and his partner's abilities and expertise were success factors:

> It's really based on my capabilities which were English, Australian and Hong Kong law and my studies in China and then the next person, Dr F, who was a Chinese national who studied in Beijing, the world's leading female arbitrator, so she's my secret weapon. So it was kind of built around our skills.
>
> (Case 31: Arbitration Co)

The following statement expresses the owner's skills and experience and how decision-making can play a key role:

> I suppose it's partly me and the way I think and the way I experience things. I think you use part of your own skills and attitudes obviously and then you can leverage your connections and other peoples' skills.
>
> (Case 33: Investment Co)

Ten SMEs pointed out that their owner's capabilities were a key factor for their survival in the Chinese market. These SMEs were of this opinion because the continued involvement of a firm's CEO in business operations and decision making process have a critical impact on the firms' performance in internationalisation. The below quote indicates a CEO's role which is a firm's unique capability:

> M, who is the CEO of the group and owner of the company, is very hands-on, very active, goes to China as many times as I do, five, six times a year I suppose.
>
> (Case 1: Furniture Co)

The manager of the importer SME believes he has had an additional advantage in dealing with China due to his wife having an Asian background who speaks two Chinese languages:

> In fact we probably have maybe six Mandarin speaking people in the company at different levels. The advantage we have is my wife speaks Mandarin and Hokkien Cantonese. It helps if you can communicate with people in their own language.
>
> (Case 2: Rubber Co)

The development of the firm's managerial capabilities can facilitate a successful international expansion (Boeker and Karichalil, 2002). Further, successful international expansion requires the managerial capabilities necessary to configure and leverage a firm's resources in the international marketplace, although the managerial capabilities of SMEs can lag in this requirement, particularly for high levels of internationalisation (Graves and Thomas, 2006).

The SMEs in this study made extensive use of their owners/manager in the Chinese operations. The personal skills and capabilities of owners and managers and their commitment to the business success played a vital role in the internationalisation process to China. Scullion and Starkey (2011) found that international firms focused on senior management development, succession planning and developing a cadre of international managers. Previous studies have indicated that management commitment to internationalisation has a significant impact on export performance (Kuivalainen et al., 2004). Javalgi and Todd (2011) suggested also that the management commitment to internationalisation is also positively related to the degree of internationalisation of SMEs.

The participants representing the SMEs in the study also expressed the opinion that their manager's abilities and expertise were essential factors for success in business in China's market. They believed that managers with education and training in Australia and working experience in Asia helped them to create a successful business in China. The relationship between education and experience of entrepreneurs or managers has been studied extensively (Cooper, Gimeno-Gascon, and Woo, 1994). Tihanyi et al. (2000) and Javalgi and Todd (2011) found that there is a positive relationship between the top management's level of education and experience, and internationalisation. The results indicate that all BIC SMEs' managers/owners possess previous international experience. The human and social capital of organisations usually results from international business skills acquired through the entrepreneurs' and managers' professional experience in foreign markets while, in terms of previous occupations and schooling, it has also been associated with internationalisation (Ruzzier, Antonèiè and Koneènik., 2006). This was based on the assumption that such accumulated experience exposes the decision-makers to information, knowledge, resources and contacts relating to foreign markets and enhances the likelihood of international business engagement and expansion (Reid, 1983). This is particularly true when professional experience has been attained in an international setting through involvement, for example, in multinational corporations or international organisations (Ruzzier, Antonèiè and Koneènik, 2006).

The participants representing the SMEs in the study indicated that not only the personalities of the owners/managers were important factors for successful business operations in the Chinese market, a critical decision making ability was also important. According to Cerrato and Piva (2010), management competencies and human resource skills play a significant role if opportunities for international development are to be fully exploited. Specifically, a limited endowment in terms of human capital is a relevant constraint to international development (Cerrato and Piva, 2010). Reuber and Fischer (1997) concluded that the ability of a firm to successfully manage international growth is influenced by the behavioral integration of the management team. Qian (2002) proposed that entrepreneurs with little previous foreign involvement and international experience should compensate for these weaknesses when competing in the international arena. According to the results of this study, the owner/manager's international experience positively affects the establishment of BIC type SMEs. Ruzzier, Antonèiè and Koneènik (2006) argued that because of the increasing number of internationally experienced entrepreneurs who are able to recognise the required amount and type of critical resources for international activities, the number of internationalised SMEs that are from their early beginnings 'born-global firms' (McDougall, Shane and Oviatt, 1994), is growing. Ruzzier, Antonèiè and Koneènik (2006) pointed out that critical resources for international activities are valuable for entrepreneurs seeking to start with internationalisation, but who do not have international experience, albeit the decision to internationalise is clearly multi-faceted and a successful internationalisation strategy should be based on more resources than just the experience, education and personal knowledge of the owners/founders.

Further, Ruzzier et al. (2007) argued that the entrepreneur's human capital relates positively and directly to the degree of internationalisation of the firm, as reflected in time spent in international activities, mode of market, degree and product. In addition, they stated there is a direct effect between individual dimensions of human capital of the firm's entrepreneur and firm internationalisation. Ruzzier et al.'s (2007) findings regarding the entrepreneurs' human capital suggest that the owner/founder acquires a broader international perspective through experience, which reduces their perceptions of risk associated with selling in foreign markets and increases knowledge of how best to sell in these markets.

Some of the participants representing the SMEs in the study suggested that an owner/manager's personal level relationships, for example being married to a local woman, assisted them with establishing and running a business in China. They were of the opinion that such personnel level attributes are vital in dealing with the language and cultural barriers they experience in China. Ruzzier et al. (2007), while supporting the notion that the personal attributes of an SME's chief entrepreneur are associated with SME internationalisation, also found that some attributes are more important in this regard than others. Entrepreneurs who are most exposed to foreign cultures through travel or residence likely accumulate experiential knowledge of international market characteristics which benefits them when internationalising their firms (Ruzzier et al., 2007).

External consultants

Some SMEs had employed external consultants for specific functions of business operations. The firm below uses co-operation agreements with advisory firms in Australia to co-operate in terms of client feeding which enhances their capacity and capabilities:

> We've got 12 co-operation agreements with advisory firms in Australia to co-operate in terms of client feeding. We've probably got four or five

co-operation agreements here in Shanghai so their capability becomes our capability. We get a small percentage, they bill the client, we can either put them in touch but ultimately we're maintaining our relationship with the client.

(Case 28: Consult Co 1)

Using external professionals in China was an important resource for SMEs, especially those ones who had a small size and limited financial capacity:

We have part time bookkeepers; we have an external accounting company who can do books into Chinese and English for our Australian finance team. It's quite simple.

(Case 13: Vehicle Warranty Co.)

Mainly, the consultants or external organisations were used by the SMEs for internationalisation and assistance with day-to-day activities, such as bookkeeping. Although these external consultants were less likely to be used for the innovative activities of the firm, the interviews provided some mention of this, for example noting that they had assisted with the preparation of innovation grants:

Again we're looking at what government programmes are available to support us. Where there is none or where I can't identify or don't know of, I use some consultants who are specialists in grants.

(Case 9: Biotech Co 3)

The development of the firm's resources, such as relationships with various expert organisations, research institutions or universities, represented external firm-oriented resources (Ruzzier, Antonèiè and Koneènik, 2006). Ahokangas (1998) determined that SMEs are dependent on the development potential of not only internal resources, but also external resources, which can be developed within and between firms and their environments. The research results indicate that the SMEs in the study use government agencies, research institutes and external consultants for their business activities for different purposes and occasions. External consultants helped the SMEs in two ways – for specific business operations, using their expertise, knowledge and experience and as a resource, especially for the smaller SMEs in the study with limited staff and financial capacity. Networking with other organisations can also be treated as external resources and forming joint ventures are other forms of external resources used by SMEs for the business purpose.

Owners/managers' Chinese background

The participants indicated that a Chinese background was an important resource for the owners and managers of these organisations. Some of the owners/managers of the SMEs represented in the study were born in China, and then had migrated to Australia, grown up in Australia, were educated in Australia, started their business in Australia and internationalised their business to China to access the opportunities there. They found that their Chinese background gave them an advantage:

> I guess being a Chinese background, it helps, but even with that being the case, I'm an overseas kind . . . so even my perceptions of the culture are slightly slanted so it still is a challenge. The benefits are probably that I have some insight into the basis for where the extremes are.
>
> (Case 3: Chemical Co)

Similar to the effect of Chinese *Haigui* employees, an owner with a Chinese background assisted the SMEs to understand the culture, speak the language and design strategies for the Chinese environment. There was no evidence, however, that a Chinese background increased the innovation performance of the SMEs.

Organisational resources and capabilities

The next major thematic area identified in the analysis was the organisational resources and capabilities that helped the SMEs to be successful in China (See Table 6.4).

Organisational resources are referred to as the structures, processes and systems in organisations which permit flows of information and training and which motivate organisational members (Andrews, 1971). Organisational resources in SMEs include the policies, management systems, funding structures, planning and control systems and the culture of the firm. SMEs identified organisational resources from a wide perspective, for example they include specific knowledge and experience in the industry, market trends and products/services in demand in their business areas and adopting current technologies in the business process.

Table 6.4 Organisational resources and capabilities

Organisational resources	Number of SMEs	Importer	Exporter	WOFE	BIC
Resources					
Technology/ Technical expertise	15	1	3	8	3
Capabilities					
Online presence	15	2	1	7	6
Chinese language capability	20	2	3	8	7
Flexibility, agility and size	14	1		7	6
Thinking, developing *new* ideas and things	31	2	3	17	9

Technology/technical expertise

Some SMEs believed that using current technology in their business provided them with additional advantages in comparison to their competitors as their competitors did not utilise such technology in their operations, for example:

> We use some really interesting accounting and inventory software to manage our company in the cloud and I think we're ahead of the game.
>
> (Case 25: Milk Co)

Technical expertise was also helpful for the SMEs and was used mainly to support innovation, as Print Co (Case 25) had suggested:

> It's quite difficult, the sublimation process. People think it might just be something very simple, printing on to garments, but it's a very technical process and if you're not doing it right you can have a lot of problems with it and actually lose a lot of money.

Previous research indicates that technology is a key resource that facilitates entry into international markets (Dhanaraj and Beamish, 2003; Ozcelik and Taymaz, 2004; Roper and Love, 2002), and it has also been said that it assists with further internationalisation (i.e. export intensity). It was apparent in this study that having this technical expertise, in any form, was important in facilitating the success of the SME in the Chinese market.

Online presence

Developing an online presence was also found to be an important organisational capability. Thirteen SMEs out of 35 studied, including two importers, one exporter, four WOFEs and six BIC SMEs, used an online presence and social media in the Chinese market, and they considered this to be one of their key capabilities that helped them. The SMEs investigated had their websites translated into Chinese and used Chinese social media tools and digital media for marketing purposes. The participants indicated that an online presence was important, however many commented that local versions of social media were the most effective way of marketing in China, particularly if targeting Chinese customers/clients:

> I think it's a matter of establishing an online presence, making a good Chinese based site, an Australian translated site into Chinese. Because we're the end distributors, you can go online and buy all these bits.
>
> (Case 6: Pneumatic Co)

Online presence appeared to be an important resource for the participants. Ravichndran and Lertwongsatien (2005) argued that a firm's performance can be explained by how effective the firm is in using information technology (IT) to support and enhance its core competencies; the results suggest that variation in firm performance is explained by the extent to which IT is used to support and enhance a firm's core competencies.

Chinese language capability

Chinese language capability was of great importance to the SMEs in the study. A large portion of the Chinese people that the participants dealt with did not speak English, making it important for the SMEs to have a good Chinese language capability. Twenty out of the 35 SMEs had alluded to this, with WOFEs (8) and BIC firms (7) stating this to be the case. Chinese language capability may be more important for SMEs that are located in China. In addition, employing staff who could speak both languages was important:

> Like, we've got a couple of senior principal Chinese engineers but definitely the team here is younger and that was a conscious decision. One was for language, one was also for that they are probably willing to accept new ideas and new ways to take things on and it won't just be the standard way.
>
> (Case 16: Processing Co)

Flexibility, agility and size

Flexibility, agility and size was also identified to be a unique capability that the SMEs used to their advantage because agility and size facilitated fast decision making and lower overhead costs:

> I think our biggest advantage has been our agility, being from a smaller town too in Australia. I think our size has been a huge help too.
>
> (Case 24: Milk Co)

Along similar lines, some of the participants expressed the opinion that their flexibility was a unique capability making them appear different to their customers/clients:

> Our whole push to establish ourselves was based on flexibility I suppose. You have to be seriously flexible, so you have to allow designing it more than once.
>
> (Case 34: Architect Co 3)

Resources Co (Case 15) expressed a similar opinion:

> If you had someone who came in who was very process driven and dogmatic, yes, they would really struggle. You have to be flexible and adaptable.

This suggests that SMEs need to be flexible and adaptable in the Chinese market to succeed in international business in the Chinese market.

Thinking, developing "new" ideas and things

Some of the SMEs in the study had gained an advantage in the Chinese market by seeking to offer something new, something that was not offered in the industry yet:

> The corporate training market in China was relatively new. When we set up our company, we were actually illegal because you couldn't register a training firm in China because the training shall be a government regulated function.
>
> (Case 26: HR Consult Co)

They also developed new ways of thinking, or new ways of doing things. Interestingly, the reference to "new" mainly related to the use of new technologies, and processes.

This newness and new thinking was articulated by most of the SMEs (31 to be exact), and highlighted that having a 'new mindset' was a very interesting resource that appeared to be helpful for SMEs in the market:

> We try to give them some more interesting and new ideas if they're looking for new ideas and we also want the right people working with that. If you want just to copy exactly the traditional way you'll find both parties are not happy so it's the way we're trying to lead them to a more contemporary way.
>
> (Case 34: Architect Co 3)

According to Helfat et al. (2007), organisational capabilities (Teece and Pisano, 1997) are important as the firm can apply them to "*create, extend, or modify its resource base*", and as the interviewees quotes demonstrate above, they can also give the firm the ability to compete better, more advantageously, and give customers what they want. The literature offers a few examples of resource-based or capabilities-based studies of SME internationalisation, which include Roth's (1995) study and a model produced by Ahokangas (1998). The research results identified a range of organisational capabilities and among them the ability to interface between Western and Asian ideas, agility, flexibility and thinking 'new' are unique. Ahokangas (1998) determined that SMEs are dependent on the development potential of key internal and external resources, which can be developed within the firm and between firms and their environments. The internal firm-oriented resources adjustment can be seen as the development strategy of a firm that tries to develop the critical resources needed for internationalisation by entering into international activities and learning from experience, without a dependence on externally available resources (Ahokangas, 1998).

Flexibly was identified as a key factor of success in the internationalisation process, highlighting the importance of dynamism in defining the set of resources

Table 6.5 Resources used by different entry modes

Low commitment	*Importing*	*Exporting*
	Parent company support	Parent company support
	Location in China	Presence in China
	Hong Kong	**Location in China**
	Brand	**Hong Kong**
	Reputation	Brand
	Experience	**Reputation**
	Knowledge	Australian Origin
	Chinese local staff	**Experience**
	Owner/managers/ employees' capabilities	Sea turtles
	External consultants	**Owners/managers/ employees' capabilities**
	Owners/managers' Chinese background	**External consultants**
	Technology/technical expertise	**Technology/technical expertise**
	Online presence	**Online presence**
	Chinese language capability	**Chinese language capability**
	Flexibility/agility/size	**Thinking "new"**
	Thinking "new"	
High Commitment	*BIC*	*WOFE*
	Presence in China	Parent company support
	Location in China	Presence in China
	Hong Kong	**Location in China**
	Brand	**Hong Kong**
	Reputation	**Reputation**
	Experience	Australian origin
	Knowledge	**Experience**
	Sea turtles	Knowledge
	Chinese local staff	Sea turtles
	Owner/managers/ employees capabilities	Chinese local staff
	External consultants	**Owner/managers/ employees' capabilities**
	Technology/Technical expertise	**External consultants**
	Online presence	Owners/managers' Chinese background
	Chinese language capability	**Technology/technical expertise**
	Flexibility/agility/size	**Online presence**
	Thinking "new"	Chinese language capability
		Flexibility/agility/size
		Thinking "new"

and competences that are required to face a challenging competitive environment (Santini and Rabino, 2011). Grant's (1991) findings suggested that organisational capabilities become important when they are combined in unique combinations, which create core competencies, which have strategic value and can lead to competitive advantage. The analysis of the results determined that the combination of unique capabilities can be treated as a critical aspect of the internationalisation process, and some of these were highly relevant for innovation as well.

Chapter summary

This research determined that adopting an internationalisation strategy must include access to market appropriate resources. The internationalisation of SMEs is a process that combines different resources and capabilities to develop strategies in the environment. It uses resources to take advantage of opportunities and minimise risk. Each enterprise has its own internationalisation process realised by the construction of resources and competences in different ways: certain SMEs progressively combine the resources and competences, going to foreign markets by steps; others grasp the combination of resources and competences from the very beginning of their foundation and therefore become international immediately and rapidly. The development of resources and competences for internationalisation not only relies on the exploration of an enterprise's internal resources but also takes into account the specific characteristics of the foreign business environment. The success of an SME's internationalisation depends both on an enterprise's available resources and the ability of the organisation to exploit these resources in a new environment. *Table 6.5* Resources used by different entry modes

A summary of the role of different resources for different entry modes is presented in Table 6.5. The figure demonstrates that some resources are necessary for all entry modes (shown in bold), and other resources are necessary for specific entry modes. Different resources are required for different entry modes due to the nature of the commitment to the market and the requirements of the organisation that this will entail. Internationalising SMEs need to consider the entry mode carefully, because the choice creates important constraints for the resources that are needed to effectuate their business strategies and achieve competitive advantage in the market. In particular, the ability to "think new" was identified as an important resource for differentiation in the market and should be a consideration in the design of internationalisation strategies and internationalisation resource development.

References

Ahokangas, P. (1998). *Internationalisation and Resources: An Analysis of Processes in Nordic SMEs*. Doctoral dissertation, Universitas Wasaensis, Vaasa.

Amit, R., and Schoemaker, P. J. H. (1993). Strategic assets and organizational rent. *Strategic Management Journal*, 14(1), 33–46.

Andrews, K. (1971). *The Concept of Corporate Strategy*. Homewood, IL: Dow Jones-Irwin.

Autio, E., Sapienza, H., and Almeida, J. (2000). Effects of time to internationalisation, knowledge intensity, and imitability on growth. *Academy of Management Journal*, 43(5), 909–924.

Barney, J. B. (1991). Firm resources and sustained competitive advantage. *Journal of Management*, 77(1), 99–120.

Bausch, A., and Van Tri, D. L. (2007). *Internationalisation of German Companies Into the Chinese Market – an Event Study on the Consequences on Financial Performance From an RBV Perspective*. Jena Research Papers in Business and Economics, Working and Discussion Paper Series School of Economics and Business Administration Friedrich-Schiller-University.

Boeker, W., and Karichalil, R. (2002). Entrepreneurial transitions: Factors influencing founder departure. *Academy of Management Journal*, 45(4), 818–826.

Camisón, C., and Villar-López, A. (2010). Effect of SMEs' international experience on foreign intensity and economic performance: The mediating role of internationally exploitable assets and competitive strategy. *Journal of Small Business Management*, 48(2), 116–151.

Cerrato, D., and Piva, M. (2010). The internationalisation of small and medium-sized enterprises: The effect of family management, human capital and foreign ownership. *Journal of Management and Governance*, 16:4: 617–644.

Chandler, G. N., and Hanks, S. H. (1994). Market attractiveness, resource-based capabilities, venture strategies and venture performance. *Journal of Business Venturing*, 9:4, 331–349.

Chang, S. J., and Rhee, J. H. (2011). Rapid FDI expansion and firm performance. *Journal of International Business Studies*, 42(8), 979–994.

Collins, D. (1994). Research note: How valuable are organizational capabilities? *Strategic Management Journal*, 15(Winter), 143–152.

Cooper, A. C., Gimeno-Gascon, F. J., Woo, C. Y. (1994). Initial human and financial capital predictors of new venture performance. *Journal of Business Venturing*, 9:5, 371–395.

Cuervo-Cazurra, A. (2007). Sequence of value-added activities in the internationalisation of developing country MNEs. *Journal of International Management*, 13:3, 258–277.

Dhanaraj, C., and Beamish, P. W. (2003). A resource-based approach to the study of export performance. *Journal of Small Business Management*, 41:3, 242–261.

Falize, M., and Coeurderoy, R. (2012). The network approach to rapid internationalisation among Born Global and Born Again Global firms: The case of the 'Global Innovation Network. Research in Entrepreneurship and Small Business XXVI Conference', November 2012, Lyon.

Filatotchev, I., and Piesse, J. (2009). R&D, internationalisation and growth of newly listed firms: European evidence. *Journal of International Business Studies*, 40:8, 1260–1276.

Foss, N. J., and Eriksen, B. (1995). Competitive advantage and industry capabilities'. In Montgomery Cynthia, A. (Ed.), *Resource-Based and Evolutionary Theories of the Firm: Toward a Synthesis*. Boston: Kluwer Academic Publishers, 43–69.

Gilbert, B. A., McDougall, P., and Audretsch, D. B. (2008). Knowledge spillovers and new venture performance: An empirical examination. *Journal of Business Venturing*, 23:4, 405–422.

Grant, R. M. (1991). The resource-based theory of competitive advantage: Implications for strategy formulation. *California Management Review*, 33:3, 114–135.

Graves, C., and Thomas, J. (2006). Internationalisation of Australian family businesses: A managerial capabilities perspective. *Family Business Review*, 19:3, 207–224.

Hambrick, D., and Mason, P. (1984). Upper echelons: the organization as a reflection of its top managers. *Academy of Management Review*, 9:2, 193–206.

Hao, J., and Welch, A. (2012). Tale of Sea Turtles: Job-seeking experiences of Hai Gui (high-skilled returnees) in China. *Higher Education* Policy, 25(2), 243–260. doi:10.1057/hep.2012.4.

Helfat, C. E., and Peteraf, M. A. (2003). The dynamic resources-based view: Capability life cycles. *Strategic Management Journal*, 24:10, 997–1010.

Javalgi, R. G., and Todd, P. R. (2011). Entrepreneurial orientation, management commitment, and human capital: The internationalisation of SMEs in India. *Journal of Business Research*, 64:9, 1004–1010.

Johanson, J., and Vahlne, J-E. (1977). The internationalisation process of the firm-a model of knowledge development and increasing foreign market commitments. *Journal of International Business Studies*, 8:1, 23–32.

Johanson, J., and Vahlne, J-E. (1990). The mechanism of internationalisation. *International Marketing Review*, 7:4, 11–25.

Keller, K. L. (1993). Conceptualizing, measuring, and managing customer-based brand equity. *Journal of Marketing*, 57:1, 1–22.

Knight, G. (2001). Entrepreneurship and strategy in the international SME. *Journal of International Management*, 7:1, 155–171.

Kuivalainen, O. (2003). *Knowledge Based View of Internationalisation – Studies on Small and Medium Sized Information and Communication Technology Firms*. Doctoral Thesis, Lappeenranta University of Technology, Finland.

Leonidou, C. L., and Theodosiou, M. (2004). The export marketing information system: Sn integration of the extant knowledge. *Journal of World Business*, 39:1, 12–36.

McDougall, P. P., Shane, S., and Oviatt, B. M. (1994). Explaining the formation of international new ventures: The limits of theories from international business research. *Journal of Business Venturing*, 9:6, 469–487.

Mishina, Y., Pollock, T. G., and Porac, J. F. (2004). Are more resources always better for growth? Resource stickiness in market and product expansion. *Strategic Management Journal*, 25:12, 1179–1197.

Morck, R., and Yeung, B. (1991). Why investors value multi-nationality. *Journal of Business*, 64:2, 165–187.

Nelson, R. R., and Winter, S. G. (1982). *An Evolutionary Theory or Economic Change*. Cambridge, MA: Harvard University Press.

O'Cass, A., and Weerawardena, J. (2009). Examining the role of international entrepreneurship, innovation and international market performance in SME internationalisation. *European Journal of Marketing*, 43:11/12, 1325–1348.

Özçelik, E., and Taymaz, E. (2004). Does innovativeness matter for international competitiveness in developing countries: The case of Turkish manufacturing industries. *Research Policy*, 33:3, 409–424.

Peng, M. W. (2001). The resource-based view and international business. *Journal of Management*, 27:6, 803–829.

Penrose, E. (1959). *Theory of the Growth of the Firm*. New York: Oxford University Press.

Perdomo-Ortiz, J., Gonzalez-Benito, J., and Galende, J. (2009). An analysis of the relationship between total quality management-based human resource management practices and innovation. *The International Journal of Human Resource Management*, 20:5, 1191–1218.

Pinho, J. C., and Martins, L. (2010). Exporting barriers: Insights from Portuguese small-and medium-sized exporters and non-exporters. *Journal of International Entrepreneurship*, 8, 253–272.

Qian, G. (2002). Mutinationality, product-diversification, and profitability of emerging US small and medium-sized enterprises. *Journal of Business Venturing*, 17:1, 611–633.

Ravichndran, T., and Lertwongsatien, C. (2005). Effect of information systems resources and capabilities on firm performance: A resource-based perspective. *Journal of Management Information Systems*, 21:4, 237–276.

Reid, S. D. (1983). Firm internationalisation, transaction costs, and strategic choice. *International Marketing Review*, 1:2, 45–56.

Reuber, R. A., and Fischer, E. (1997). The influence of the management team's international experience on the internationalisation behaviours of SMEs. *Journal of International Business Studies*, 2:4, 807–826.

Roper, S., and Love, J. H. (2002). Innovation and export performance: Evidence from the UK and German manufacturing plants. *Research Policy*, 31, 1087–1102.

Roth, K. (1995). Managing international interdependence: CEO characteristics in a resource based framework. *Academy of Management Journal*, 38:1, 200–231.

Ruzzier, M., Antoncic, B., Hisrich, R. D., and Konecnik, M. (2007). Human capital and SME internationalisation: A structural equation modeling study. *Canadian Journal of Administrative Sciences*, 24:1, 15–29.

Ruzzier, M., Antoncic, B., and Konecnik, M. (2006). The resource-based approach to the internationalisation of SMEs: Differences in resource bundles between internationalised and non-internationalised companies. *Zagreb International Review of Economics & Business*, 9:2, 95–116.

Santini, C., and Rabino, S. (2011). Internationalisation drivers in the wine business: A RBV perspective. *International Journal of Business and Globalisation*, 8:1, 7–9.

Scullion, H., and Starkey, K. (2011). In search of the changing role of the corporate human resource function in the international firm. *The International Journal of Human Resource Management*, 11:6, 1061–1081.

Sharfman, M. P., Woff, G., and Chase, R. B. (1988). Antecedents of organizational slack. *Academy of Management Review*, 13:4, 601–614.

Stinchcombe, A. L. (1965). Social structure and organizations. In March, J. G. (Ed.), *Handbook of Organizations*. Chicago: Rand McNally & Firm, 142–193.

Tan, H-P., Plowman, D., and Hancock, P. (2007). Intellectual capital and financial returns of companies. *Journal of Intellectual Capital*, 8:1, 76–95.

Tan, J., and Peng, M. W. (2003). Organizational slack and firm performance during economic transitions: Two studies form an emerging economy. *Strategic Management Journal*, 24:13, 1249–1263.

Teece, D. J., Pisano, G., and Shuen, A. (1997). Dynamic capabilities and strategic management. *Strategic Management Journal*, 18:1, 509–533.

Tesfom, G., and Luts, C. (2006). A classification of export marketing problems of small and medium sized manufacturing firms in developing countries. *International Journal of Emerging Markets*, 1:3, 262–281.

Tihanyi, L., Ellstrand, A. E., Daily, C. M., and Dalton, D. R. (2000). Composition of the top management team and firm international diversification. *Journal of Management*, 26:6, 1157–1177.

Tseng, C., Tansuhaj, P., and Rose, J. (2004). Are strategic assets contributions or constraints for SMEs to go international? An empirical study of the US manufacturing Sector. *Journal of American Academy of Business*, 5:1/2, 246–254.

Weerawardena, J., Mort, G. S., Liesch, P. W., and Knight, G. (2007). Conceptualizing accelerated internationalisation in the born global firm: A dynamic capabilities perspective. *Journal of World Business*, 42, 294–306.

Wernerfelt, B. (1995). The resource-based view of the firm: Ten years after. *Strategic Management Journal*, 16:3, 171–174.

Winter, S. G. (1995). Four Rs of profitability: Rents, resources, routines and replication. In Montgomery Cynthia, A. (Ed.), *Resource-Based and Evolutionary Theories of the Firm: Toward a Synthesis*. Boston: Kluwer Academic Publishers, 147–178.

Zahra, S. A., Ireland, R. D., and Hitt, M. A. (2000). International expansion by new venture firms: International diversity, mode of market entry, technological learning, and performance. *Academy of Management Journal*, 43:5, 925–950.

7 The barriers, liabilities and costs of operating in China

Introduction

Small and medium-sized enterprises (SMEs) face many challenges when internationalising. In addition to the limited strategic resources and knowledge that they have available to support their internationalisation (relative to large organisations), they usually have access to smaller networks and are more exposed to opportunity costs and the issues that present themselves in the foreign market. Having made a decision to internationalise to one location reduces the opportunities to internationalise to other locations to a much greater extent for SMEs than for large organisations.

The barriers that all organisations face when internationalising manifest themselves in different forms for SMEs. The barriers which are particularly significant for SMEs when entering China can be described as the liabilities of foreignness (LOF) (Zaheer, 1995), liabilities of smallness (LOS) (Aldrich and Auster, 2011), liabilities of newness (LON) (Stinchcombe, 2012), liabilities associated with outsidership (LOO) (Johanson and Vahlne, 2009) and industry specific liabilities (Panibratov, 2015), such as the difficulties financial and advisory organisations experience in gaining critical industry specific registrations in foreign markets. Organisations may also experience liabilities as a result of their home-based disadvantages, called the liabilities at home (LAH). To date, however, the literature has not identified the liabilities for foreign SMEs from western countries entering foreign markets, such as China, which is characterised by rapidly changing and developing business and economic conditions. It is possible that the market conditions may create different liabilities or reduce the impact of liabilities which have been identified for entry into mature markets.

This chapter reviews the state of the extent literature that considers how each of these barriers affects the internationalisation of SMEs. These constructs are then compared with the constructs identified from the analysis of the data provided by the SMEs interviewed for this book to identify whether they apply to entry from a western country into the Chinese market and whether other liabilities not previously identified also affect the internationalisation process. The SMEs that participated in the study, the data collection and analysis technique and the objectives of the study are described in the introduction chapter.

Literature review

The review of the literature will consider the four primary sources of barriers to internationalisation for SMEs in China – LOF, LOS, LON and LOO. LOF applies to the internationalisation of all organisations, however, both the psychic distance between Australia and China and the limited resources available to SMEs means that this liability is likely to have a substantial effect and that new perspectives on this construct may result from examining the experiences of SMEs in this context. LOS is clearly important for SMEs, however, the huge scale of organisations in China means that the size differential between these SMEs and large companies in their home country is much less than it would be in China. In a similar manner, an SME entering a mature market will experience LON, however the rapid rate of development and change in China will exacerbate the LON and the analysis may identify new dimensions of LON that apply to SMEs under these conditions. The increased difference in size between large organisations and these SMEs in China may identify new dimensions of LOS. Finally, LOO will be significant in the case of internationalisation to China, however, the literature considering the effect of LOO under large psychic distances for SMEs is very limited. The analysis of the findings from this study may introduce new constructs to this area. The review of the literature will conclude with a summary of the key constructs for these barriers that have been identified as being applicable to the internationalisation of an SME from a western country to China.

Liabilities of Foreignness (LOF)

The liability of foreignness is one of the most significant barriers to internationalisation success. LOF results from domestic organisations enjoying more location-based advantages than foreign organisations (Jiang, Liu and Stening, 2014). Research in this area commenced in the 1970s and is well developed. In this literature Hymer (1976: 34–35) defined it as "the social and economic costs that organisations face when they operate in foreign markets", and which domestic organisations do not experience. Hymer's original contention was that organisations in foreign markets experienced disadvantages relative to the local organisations, due to the costs associated with gaining cultural knowledge and dealing with legal process and language differences. Hymer also suggested that organisations do not incur these costs on an ongoing basis. Discrimination, however, by governments, suppliers and consumers can generate ongoing costs. Zaheer (1995: 343) then suggested that LOF can be measured by considering: a) the spatial differences (travel, transportation and coordination costs), b) the unfamiliarity with the local environment, c) the discrimination faced by foreign organisations and finally d) the restrictions from the home country. More recently Yu and Kim (2013) suggested that these costs were caused by the spatial distance, unfamiliarity and lack of legitimacy in Asian host country markets.

The extant literature has focused primarily on the capabilities used to overcome these costs and internationalisation to developed markets (Barnard, 2010; Denk,

Kaufmann and Roesch, 2012). There is some challenge in the extant literature regarding whether the LOF literature has been superseded by the institutional theory literature (Denk, Kaufmann and Roesch, 2012; Panibratov, 2015). Institutional theory applies constraints, such as the need to imitate the practice of domestic organisations and thus predicts some of the limitations identified by liability theory. This debate is not yet resolved, however, and literature is still identifying evidence for the need for the LOF perspective (Lindorfer, d'Arcy and Puck, 2016; Panibratov, 2015; Wu and Salomon, 2016). In the case of foreign organisations internationalising from developed countries to countries with rapidly developing markets, in which the business environment is experiencing a rapid rate of change and cultural factors have a dominant effect, the LOF is still appropriate for explaining the costs associated with these liabilities (Yu and Kim, 2013) and the subsequent effect on internationalisation performance. The LOF research relevant to the Chinese context commenced 20 years ago, when significant numbers of organisations started to internationalise into the Chinese market specifically to trade there (2014). This literature is rapidly evolving in response to the changing nature of the Chinese business environment (Jiang, Liu and Stening, 2014), especially Chinese businesses' rapid adoption of international laws, practices and management approaches. LOF is less of a barrier to internationalisation in dynamic foreign markets, such as China, due to the high rate of change and environmental turbulence. These factors reduce the knowledge asymmetry between foreign and domestic companies and home country advantages of domestic competitors (Jiang, Liu and Stening, 2014). There is evidence, however, that even in rapidly expanding markets, LOF exists and has similar effects to LOF in mature markets (Acheampong and Dana, 2017).

The LOF for SMEs results from the difficulty in building social capital (Prashantham, 2011), difficulty of transferring resources that are located in the home country (Schweizer, 2013), institutional distance, cultural distance, volatility and channel competition (Gorostidi-Martinez and Zhao, 2017). According to the literature, these liabilities can be overcome in the same way that large enterprises overcome their LOFs, through strategy, partnership, knowledge acquisition and social capital (Acheampong and Dana, 2017; Bengtsson and Johansson, 2014; Hollender, Zapkau and Schwens, 2017; Jiang, Liu and Stening, 2014; Yu and Kim, 2013; Zhou and Guillen, 2016). Few of these studies, however, have considered the case of resource constrained organisations responding to rapidly changing sources of LOF (foreign SMEs in China) and, under these circumstances, the impact and responses to LOF may well be different. This chapter will contribute to this literature by identifying both the sources and responses to LOF for foreign SMEs in China.

The main cause of LOF being the location-based advantage of domestic competitors makes internationalisation partnerships attractive for foreign companies entering markets such as China (Bengtsson and Johansson, 2014; Wei and Clegg, 2015). LOF also results from reduced levels of trust, commitment and shared knowledge about the business and cultural practices of both parties (Panibratov, 2015). These factors can result from the organisation's type of ownership, the foreign country market characteristics and internationalisation mode selected (Zhou and Guillen, 2016). Whilst LOF can manifest itself as a reduction in business opportunities (Barnard, 2010), it can also result in more significant barriers to success such as crimes committed against the organisation or difficulties in raising capital in the foreign market (Acheampong and Dana, 2017; Li, Bruton and Filatotchev, 2016; Lindorfer, d'Arcy and Puck, 2016). Larger organisations will have a larger level of aggregate experience with the foreign markets through their larger staff base and the personal contacts this provides. In many cases, larger organisations can build their knowledge and profile in the foreign market by maintaining a limited presence over an extended period. SMEs, on the other hand, find it difficult to support an extended period in the market, solely to acquire knowledge and profile (Tiwari, Sen and Shaik, 2016). Their need to generate cash flow from all activities makes it difficult to sustain extended non-profit generating activities. Larger organisations may also be able to employ more foreign country nationals in their Chinese operations to reduce their LOF than is possible for SMEs due to resource constraints.

Factors which moderate the LOF

All foreign enterprises seek to reduce the impact of the LOF as it increases the cost of business in the foreign market (Acheampong and Dana, 2017; Gorostidi-Martinez and Zhao, 2017). When first entering the market, behaving in a similar manner to the local companies (adopting an isomorphism strategy) in the foreign market reduces the LOF, although the benefits of this approach are greater for foreign companies with limited experience of the foreign market. Companies with greater market experience can find alternative ways to reduce the effect of LOF that take advantage of their foreignness (Wu and Salomon, 2016). As the market develops, the increased availability of local resources to assist the foreign organisation can reduce the LOF (Yildiz and Fey, 2012). For example, knowledge gained from suppliers or from co-locating with other foreign organisations can be used by foreign organisations to reduce their LOF (Barnard, 2010; Lamin and Livanis, 2013).

Superior competitiveness resulting from market relevant advantages and international operations are also factors which reduce the effect of the LOF (Boehe, 2011; Jiang, Liu and Stening, 2014; Zhou and Guillén, 2015). From a social integration perspective, there is evidence to suggest that the LOF is reduced by engaging in positive social responsibility activities, but that the LOF is increased when the foreign organisation does not engage in these activities (Crilly, Na and Yuwei, 2016; Moeller, 42013). Under certain circumstances, foreignness can provide a competitive advantage (Jiang, Liu and Stening, 2014). For example, a foreign bank offering foreign trade services can use this as a point of differentiation, making the organisation more attractive than foreign trade services provided by domestic companies (Boehe, 2011). Of course, this would not stop the organisation from experiencing other liabilities of foreignness, such as discrimination (Yu and Kim, 2013). The advantages resulting from foreignness are best considered from the resource-based perspective in which valuable resources possessed by the organisation, such as those located in a different country, provide a competitive advantage (Boehe, 2011; Denk, Kaufmann and Roesch, 2012; Wei and Clegg, 2015).

Liabilities of Smallness (LOS) and Newness (LON)

The literature considering LOS and LON is relatively limited (Aldrich and Auster, 2011; Ko and Liu, 2016), although the articles that deal with these liabilities identified strong relationships between the size and newness of a foreign subsidiary and its likelihood of success (Hollender, Zapkau and Schwens, 2017). The greater likelihood of smaller foreign operations failing has also been shown to associate with their likelihood of newer (less legitimate and experienced) organisations failing in a foreign market (Arditi and Kale, 1998). The LOS tends to result in reduced legitimacy and credibility and is often caused by a lack of flexibility (due to limited resources) and unfavourable relationships with larger organisations (Bengtsson and Johansson, 2014). The LON also results in a lack of legitimacy and brand and is probably caused by a lack of host country relevant certifications, knowledge and organisational learning (Djupdal and Westhead, 2015), as well as scarcity of resources, limited product differentiation and limited managerial and operational capabilities (Arditi and Kale, 1998). Generating significant revenue in a foreign market can also mean that small companies are particularly subject to the effects of foreign exchange rate variations (Kim, Tesar and Zhang, 2015). Whilst the variation in exchange rates will affect the profitability of an international transaction for organisations of any size, internationalised SMEs are likely to have a significantly greater proportion of their sales occurring in the foreign market than large companies (Hollenstein, 2005).

Factors which moderate the LOS and LON

Not surprisingly, international experience and product adaptation capability moderate the effect of LOS and LON (Hollender, Zapkau and Schwens, 2017). In China, it has been found that small domestic organisations increase their legitimacy using guanxi (Ko and Liu, 2016) (relation based networks) and this is one of the advantages of small local organisations that creates a liability for small foreign organisations. Building guanxi is more difficult for a foreign SME due to the cultural knowledge required and therefore building legitimacy in this way comes at a greater cost for foreign SMEs. Co-opetition can moderate LOS and LON (Kock, Nisuls and Soderqvist, 2010). When collaborating with large competitors in the foreign market, SMEs learn how to sustain their independence and balance their relationships, more rapidly developing their legitimacy (Bengtsson and Johansson, 2014). Certification also provides an increased level of legitimacy in a foreign market, which reduces LOS and LON, although mainly for very new and very small organisations (Djupdal and Westhead, 2015). Host country relevant or recognised international certification, such as distributor certification in

China, provides a symbol of credibility and reliability (Minard, 2016). LOS is also moderated by power or information asymmetries in the market when they favour the SME, however, they create more LOS when they are not biased towards the SME. For example, a small organisation may occupy a position of power in a global supply chain, acting as a critical link, by controlling a key resource or acting as a gateway (Kalantaridis and Vassilev, 2011). This condition will give the SME influence at a level disproportionate to the organisation's size and resources and so reduces its LOS.

Liabilities of outsidership (LOO)

LOO is closely related to LOF, but is primarily due to social network factors (Johanson and Vahlne, 2009; Schweizer, 2013), whereas LOF can be due to institutional factors as well. LOO is strongly connected to LOF (Johanson and Vahlne, 2009) and is often an extension of LOF. Although liability of outsidership produces uncertainty resulting from a lack of network membership (Schiavini and Scherer, 2015), rather than a lack of credibility due to psychic distance represented by LOF, both the causes and approaches for dealing with LOO are very similar to the approaches for dealing with LOF. These involve establishing guanxi or alternative business support networks (such as business association membership) to increase knowledge and business profile, so as to reduce uncertainty and/or increase opportunities. For example, Chinese internationalising organisations use their guanxi network building skills in foreign countries to establish new networks and overcome the LOO (Chen, 2017). Foreign SMEs in China, by comparison, may be unable to establish guanxi quickly and will need to use different paths to create networks to reduce their LOO (Schiavini and Scherer, 2015). The establishment of networks by any pathway can take time and will delay dealing with the uncertainty resulting from LOO. The LOO will remain until business conditions which reduce uncertainty, such as increased trust and knowledge, are generated (Johanson and Vahlne, 2009; Schweizer, 2013).

Putting it all together

The literature reviewed above suggests that LOF results from the domestic organisation's home country advantages and their relevance to the foreign market. LOF results in reduced trust, commitment and shared knowledge and it is moderated by the rate of change in the foreign market (although the rate of change in China can result in some disadvantage for domestic organisations as well). It is also moderated by isomorphic behaviours (responding in the same way that other organisations in the market would respond in order to maximise the legitimacy achieved) in the early stages of market entry, accessing foreign market resources such as knowledge, market relevant advantages and international operations capabilities and positive social contributions (Barnard, 2010; Boehe, 2011; Crilly, Na and Yuwei, 2016; Denk, Kaufmann and Roesch, 2012; Gorostidi-Martinez and Zhao, 2017). LOO is due to similar causes to LOF, however, LOO results in uncertainty, rather than lack of credibility. It is moderated by the same behaviours as LOF. LOS and LON result from limited resources, product differentiation and managerial capability in the host country, which reduces the rate with which the foreign SME adapts to the local environment. They are moderated by international experience and product annotation capabilities, network capabilities, collaboration with large enterprises in the foreign market and power asymmetries.

This suggests that the interview participants should be expected to identify liabilities resulting from foreignness, outsidership, smallness and newness. In addition, the participants can be expected to display attention to building networks, knowledge, credibility, trust, making social contributions, acquiring access to more resources and building management capability. They can be expected to have adopted isomorphic and network development behaviours, considered making social contributions and focused on accessing foreign market resources, product adaptation and leveraging their market relevant advantages and collaboration with large organisations in the market.

Interview findings and analysis

This section presents the findings of the analysis of the interviews with the representatives of the 35 participating companies. It considers the types and sources of internationalisation barriers, liabilities and costs identified by the interview participants. This section considers all of the liabilities together, rather than assuming the constructs identified will divide automatically into the different liability literature domains. The next section 'Comparison of the findings to the literature', identifies the liabilities as LOF, LOO, LOS or LON and considers how the findings contribute to these specific areas of the liability literature. This section also considers how the participants responded to these liabilities and how these responses relate to the liability literature.

The consolidated findings from all of the participants are considered in this analysis section, as well as the distribution of responses across the industry sectors represented by the sample, to determine whether the comments were more relevant to particular industries. The industry distribution for categories with small numbers of respondents has not been considered. These constructs were not considered to be representative of the entire sample, but were included because of the strong evidence provided by the participants that did comment.

The higher order constructs that related to liabilities identified in the responses were business, competitive and economic factors. Business factors were found to be comprised of the constructs of social factors, dealing with regulations, lack of networks and lack of partnerships. The social factors construct was found to be comprised of legitimacy, which was in turn comprised of the need to be adaptive and build trust, together with the constructs of understanding culture and language, building social relationships, meeting partner and customer expectations and customer and partner transparency. The competitive factors construct was found to be comprised of logistics and infrastructure constructs and resources constructs and the economic factors construct was found to be comprised of constructs of limited access to capital, international business costs and income challenges.

With one exception, there was no evidence that the identified liabilities applied more strongly to one industry group in the sample than others. Participants from the services, manufacturing, technology and finance sectors of the sample made comments fitting into 10 or more of the 15 identified constructs, suggesting that the majority of constructs applied to all of the industries in the study. Four of the eight companies which commented on 10 or more of the constructs were from the service area, which was consistent with their numbers in the total sample. The companies offering the greatest number of comments relating to these things were similarly distributed. Ten of the participants that offered 20 or more comments each regarding the categories came from the services, manufacturing, technology and finance areas. Four of these 10 participants came from the service sector of the sample.

Overview: liabilities/barriers identified by the participants

The findings were categorised into the structure shown in Figure 7.1. The figure indicates that the higher order construct of business practices and the construct of social practices received the most numerous and varied responses from the participants, whilst the range of responses relating to the higher order constructs of competitive factors and economic factors were both fewer in the number of constructs of which they were comprised and number of comments. This is consistent with the theory considered in the literature review section of this chapter which determines that the liabilities of foreignness, outsiderness, smallness and newness arise from a lack of resources, trust, networks, adaptation and collaboration (Barnard, 2010; Gorostidi-Martinez and Zhao, 2017; Johanson and Vahlne, 2009; Schiavini and Scherer, 2015; Schweizer, 2013).

A particularly interesting finding was the very large number of comments relating to LOF resulting from a lack of understanding of Chinese culture and language, as shown in Figure 7.2. Closely related to this was the relatively large number of comments relating to the role of social relationships in increasing this understanding and reducing the corresponding LOF. Conversely, the LON resulting from the need to be adaptive and achieve credibility in the Chinese market attracted a significant number of responses, but only a small number of participants actually provided the responses. The same applies to the LOF and LOO resulting from the need to meet partner and customer expectations and regulations. The number of responses for each of the categories shown in Figure 7.1 are displayed in Figure 7.2.

The total number of responses which related to all liabilities was 147. The participants provided only one response relating to LOS (due to limited income). Only a small number of responses related to LON due to a lack of logistics and infrastructure arrangements and a lack of knowledge were also limited, but have been included because of the logical merit. The item identifying a LOF resulting

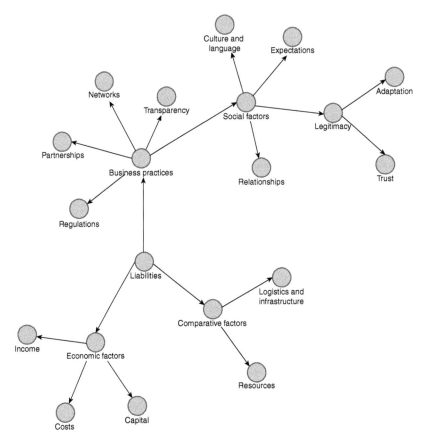

Figure 7.1 Structure of relationships relating to liability

from the costs of international transactions, combined with the rising operating costs in China, was the most frequently identified out of the liabilities resulting from economic and competitive factors conditions and was identified by eight participants. By comparison, the LOF resulting from not understanding cultural and language factors was identified by 15 of the 35 participants. Table 7.1 shows the number of participants and the number of responses received for each of the categories. The highlighted categories have been included for the purpose of structure and the remaining categories contain the responses. The number of participants and comments for each of the highlighted categories represents the total of its subordinate categories.

Details of the findings

This section describes the findings relating to each of the categories and presents examples from the interviews. The relationship between these findings in the

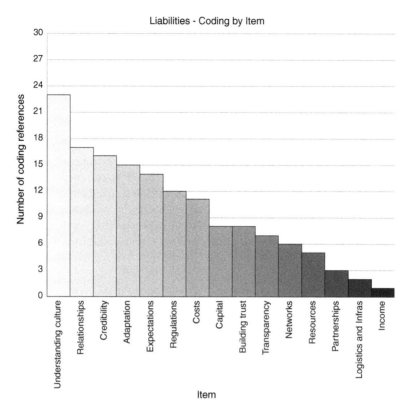

Figure 7.2 Frequency of responses to each of the identified categories

Table 7.1 Numbers of participants and number of responses for each category

Category	Number of participants	Number of comments
Liabilities	28	147
Business Practices	28	121
Networks	3	6
Partnerships	3	3
Regulations	10	12
Social Factors	24	100
Expectations	8	12
Legitimacy	13	42
Adaptation	7	15
Building trust	5	9
Credibility	9	15
Relationships	10	15
Transparency	5	8
Understanding culture and language	15	22
Competitive Factors	6	7
logistics and Infrastructure	2	2
Resources	4	5
Economic Factors	13	19
Capital	6	8
Costs	8	10
Income	1	1

extant literature will be considered in the next section. The participants tended to identify liabilities in general terms and focus on their specific causes in their comments. To better capture this information, the constructs were developed around the causes and the discussion in this section follows that format.

Lack of networks

As shown in Table 7.1, the construct relating a lack of networks to the liability of a lack of credibility (an LOF or LON) only received six comments from three participants. All of the comments described responding to a liability (of foreignness or newness) resulting from a lack of credibility by establishing networks. Two of the participants made the observation, however, that liabilities resulting from an absence of networks are equally present in most countries. For example one participant noted that, in dealing with liabilities:

> For me, for a business in Australia, I think you do need networks. If you do business in America you also need networks so why is China different?
>
> (Case 10: Biotech Co)

Others indicated that the absence of a network immediately leads to a liability (of newness), due to a lack of credibility for the participants entering China. They suggested that responding to this liability required building networks, for example "networking and finding the right channels to grow your business to get the clients in is still the biggest challenge for us".

Lack of partnerships

The effect of lack of partnerships were only identified by three participants. These participants all indicated that there was a liability (of foreignness) due to a lack of knowledge, which affected the success of their operations. These participants concluded that they needed to form partnerships to respond to this LOF. For example, one participant noted that his organisation entered a joint-venture because the organisation was concerned about the liability resulting from the lack of knowledge about registration processes in China which was directly attributed by the participant to not having a partnership:

> I was scared of the regulatory requirements as I understood them and I shouldn't have [been]. So I should have got good advice, I should have got better advice at the time.
>
> (Case 11: Recruitment Co)

The participants also noted that this response represented a cost, in relation to dealing with the identified liability. They would have preferred not to have had a partnership if the liability had not existed because of the difficulty of coordinating with the Chinese partner, representing a LOF (due to cultural barriers) and LOS (due to having insufficient resources to properly manage communication and the relationship with partners in a different country). Another participant noted that "If we can get where we want to be without giving up any ownership of our company that would be our preference". This identifies achieving partnerships through sharing equity in the Chinese operations with local organisations as a moderator for LOF, but a 'cost' as well.

Dealing with regulations

The liabilities associated with dealing with regulations were identified relatively frequently, with 12 comments received from 10 participants. Five responding participants were from the service industry, two participants from agribusiness, two participants from manufacturing and one participant from the technology industry, suggesting that the identified liabilities had relevance across the sample. One of the aspects of this construct was that the difficulty for foreigners of understanding Chinese business regulations was a liability (of foreignness and newness), but that the regulations had become easier to understand over the last 10 years and was a cost of doing business there. For example, one of the participants noted that:

> The regulatory environment here [is] different to Australia, but it's not onerously different. In some ways it's easier, sometimes it's harder depending on which element it is that you're working in, but it is what it is and you work with it.
>
> (Case 11: Recruitment Co)

One of the major contributors to the liability associated with the effect of Chinese regulations was that Chinese law was more open to interpretation than the participants' home country law. For example, one participant noted that "It's different to Australian law which may be very detailed, but in China the law is very vague. They drafted it that way to allow you to have further interpretation so it's a very different system". The difference increased the cost of business for their Chinese operations by requiring them to acquire the necessary skills to accommodate the different regulatory environment and allocate management resources to managing the difference. One participant summed up some of these costs by noting that:

> trademark law is different in China to Australia. . . . It's difficult to understand and a bit of a barrier to business in China . . . before you do business in China, you have to and understand how the trademark system works and spend $10-20,000 on trademarks.
>
> (Case 24: Meat Co)

This can be interpreted as a LOF which would be particularly significant for SMEs due to the identified management costs.

Meeting Chinese business partner and customer expectations

This construct also attracted 12 comments from eight participants. The participants included four manufacturing companies, one agribusiness company, two service companies and a technology company, suggesting that the identified liabilities applied across the sample. It covered a wider range of forms and sources of liability than the previous constructs, however, they were all LOFs which the participant needed to respond to increase the SME's legitimacy. Sources of this liability included cultural norms and government policies and the isomorphic behaviours that were required to overcome them and gain legitimacy. The isomorphic behaviours required included social behaviours such as entertaining, symbols, such as impressive business facilities, specific forms of product features, such as technology innovation and the need to provide more evidence in order to gain trust. One example was: "it's all tailor made so people can walk in here and go this is very, very serious business". Another example was:

> So the Chinese way of saying please don't talk about the deal, tell me about your wife, when are you having children and doing that three or four times and actually calling that a KPI that I've actually got some traction with this family and he or she feels that I've shared some of my home life. Now I'm ready to talk about going somewhere together because they know that I like this wine.
>
> (Case 28: Consult Co 1)

The comments from the participants relating to this construct varied considerably regarding the isomorphic behaviours that needed to be adopted. For example, some indicated that the isomorphic behaviour of accepting corruption was not necessary: "it's certainly possible to do business in China legally". Although some respondents identified both interest and engagement in innovation amongst Chinese customers, other respondents identified a resistance to directly adopting new technologies. For example, one respondent noted that "There's a degree of discomfort with accepting something that no-one's used before". Some participants identified liability (of outsidership) associated with introducing new technologies not available in the market and experienced this liability in specific industries. Other participants, however, found that different industries had expectations of innovation and that introducing new technologies reduced the LOO. In each case, however, there was a LOO associated with technology levels and responding to those required, in one case, not taking advantage of an existing innovation and, in the other case, investment in innovation.

Need to be adaptive

Seven participants commented on this construct, providing a total of 15 relevant comments. Three service companies, one agribusiness, one manufacturing, one finance and one technology company responded, suggesting that the identified liabilities had relevance across the sample. The need to be adaptive experienced by the participants created liabilities (of foreignness or outsidership). When the expectation was not met, it resulted in concomitant isomorphic behaviours from the participants. For example, one participant indicated that:

> we've focused just on a select few, a couple of products here to understand what does it need to look like and we've already . . . I think one of those products is already on its fourth evolution. We had to change and adapt to that very quickly, changing our logos, our colours, our wording, terminologies.
>
> (Case 13: Vehicle Co)

Reducing the effect of these liabilities represented a significant cost for the SMEs, as the following example indicates: "We try to schedule it in but because we're quite limited with our resources, we have to be structured in understanding and responding to, I guess, market opportunities". Isomorphic responses to these liabilities revealed LOS which added further costs. This finding suggests that LOS can be related to responding to LOF.

One of the partners described an interesting approach that their organisation had taken to reduce the LOS experienced in responding to partner and customer expectations of innovation. This participant's organisation sought out Chinese organisations that already responded to the expectations of innovation by creating unique innovations. The participant's organisation planned to partner with organisations that had already developed the capabilities that reduce this liability in order to reduce their own exposure. This was described by the participant as follows:

> Their growth in China was to bring a very large part of their R&D capability into China and then to have business developers out in the countryside looking for particularly innovative Chinese manufacturers in a niche that might fit into their business, to look at them as potential acquisitions or partners and to then put that innovative product into their R&D department as an incubator because these guys were innovative.
>
> (Case 11: Recruitment Co)

Building trust

Lack of trust was identified as a liability (of foreignness and newness) by seven of the participants, offering nine comments. The isomorphic response described by these participants was not unique to China and was considered by the participants to be a LOF for any foreign market. The isomorphic response to this LOF was described by one participant as developing "a deep and meaningful partnership or relationship built on trust and mutual respect and benefit". There was some indication of an advantage of foreignness for certain industries, which counted the LOF in those industries for the foreign SMEs. The literature also identifies some evidence for this phenomena (Boehe, 2011). For example, one participant noted that:

> Absolutely, yes, and it's financial services so we were told in this sort of sector Chinese people would trust a government owned company or a foreign owned company that is substantial, probably not a new Chinese owned business because that potentially could be dodgy.
>
> (Case 13: Vehicle Co)

The Chinese business environment also provided opportunities for isomorphic responses in order to gain trust and reduce the LOF. For example, some participants utilised the Chinese online payment system, Alipay, which provided some guarantees to Chinese customers that increased their level of trust in the transaction. One participant described the process of adopting this online pay system:

> Alipay [is] the PayPal of China, the debit card facility. So I think it's necessary to cater to the different markets but it's taken us a long time, especially to get Alipay up and running, but I think it's vital. You need to respect the local customs and work with it and to, I guess, close a circle as a business that starts up here and pitfalls, you learn from what other people have done and how they've succeeded. If you can't sell your product online that cuts out a lot of market share right there in China.
>
> (Case 14: Office Co)

Trust was also one of the items that required reciprocal compliance. The participants also needed to trust their partners, for example: "The biggest issue is having to put ourselves completely at the mercy of people who we didn't know previously". This is another form of LOF. Whether the trust is required by a customer in China or by the foreign SME, its absence interferes with business transactions and represents a cost. Increasing trust will reduce this source of LOF.

Building credibility

The LOF, LON and LOS resulting from the need for credibility in China for the SMEs was the third construct for creating legitimacy and created significant costs for the participants. Eighteen comments were provided by 11 participants for this construct. Five service industry participants, two manufacturing industry participants, two finance participants and two agribusiness participants responded, suggesting that the identified liabilities had relevance across the sample. The participants with customers that were large organisations observed that it was difficult to gain responses from these companies. This would have been a LOS, as the following example indicates "if you're small you have very little chance of having your voice heard".

The same condition, however, may have applied to these participants in their home country market as well. The parallels with LOS in the home country market for this SME were supported by comments from other participants. They observed that they responded to this LOS by gaining credibility using the same activities in which they would have engaged in their home country to gain credibility. One of the activities was increasing the public profile of the organisation, as the following example illustrates:

> It's an industry lobby group that talks to government and not only talks to government but does that through lots of advocacy things and I get invited to speak at different forums or I get to do some media in China and other things like that . . . my personal brand and the company brand is enhanced as a result.
>
> (Case 11: Recruitment Co)

Approaches for increasing credibility included registering the SME on Wechat (a Chinese social media platform). This last activity could be considered to be an isomorphic response as most Chinese companies also are registered on Wechat to increase their profile. Several participants also identified country of origin and international reputation characteristics as valuable contributions to their credibility in the market which was generated by their foreign background. This finding was also consistent with the literature which observes that international capability and foreign competencies can reduce LOF (Jiang, Liu and Stening, 2014; Zhou and Guillén, 2015).

Building social relationships

The LOF and LOS resulting from a lack of social relationships were also frequently identified, generating 15 comments from 10 participants. Comments came from three manufacturing companies, two service companies, two finance companies, two technology companies and one agribusiness, suggesting that the identified liabilities were relevant across the sample. One of the most important conditions for this source of liability was that cultural conditions varied widely across China and that even immediately outside a major capital city, the culture could be significantly different. This meant that the value of social relationships varied across geographical areas. The LOF resulting from the need for local social relationships meant that the SMEs experienced a new LOF every time they moved to a new region. One participant explained this as follows:

> if I storm into Chungdu or into the north east as a Shanghai person I won't be listened to. I need to be accepting that I'm in a different part of the country and they do things a little bit differently there. Having strong relationships or guanxi or whatever it might be called in Beijing or in Shanghai, it won't get me terribly far in those cities. I need to have good relationships in those cities and understand why it's important.
>
> (Case 11: Recruitment Co)

The participants observed that this created a liability for domestic companies as well and so cannot be considered a source of LOF. The participants did note, however, that although guanxi was, for their purposes, becoming more comparable to international business professional relationship building, it was very useful for some of the participants in enabling them to conclude negotiations with large organisations that might otherwise ignore them due to their size (see section on Building Credibility). For example, one construction industry participant needing to negotiate fire codes observed that guanxi was useful in enabling them to "meet the head of the fire bureau so we need a relationship just to get the appointment". This type of social relationship enabled this participant to overcome the LOF.

Customer and partner transparency

Unlike most of the other constructs, this LOS was the result of the characteristics of some of the domestic organisations in China. Subsequently, it did not require an isomorphic response, although it still represented a liability to some of the participants. Eight comments were received from six participants on this construct. This liability related to the previously mentioned LOS resulting from a lack of credibility when dealing with large enterprises, although there was no evidence of the situation being different for domestic SMEs in the previous case. For example, one manufacturing participant observed:

> We're trying to avoid disputes of course but the bigger companies, they're too big to get their attention, so sometimes you've got to threaten arbitration or something and then they'll come and talk to you again and solve something.
>
> (Case 17: Metal Frame Co)

This condition appeared to apply equally to participants from different industries including manufacturing, finance and service. Interestingly, one of the participants had set up an arbitration service specifically to resolve disputes between Chinese and multinational companies. It is possible that this represented a LOF, as a domestic company may not have had the same expectations as the participants who made these observations.

Understanding culture and language

This construct attracted the greatest number of responses (23) of any construct, from the greatest number of participants (16). Responses were received from eight service companies, four manufacturing companies, two technology companies and two finance companies, suggesting that the identified liability was relevant to the different industry groups making up the sample. Most of the participants were very familiar with the LOF resulting from the lack of knowledge of culture and language. For example, one participant noted: "How the culture affects the business is quite interesting. Sometimes it's just communication, it's the challenge of communicating and understanding". The costs associated with this liability were quite substantial. As one participant noted:

> one of the biggest barriers still is the language barrier, that can be difficult sometimes and sometimes the difference between dealing with a company and not is they don't have good English, you're going to need to bring in an outside party and, one, it adds to the cost but, two, it just makes things more difficult.
>
> (Case 1: Furniture Co)

The respondents indicated that these barriers were also diminishing as the Chinese acquired more Western cultural knowledge and English language proficiency. For example, a larger participant (categorised as a medium organisation) observed that it was less of a liability, as the following example indicates: "Everyone always says everything is different in China but it really isn't if you keep your eyes open, maybe just a different culture but the emotions of people, I think, that's not so hugely different". In addition, the first quoted participant also noted:

> Probably not as important as they used to be. Five to 10 years ago they were certainly very important because it was difficult to deal direct with factories certainly because of the language barrier. So nine times out of 10 you would go through an agent and the majority of the time that agent was Taiwanese. They would be the agents and they would take you to some Chinese factories and show you around and all that sort of thing.
>
> (Case 1: Furniture Co)

Apart from the potential to lose out on valuable business deals due to language and cultural barriers, the costs associated with adaptation to different languages and cultural behaviours is also a significant cost. As one participant observed: "I will do things in one way and the team will do it another way. It sometimes can be a headache trying to understand why are things done this way but we have to work with it and change the way we do things to work with the cultural differences".

Logistics, infrastructure and resources

These two categories were both considered to be LOOs due to competitive forces and attracted a small number of responses, so they will be dealt with together. Seven responses from six participants were received for these two categories in total. The participants observed that infrastructure was developing rapidly in China and the LOO due to difficulties that the SMEs had in managing the Chinese logistics and infrastructure had reduced over time. In addition, some of the participants reported relying on foreign resources as well as Chinese resources in China for logistics and infrastructure activities. The combination of these resources may have reduced these problems to a level lower than experienced by domestic Chinese companies and generated an advantage of foreignness for these organisations. For example, one participant noted that: "our senior management team are from different Western countries, Australia, UK or United States, but we use the resources in China so it's the best of two worlds". This observation is consistent with the literature which identified the value of foreign located resources for foreign enterprises in China (Jiang, Liu and Stening, 2014; Zhou and Guillén, 2015).

The difficulty of managing logistics and infrastructure in China, however, still created a LOS for the smaller participants who observed that a lack of resource availability in China slowed their rate of growth. One participant explained this as follows:

> We are working very slowly because we don't have a lot of labour resources here to do that and we don't have a full time marketing senior to support us.
>
> (Case 12: Accounting Co)

Limited access to capital

LOS resulted from difficulties of accessing capital for some of the SMEs as a small organisation with limited collateral. This interfered with their rate of growth or stopped them from performing operations necessary to be successful in the market. It can also be considered to be a LOF because foreigners find it more difficult to attract capital in China than local companies due to legislation. Eight comments were received from six participants regarding the challenges associated with capital in the Chinese market. The conditions around this appeared to be unchanging, with the small organisations being unable to generate capital from the Australian capital market for their activities in China and unable to generate capital in the Chinese market because of a lack of collateral. Some of these organisations relied on capital from relatives, whilst others relied on government development grants to assist with their internationalisation to China. For example, one participant noted: "It's not easy to get money here. We have no collateral". The lack of capital created a major motivation for having a Chinese partner, as one participant noted, "I think a Chinese partner adds a lot. Access to capital is something that they have in spades".

International business costs and income challenges

Foreign SMEs in China experience two sets of costs – the costs of operations in China, as well as the costs of operating a foreign enterprise, which results in a number of extra costs that domestic organisations do not have to bear, such as the cost of repatriating funds to the home country. These costs result in an LOF. The construct of international business costs generated 10 responses from eight participants. One comment was also received regarding the construct of income challenges which reflected the LOF resulting from the greater difficulty that foreign SMEs experience in collecting payments from customers in China. This construct was included because of its natural association with the construct of international business costs. Responses were received from six service companies, two manufacturing companies and one agribusiness. The greater frequency of responses from the service companies suggests that the liabilities identified were more relevant for the service industry participants than for the other participants in the study. It was particularly interesting that there were only two comments from the manufacturing participants regarding costs and income, as the liabilities identified would have been more significant for manufacturing companies than for the service companies. The service companies, however, were generally smaller than the manufacturing companies, so liabilities relating to cash flow may have been more significant for these participants.

The participants indicated that costs in China were increasing although this did not create an increase in the LOF as domestic companies would have experienced the same costs. Foreign SMEs, however, are probably more exposed to price rises in China due to the need to lease all of their property, rather than owning some property, as would be the case for some domestic competitors. The greater exposure to cost increases in China for foreign SMEs would mean that cost increases would generate a LOF. In addition, the SMEs operating as subsidiaries in China would also have options as to where to invest their resources. If the ability to generate an income from China was reduced, the organisation would have less justification for operating in China, which creates another LOF for the Chinese operations.

Summary of findings

The findings provide examples of each of the forms of liability identified in the literature review and demonstrate that liability theory provides an effective basis for categorising the barriers of entry of SMEs into China. The most common form of liability identified was LOF, followed by LOS. The LOF was generated by a range of conditions including a lack of credibility, knowledge, ability to interpret regulations, culture and language, social norms, trust, social relationships, access to capital and carrying international business costs. LOS was generated as a result of: insufficient credibility with large customers; a shortage of the resources required to properly manage adaptation and activities in the local market, such as international partners and Chinese logistics; access to capital with limited equity and limited number of social relationships. The comments identified provided little evidence for the effect of institutional forces on the participants, with the exception of the costs of adapting to meet cultural business norm expectations and regulatory requirements.

Table 7.2 categorises and summarises the forms of liability identified in relation to each of the identified constructs. Table 7.2 also shows that there is no apparent relationship between the number of comments received (an indication of the level of significance of the construct for the participants) and the evidence provided by the participants for the causes of that liability.

Table 7.2 Liabilities represented by the different identified categories

Category	Liability type	No. of comments	Comment
Networks	LOF and LON	6	No network is a liability and when established is a benefit
Partnerships	LOF	3	No partnerships is a liability and when established is a cost
Regulations	LOF and LON	12	Effect of regulations is reducing, but is still a business cost for SMEs
Expectations	LOF and LOO	12	Leads to isomorphic behaviour, but the level of liability varied by industry sector
Adaption	LOF and LOS	15	Required in isomorphic behaviour, created a cost for entry but could also create a benefit
Building trust	LOF and LON	9	Considered to be reciprocal and similar requirements in other markets
Credibility	LOF, LOS and LON	18	Country of origin or international profile credibility factors were significant with some indications of possible liability for micro size organisations
Relationships	LOF and LOS	15	Guanxi offered advantages in specific instances, but was otherwise viewed as similar to professional business relationships
Transparency	LOS	8	Some indication of disadvantage resulting from transparency issues that may not have applied to domestic SMEs

Culture and language	LOF	23	The effect would only be a significant liability for small organisations
Logistics, infrastructure and resources	LOO	2	Participants expressed a desire for more logistics and infrastructure and evidence of competitive advantage from foreign resources
Capital	LOF	8	Unchanged and requires that small enterprises require government support or a partner to assist with internationalisation
Costs and income	LOF	11	Increased costs in China and difficulty in ensuring payment was a liability for small organisations, exacerbated by their foreignness. Was more frequently identified by the service sector than other sectors in the sample

Comparison of the findings to the literature

This section considers how the experiences and behaviours of the interview participants compares to the observations in the literature and where this supports, extends or challenges current thinking. One of the most important findings from this research was that the barriers to internationalisation were frequently directly expressed as liabilities (147 relevant comments were received from the participants). The references to institutional forces mainly focused on the difficulty associated with interpreting regulatory forces and responding to social norms. This provides evidence to counter the recent assertions in the literature that institutional theory has supplanted liability theory as an effective explanation for the behaviours and performance of internationalising SMEs (Denk, Kaufmann and Roesch, 2012; Panibratov, 2015).

The constructs that generate forms of liability identified from the interview analysis did not identify any new forms of liability for the foreign SMEs in the sample. Table 7.2 shows, however, that the constructs attracting the greatest number of comments represented a cause of either an LOF or LOS. A LOO was identified in relation to meeting customer and partner expectations, as well as managing logistics infrastructure and resources, however, only eight of the participants commented on these two constructs. A LON was identified in relation to four constructs (lack of networks, understanding regulations, building trust and creating credibility) and by 17 participants. The large number of constructs identified that represent causes of LOF is a logical finding for foreign SMEs. Such organisations will have less total experience with internationalisation than large organisations which may employ hundreds of staff with foreign country knowledge and so will be more exposed to sources of LOF. The number of constructs that identify causes of LOS for the sample are logical, given that the organisations are characterised by their limited resources being small to medium sized organisations.

The limited number of constructs identified that generate LOO and LON was an interesting finding. This suggests that the participants were able to overcome the constraints of their limited resources when it came to causes of liabilities resulting from outsidership or newness. This may reflect the strong long-term relationship between Australia and China and experience of the entrepreneurs who had established these organisations, which enabled them to reduce the relationship and knowledge based causes of LOO and LON. This would have reduced the structural causes of LOF for the participants, such as the need to build networks, adapt the organisation and have detailed technical understandings of Chinese regulations, or of the resource constraints associated with being an SME in China.

Another interesting finding was that foreignness, whilst being a direct liability, was also identified as a contributor to generating credibility by the participants. Foreignness, in certain industries such as the agricultural industry, engendered greater trust than domestic organisations in the same industry achieved. In these instances, this reduced or even eliminated LOF. This finding demonstrates that the factors that cause a liability can also be a reason for the absence of a liability and that changes to the conditions in the country can change the liabilities that organisations experience in that country. The findings also indicated that this effect varies from industry to industry. In the case of innovation, for example, it was found that innovation led to a LON in some traditional Chinese markets that did not want innovation, whilst it was an expectation in other Chinese markets. No liability reducing factors were identified for the LOS, however. It could be hypothesised that an SME has the capacity to change more quickly than a large organisation, reducing the cost of adaptation because of LOS, however, this capacity would also be true for all domestic SMEs. This extends the SME internationalisation literature. This literature has identified the value of home country based resources in mitigating the liability of outsidership (Bengtsson and Johansson, 2014; Hollender, Zapkau and Schwens, 2017; Schweizer, 2013), but has not identified home country factors which reduce the causes of LOF.

The analysis determined that partnerships reduced the LOF and LOO resulting from a shortage of knowledge in the short-term, but provided a disadvantage in terms of the cost of managing the cross-country partnership for the SME and splitting profitability. This finding provides a valuable extension to the SME literature considering LOF and LOO by introducing the concept of diminishing returns on the benefits of partnerships for foreign SMEs in China. The literature has identified the moderating effect of partnerships on the LOF and LOO, but does not consider the long-term value of these relationships (Dias and Lopes, 2014; Merino and Grandval, 2012). Dias and Lopes (2014) determined that partnerships increase the rate of internationalisation of SMEs by providing market knowledge. Once the market knowledge has been assimilated by the SME, however, future knowledge and resource asymmetries in the partnership may become a disadvantage for the SME in the foreign market. This may be the reason why the participants found that partnerships represented a cost in the long term. Merino and Grandval (2012) hint at this by noting that, in addition to the value of market information for partnerships established by foreign SMEs, it is important that a sustainable management of partnership resources be established.

The finding that the development of trust was a reciprocal issue for the participants and Chinese partners and customers – a liability was generated when either the partner or customer did not trust the foreign SME or when the foreign SME did not trust the partner or customer – adds an interesting construct to the SME internationalisation literature. The SME internationalisation literature focuses on the externalisation of trust as a component of establishing credibility with foreign customers and partners (Fiedler, Fath and Whittaker, 2017; Ratajczak-Mrozek, 2014; Rodrigues and Child, 2012; Udomkit and Schreier, 2017). It does not mention, however, the importance of the SME's trust in its foreign market. The findings from this study identified causes of LOF arising from either a lack of trust on the part of the foreign SME or on the part of the SME's customers and partners. This suggests that mutually established trust, particularly the facilitation of coordinated processes such as contracts and development of innovation, could reduce one of the causes of LOF.

Fiedler, Fath and Whittaker (2017) determined establishing the trust of market actors with the SME as an important mechanism for market entry. The importance of establishing the trust of market actors for the long term performance of the SME was not, unfortunately, identified from the data analysis. The findings in this project suggest that establishing the trust of market actors to establish credibility in a foreign market is not sufficient for SME internationalisation success; the SME should expect trust to be established reciprocally. As one participant noted, "don't ever trust the business relationship". In a similar way, Ratajczak-Mrozek (2014) externalises the trust process as a source of opportunity for the SME, but does not identify trust as a method of controlling the effect of external relationships on the SME. Udomkit and Schreier (2017) identify the trust pre-condition for SMEs joining and maintaining membership of networks. Although these authors do not identify the effect of the SME's trust of its network actors, they do identify the need for a more reciprocal form of trust for SMEs in network relationships. The authors refer to this as "friendship", in which the mutual benefits of both parties are a precondition for this type of trust.

The liability of transparency of market actors was closely related to the liability of the effect of trust on the participant's internationalisation success. The literature does not consider the effect of transparency of market actors on the success of SME internationalisation. The participants noted that a lack of transparency of market actors had a significant impact upon their ability to manage their relationships in China. Examples indicated that transparency of market actors reduced the participant's ability to secure payment for work. The participants suggested that, although the relationship development in China had become more similar to normal international business relationship development processes, dealing with transparency was an important area in which guanxi had a significant value for the participants.

The findings in relation to the culture, language, costs and income constructs also make a valuable extension to the SME internationalisation literature, by identifying the impact of these factors on small organisations, compared to the impact on SMEs. Whilst the larger SMEs involved in the study experienced a relatively limited increase in liability from these constructs, the small company participants indicated that these constructs created significant liabilities. The limited resources of small international businesses causes increased internationalised operation expenses, income interruptions and the costs associated with adapting to culture and language differences created substantial LOFs. This finding contributes to the emerging literature on this topic which has determined that small organisations internationalise to seek opportunities and knowledge through which to compete (Bilas, Franc and Kvaternjak, 2013; Gonçalves Cunha and De Campos, 2012; Wąsowska, 2017). This literature does not consider, however, the effect of costs, interruptions and adaptation that could generate increased liabilities (Ibeh et al, 2004). This study has determined that causes of LOF such as cultural and language differences and international cost and income uncertainty affect the internationalisation of foreign small companies.

Conclusion

The 35 participants in this study provided a large number (147) of comments that related to causes of liabilities experienced in internationalising to China. These comments were classified into 15 constructs for the generation of liabilities, which were grouped into the higher order constructs of business practice, economic and competitive factors. The most frequently identified constructs were understanding local culture and language, adapting, achieving credibility, developing relationships and meeting customer and partner expectations and regulations. The evidence identified the capacity of these constructs to generate a liability and the effect of these liabilities on internationalisation of the foreign SMEs in the study. This provides direct evidence for the value of liability theory for explaining the behaviours and experiences of SMEs internationalising to China. The constructs provided a small amount of evidence for the value of institutional theory in explaining the behaviours of the SMEs, which was the difficulty in interpreting government regulation and responding to social norms.

The findings were used to make several extensions to the literature. The constructs that lead to the generation of LOF and LOS were most commonly identified, suggesting that SME internationalisation theory should focus on developing operational constructs for these liabilities. The findings also determined that the sources of some liabilities, such as the need for foreign SMEs to develop credibility because of their foreignness, were minimised by the credibility associated with the foreign SME's home country. This was particularly applicable to SMEs offering agricultural products or financial services for which domestic Chinese organisations had limited credibility. It was also found that using partners to moderate the effects of LOO and LON due to knowledge deficit was only effective in the short term and created organisational complexity and costs in the long-term.

The findings also extended the literature relating to the importance of trust, which currently focuses on externalising trust to reduce liabilities in the foreign market, by determining that without reciprocal trust, the behaviour of market actors can also create liabilities for the SMEs. Market actor transparency was also found to be a LOS for the participants. Some participants indicated that guanxi could reduce this cause of LOS, although the respondents did not indicate that it would reduce the other causes of liability identified in the study. The impact of understanding culture, language and the effect of cost and income inconsistencies in the Chinese market were found to be stronger causes of LOF for the smaller businesses in the study. The constructs identified in this chapter can be used in future research as a basis for extending the literature in the areas identified above.

References

Acheampong, G., and Dana, L.-P. (2017). Liability of foreignness in fast-expanding markets: Evidence from Ghana. *Thunderbird International Business Review*, 1, 51.

Aldrich, H. E., and Auster, E. R. (2011). Even Dwarfs Started Small: Liabilities of Age and Size and Their Strategic Implications. In Aldrich, H. E. (Ed.), *An Evolutionary Approach to Entrepreneurship: Selected Essays by Howard E. Aldrich*, 257–290. Cheltenham, UK and Northampton, MA: Edward Elgar.

Arditi, D., and Kale, S. (1998). Business failures: Liabilities of newness, adolescence, and smallness. *Journal of Construction Engineering and Management*, 124:6, 458–464.

Barnard, H. (2010). Overcoming the liability of foreignness without strong firm capabilities – the value of market-based resources. *Journal of International Management*, 16, 165–176.

Bengtsson, M., and Johansson, M. (2014). Managing coopetition to create opportunities for small firms. *International Small Business Journal*, 32:4, 401.

Bilas, V., Franc, S., and Kvaternjak, I. (2013). Internationalisation of micro and small enterprises in the information technology industry of the Republic of Croatia. *Economic Review: Journal of Economics & Business/Ekonomska Revija: Casopis za Ekonomiju i Biznis*, 11:1, 45.

Boehe, D. M. (2011). Exploiting the liability of foreignness: Why do service firms exploit foreign affiliate networks at home? *Journal of International Management*, 17, 15–29.

Chen, J. (2017). Internationalization of Chinese firms: What role does Guanxi Play for overcoming their liability of outsidership in developed markets? *Thunderbird International Business Review*, 59:3, 367–383.

Crilly, D., Na, N., and Yuwei, J. (2016). Do-no-harm versus do-good social responsibility: Attributional thinking and the liability of foreignness. *Strategic Management Journal*, 7, 1316.

Denk, N., Kaufmann, L., and Roesch, J.-F. (2012). Liabilities of foreignness revisited: A review of contemporary studies and recommendations for future research. *Journal of International Management*, 18, 322–334.

Dias, E. B., and Lopes, D. S. (2014). Co-operation between Large Enterprises (LE's) and SME's: An approach to overcome the stage internationalization process. *Business: Theory and Practice*, 15:4, 316–327.

Djupdal, K., and Westhead, P. (2015). Environmental certification as a buffer against the liabilities of newness and smallness: Firm performance benefits. *International Small Business Journal*, 33:2, 148–168.

Economist. (2014). Small is not beautiful; Foreign entrepreneurs in China: 66: Economist Intelligence Unit N.A. Incorporated.

Fiedler, A., Fath, B. P., and Whittaker, D. H. (2017). Overcoming the liability of outsidership in institutional voids: Trust, emerging goals, and learning about opportunities. *International Small Business Journal*, 35:3, 262.

Gonçalves Cunha, C. S., and De Campos, R. P. (2012). The internationalization of micro and small companies from knowledge-management standpoint: A multiple case study in Brazil. *Proceedings of the International Conference on Intellectual Capital, Knowledge Management & Organizational Learning*, 60–69.

Gorostidi-Martinez, H., and Zhao, X. (2017). Strategies to avoid liability of foreignness when entering a new market. *Journal of Advances in Management Research*, 14:1, 46.

Hollender, L., Zapkau, F. B., and Schwens, C. (2017). SME foreign market entry mode choice and foreign venture performance: The moderating effect of international experience and product adaptation. *International Business Review*, 26:2, 250–263.

Hollenstein, H. (2005). Determinants of international activities: Are SMEs different? *Small Business Economics*, 24:5, 431.

Hymer, S. (1976). *The International Operations of National Firms: A Study of Direct Foreign Investment*: Cambridge, MA: MIT Press, c1976.

Ibeh, K., Johnson, J. E., Dimitratos, P., and Slow, J. (2004). Micromultinationals: Some preliminary evidence on an Emergent 'Star' of the international entrepreneurship field. *Journal of International Entrepreneurship*, 2:4, 289–303.

Jiang, F., Liu, L., and Stening, B. W. (2014). Do foreign firms in China incur a liability of foreignness? The local Chinese firms' perspective. *Thunderbird International Business Review*, 6, 501.

Johanson, J., and Vahlne, J. E. (2009). The Uppsala internationalization process model revisited: From liability of foreignness to liability of outsidership. *Journal of International Business Studies*, 40:9, 1411–1431.

Kalantaridis, C., and Vassilev, I. (2011). Firm size and the nature of international relationships: The case of globally integrated small firms. *Journal of Small Business Management*, 49:4, 639.

Kim, Y. J., Tesar, L. L., and Zhang, J. (2015). The impact of foreign liabilities on small firms: Firm-level evidence from the Korean crisis. *Journal of International Economics*, 97, 209–230.

Ko, W. W., and Liu, G. (2016). Overcoming the liability of smallness by recruiting through networks in China: A Guanxi-based social capital perspective. *International Journal of Human Resource Management*, 1–28.

Kock, S., Nisuls, J., and Soderqvist, A. (2010). Co-opetition: A source of international opportunities in Finnish SMEs. *Competitiveness Review*, 2, 111.

Lamin, A., and Livanis, G. (2013). Agglomeration, catch-up and the liability of foreignness in emerging economies. *Journal of International Business Studies*, 44:6, 579–606.

Li, W., Bruton, G. D., and Filatotchev, I. (2016). Mitigating the dual liability of newness and foreignness in capital markets: The role of returnee independent directors. *Journal of World Business*, 51, 787–799.

Lindorfer, R., d'Arcy, A., and Puck, J. (2016). Location decisions and the liability of foreignness: Spillover effects between factor market and capital market strategies. *Journal of International Management*, 22, 222–233.

Merino, P. B., and Grandval, S. (2012). Partnerships between SMEs and MNEs on foreign industrial markets: A strategy to reduce the liability of foreignness. *International Business Research*, 6, 53.

Minard, P. (2016). Signalling through the noise: private certification, information asymmetry and Chinese SMEs' access to finance. *Journal of Asian Public Policy*, 9:3, 243–256.

Moeller, M., Harvey, M., Griffith, D., and Richey, G. (2013). The impact of country-of-origin on the acceptance of foreign subsidiaries in host countries: An examination of the 'liability-of-foreignness'. *International Business Review*, 22:1, 89–99.

Panibratov, A. (2015). Liability of foreignness of emerging market firms: The country of origin effect on Russian IT companies. *Journal of East-West Business*, 21:1, 22–40.

Prashantham, S. (2011). Social capital and Indian micromultinationals. *British Journal of Management*, 1, 4.

Ratajczak-Mrozek, M. (2014). The importance of locally embedded personal relationships for SME internationalisation processes – from opportunity recognition to company growth. *Journal of Entrepreneurship, Management and Innovation*, 3, 89.

Rodrigues, S. B., and Child, J. (2012). Building social capital for internationalization. *RAC – Revista de Administração Contemporânea*, 16:1, 23–38.

Schiavini, J. M., and Scherer, F. L. (2015). Overcoming liability of outsidership in China: The experience of Brazilian companies in developing Guanxi. *InternexT: Revista Eletrônica de Negócios Internacionais da ESPM*, 10:3, 44–57.

Schweizer, R. (2013). SMEs and networks: Overcoming the liability of outsidership. *Journal of International Entrepreneurship*, 11:1, 80–103.

Stinchcombe, A. L. (2012). Social structure and organizations. In Landstrom, H. and Lohrke, F. T. (Eds.), *Intellectual Roots of Entrepreneurship Research*. Elgar Research Collection. International Library of Entrepreneurship, vol. 23. Cheltenham, UK and Northampton, MA: Edward Elgar, 704–755.

Tiwari, S. K., Sen, S., and Shaik, R. (2016). Internationalisation: A study of small firms from emerging markets. *Journal of Developing Areas*, 50, 355–364.

Udomkit, N., and Schreier, C. (2017). Tie the ties: The significance of the binding networks in SMEs' internationalization process. *Journal of Asia-Pacific Business*, 18:1, 4.

Wąsowska, A. (2017). Organisational-level attributes of micro-multinationals. The evidence from European SMEs. *International Journal of Management and Economics*, 53:1, 84–98.

Wei, T., and Clegg, J. (2015). Overcoming the liability of foreignness in internationalization in emerging economies: Lessons from acquiring a Chinese firm. *Thunderbird International Business Review*, 2, 103.

Wu, Z., and Salomon, R. (2016). Does imitation reduce the liability of foreignness? Linking distance, isomorphism, and performance. *Strategic Management Journal*, 12, 2441.

Yildiz, H. E., and Fey, C. F. (2012). The liability of foreignness reconsidered: New insights from the alternative research context of transforming economies. *International Business Review*, 2, 269.

Yu, J., and Kim, S. (2013). Understanding liability of foreignness in an Asian business context: A study of the Korean asset management industry. *Asia Pacific Journal of Management*, 30:4, 1191.

Zaheer, S. (1995). Overcoming the liability of foreignness. *Academy of Management Journal*, 2, 341.

Zhou, N., and Guillén, M. F. (2015). From home country to home base: A dynamic approach to the liability of foreignness. *Strategic Management Journal*, 36:6, 907–917.

Zhou, N., and Guillen, M. F. (2016). Categorizing the liability of foreignness: Ownership, location, and internalization-specific dimensions. *Global Strategy Journal*, 6:4, 309–329.

8   How HRM contributes to innovation in China

Introduction

In general, it is argued that small and medium-sized enterprises (SMEs) tend to make less use of systematic and sophisticated human resource management (HRM) practices than large organisations, because of their lack of sufficient resources and technical knowledge necessary to implement comprehensive HRM systems (Kotey and Slade, 2005; Zheng, Morrison and O'Neill, 2006, 2009; Innes and Wiesner, 2012; Allen, Ericksen and Collins, 2013). However, it is also evident that an increasing number of SMEs have recognised the importance of implementing best HRM practices in order to assist their firms to grow, survive and sustain their businesses in the globally competitive environment (Hayton, 2003; Kotey and Slade, 2005; Newman and Abdullah, 2014; Sheehan, 2014). With support from the resource/knowledge-based theory (Grant, 1996; Barney, 2001), successful SMEs were empirically identified to have some positive human resource management outcomes such as employee competency, enhanced human capital of owners/managers, increased organisational commitment and employee wellbeing as a result of fair compensation and skill development (Georgiadis and Pitelis, 2012; Newman and Abdullah, 2014; Wu, Bacon, and Hoque, 2014). Fast growing and innovative SMEs in some European countries (e.g. Belgium, Turkey and Spain) were also found to be associated with specific HRM practices that would generate organisational learning and knowledge creation, leading to enhancing employee creativity and organisational overall innovative capability and performance (De Winne and Sels, 2010; Ceylan, 2013; Donate, Peña and Sánchez de Pablo, 2016).

For the purpose of this study, we have adopted Innes and Wiesner's (2012) definition of HRM as a set of human resources (HR) practices used to manage the workforce of SMEs, including typical HRM functions such as recruitment, selection, training and development, compensation and performance appraisal of employees (Innes and Wiesner, 2012, p. 33). According to Innes and Wiesner (2012), there have been limited studies of the HRM practices that are required for innovation and positive firm outcome of Australian SMEs. Despite having a large-scale survey of 1230 Australian SMEs with fewer than 100 employees, Innes and Wiesner (2012) argue with an inconclusive result that there exists a strong multiple clustering of practices within HRM functions in SMEs, and that the predictors of implementing HRM practices are closely associated with "the liability of firm smallness and the difficulties firms face in the absence of HR professionals" (p. 32). Although not directly focusing on examining HRM practices, Tan, Smyrnios and Lin (2014) investigated drivers of learning orientation in 253 Australian fast-growing SMEs, and found that job-related HRM practices and organisational climate are positively related to employee learning, and subsequently motivated Australian SMEs to develop a culture of innovation, creativity and entrepreneurial attitude for continuing growth. These findings suggest that Australian SMEs have, to some extent, adopted HRM practices to assist their firm development and growth, despite being somewhat constrained by the liability of smallness (LOS).

Innes and Wiesner's (2012) list of HRM practices is based on five HRM functions, 29 recruitment methods, 18 selection practices, 22 training and development programs, 19 performance appraisal techniques and 22 compensation designs (even though a clear association of these HRM practices to SME performance was not established). Tan, Smyrnios and Lin (2014) simply used two items (i.e. rewards such as bonus/incentive given to employees; and use of employee motivation mechanism) to measure job-related HRM practices. These diverse views on a vast range (2–110) of items associated with HRM practices raise an important research question: what actually constitute specific and systematic HRM practices that would have been adopted by innovative SMEs?

To answer this research question, we conducted an exploratory study of the HRM practices of 35 Australian innovative SMEs operating in China. The use of China as a context for our research investigation has two reasons: first, China represents a considerably different context both culturally and institutionally from Australia. To successfully operate in the complex Chinese market, Australian SMEs would need to be innovative, either developing new products, having to adopt some new marketing ideas to sell their goods and services with added values for Chinese customers, or creating a new organisational structure and culture that would fit into China's business culture and institutional environment. Thus, the selection of Australian SMEs operating in China would fit the criteria of innovative firms for the current research. Second, according to Shipton et al. (2017), organisations that involve exploring options for challenging the institutional parameters that may inhibit innovation must be entrepreneurial. This type of organisation is more likely to pursue a set of entrepreneurial HRM practices that offer opportunities for their employees to be exposed to new experiences, foster active awareness and critique of institutional parameters and develop a unique set of organisational capabilities and competencies different from their competitors. Therefore, the study of HRM practices of Australian SMEs operating in China would serve the purpose of assisting business owners, employees and HRM practitioners to effectively address the challenging institutional differences between Australia and China, and to help Australian SMEs further grow, survive and sustain in the Chinese market.

We start the chapter with a brief literature review. This is followed by the outline of data analysis techniques and main findings from the case analysis of HRM practices adopted by Australian SMEs operating in China. We conclude the chapter with discussion on some theoretical and practical implications and research limitations.

Literature review

The extant literature that discusses HRM practices in small innovative firms is supported by several strategic management theories, such as the resource-based view, knowledge-based theory (Grant, 1996; Barney, 2001; Mayson and Barrett, 2006) as well as institutional theory (DiMaggio and Powell, 1983; Scott, 1995; Shipton et al., 2017). In line with the resource-based view of the firm, it is widely accepted that the ability for small firms to innovate largely depends on their underlying resources and capabilities. Such resources and capabilities can be acquired, developed and retained via various HRM measures such as strategic hiring and selection, training and career development and attractive compensation with job design and teamwork, organisational culture and competent leadership (Barney, 2001; Jiménez-Jiménez and Sanz-Valle, 2008; Jiang, Wang, and Zhao, 2012; Andries and Czarnitzki, 2014; Seeck and Diehl, 2017). Similarly, from the knowledge-based view, innovation is a function of a firm's ability to create, manage and maintain knowledge, and that knowledge is created by and restored within individual employees, thus employee knowledge and creativity cultivated via effective HRM policies and practices play an important role as drivers of firm innovation (De Winne and Sels, 2010; Bronay-Barrachina et al., 2012; Ceylan, 2013; Seeck and Diehl, 2017).

Because of the size and limited resources of SMEs, institutional theory provides an additional perspective on why small firms may behave differently from large ones, and why their innovative behavior may not always be rational and expected (Shipton et al., 2017). The majority of SMEs do not follow the approach of large organisations, which frequently adopt a universalistic approach of 'best' HRM practices which drive organisational performance (Innes and Wiesner, 2012). Instead, SMEs were found to strategically choose some HRM policies and practices over the others (Zheng, Morrison and O'Neill, 2009; Cooke and Saini, 2010), because of the necessity to respond to coercive, normative and mimetic pressures (DiMaggio and Powell, 1983) in order to gain institutional legitimacy, which is defined by Suchman (1995) as "a generalized perception or assumption that the actions of an entity are desirable, proper, or appropriate within some socially constructed system of norms, values, beliefs and definitions" (p. 574). Innovative SMEs, in particular, tend to adopt a contingency and/or configuration approach of 'best fit' HRM practices that align with their organisational business strategy and internal organisational structure and culture, as well as respond appropriately to external environmental and institutional pressures (Hayton, 2003; Rosi and Mahnood, 2013; Tang, Chen and Jin, 2015).

In essence, there are no disagreements theoretically on why innovative SMEs should adopt HRM to generate employee creativity, and develop organisational capability and competitiveness, so as to maintain and sustain firm performance. But to what extent and how comprehensive HRM systems that innovative SMEs should adopt remains arguably divergent. Table 8.1 illustrates some examples of different views on HRM practices in innovative SMEs sourced from reviewing a series of relevant empirical studies derived from the existing literature. The remaining discussion will focus on explaining SMEs' innovative types and activities, and their corresponding divergent HRM practices as illustrated in Table 8.1, as well as the relationship between HRM, innovation and performance.

Innovation in SMEs and HRM practices

Within the parameter of discussing the relationship between HRM and innovation, we have adopted Seeck and Diehl (2017: 915) and Shipton et al.'s (2017: 248) definition of innovation as "the intentional generation, promotion and realization of new ideas within a work role, group or organization". At the individual level, innovation refers to employees' novel ideas, creativity and innovative actions (Shipton et al., 2017). At the organisational level, changes can be technological (with change of product, service or production process) or there can be changes in administrative activities, social and team working processes or organisational structures (Damanpour and Evan, 1984; Seeck and Diehl, 2017). Technological and administrative changes are closely in line with product, process and organisational innovation.

Four types of innovation activities identified by Ceylan (2013) are related to SMEs' product, process, organisational and marketing innovation. Product innovation activities refer to the implementation of new or significantly improved goods or services; whilst process innovation activities would engage in the implementation of new or significantly improved production or delivery methods. Marketing innovation activities are easily identified as any new marketing methods; whilst organisational innovation activities would be related to adopting new management practices and organisational cultural and structural changes (Ceylan, 2013; Seeck and Diehl, 2017). Among these four types of innovative activities, organisational innovation is regarded as the most important as it helps improve the firm's capability to implement other innovative practices (Birkinshaw, Hamel and Mol, 2008). For instance, to develop new processes such as new production or supply channels or marketing methods, employee knowledge and skills of various functions must be developed, and organisational innovation activities such as designing and implementing new HRM practices, and new organisational culture and structure help change and apply new processes by increasing various functions' capacity and generating innovative performance (Halim et al., 2014).

In the strategic HRM literature, it is suggested that configuration of HRM practices affect different types of innovation activities. For instance, Shipton et al. (2006) argue that training and performance appraisal focused on employee development and teamwork would support product innovation activities. Chen and

Table 8.1 Different views on effects of HRM practices on SME innovation

HRM practices	Innovation types, capabilities and strategy	Sources
Training and performance appraisal focused on employee development and teamwork	Product innovation	Shipton et al. (2006); Seeck and Diehl (2017)
Selection, training and performance appraisal focused on employee development, employee participation, teamwork and compensation practices	Process innovation	Chen and Huang (2009); Ceylan (2013)
High-commitment HRM practices	Organisational innovation	Seeck and Diehl (2017)
Selection, formal participation programs, trainings and performance appraisals, career development and mentoring and teamwork and compensation practices	Marketing innovation	Ceylan (2013)
Strategic staffing, employee participation and compensation	Administrative innovation	Seeck and Diehl (2017)
Training, appraisal and team work	Technical innovation	Seeck and Diehl (2017)
Strategic hiring and selection, reward, job design and teamwork	Technological innovation	Jiang, Wang and Zhao (2012)
High-profile personnel HRM practices (i.e. selective staffing, training and high compensation systems)	Human capital development	Donate, Peña and Sánchez de Pablo (2016)
Collaborative HRM practices (i.e. work autonomy, broad job design, empowerment, teamwork and group-oriented incentives)	Social capital development	Donate, Peña and Sánchez de Pablo (2016)
Training and development, suggestion schemes, employee recognition awards and quality initiatives	Innovation-oriented business strategy	Cooke and Saini (2010)

Huang (2009) suggest that selection based on a candidate's future potential, training and performance appraisal focused on employee development, employee participation, teamwork and compensation practices would enhance process innovation activities. The findings of Cooke and Saini (2010) indicate that the HRM practices most used to support innovation-oriented business strategy were training and development, suggestion schemes, employee recognition awards and quality initiatives. Jiang, Wang and Zhao (2012) show that HRM practices such as strategic hiring and selection, reward, job design and teamwork are positively related to employee creativity, which in turn contribute to technological innovation. With a survey of 103 Turkish firms, Ceylan (2013) found that commitment-based HRM systems – characterised by a bundle of strategic HRM practices such as selection that focuses on building internal labor markets and the selection of external candidates who fit the firm, formal participation programs, training and performance appraisals that emphasise human capital development, career development and mentoring, and teamwork and compensation practices that focus on group or firm performance – were the core drivers of process and marketing innovation activities. Seeck and Diehl (2017), after reviewing 35 empirical studies examining the impact of HRM on innovation published during the past 25 years (1990–2015), conclude that HRM practices fostering employee commitment, loyalty, learning and intrinsic motivation were found to be conducive to overall organisational innovation (see Table 8.1).

Arguably, any innovative firms need to adopt different types of innovation activities pertaining to all aspects of the organisation rather than a single innovation activity (Damanpour, 1991). Correspondingly, a bundle of HRM practices, instead of using a single HRM practice, are believed to be more likely to contribute to the success of implementing innovation activities (Ceylan, 2013). The bundle is often characterised as high-performance, high involvement or commitment HRM systems (Shipton et al., 2017), which are further discussed next with reference to its link to performance and innovative SMEs.

Bundled HRM practices, SME innovation and performance

Following on from Huselid's (1995) coining of the term high-performance work practices (HPWP), a significant number of empirical studies have tested the underlying relationship between high-performance HRM systems and firm performance, especially with reference to SMEs (e.g. Hayton, 2003; Zheng, Morrison and O'Neill, 2006, 2009; Allen, Ericksen and Collins, 2013; Wu, Bacon and Hoque, 2014). However, few studies have analyzed the way in which an SME may be more innovative by using a specific set of high-performance HRM practices. Recently, Donate, Peña and Sánchez de Pablo (2016) divided HPWPs into high-profile personnel HRM practices and collaborative HRM practices, and analysed the effect of these two different HRM practices on generating innovative capabilities mediated by human and social capital among 436 Spanish SMEs. The results show that high-profile personal HRM practices (i.e. selective staffing, training and high compensation systems) positively influence human capital while collaborative HRM practices (i.e. work autonomy, broad job design, empower-ment, teamwork and group-oriented incentives) influence social capital. Both human and social capitals were found to positively mediate the relationship between HRM and innovation capabilities.

A set of high-commitment HRM practices includes high pay contingent on performance, greater autonomy, and the use of teams, enhanced opportunities for training and development, and selective staffing focused on organisational fit (Allen, Ericksen and Collins, 2013). With three waves of surveying both CEOs and employees of over 200 small firms, Allen, Ericksen and Collins (2013) exam-ine the effects of high-commitment HRM practices on the performance of small businesses, mediated by employee involvement and quit rates. The authors con-firm that there was a positive HRM-performance link. However, the study did not test the link between high-commitment HRM practices and innovation.

Zhou, Hong and Liu (2013) tested the link between two HRM systems (commitment-oriented v. collaboration-oriented) and innovation with a sample of 179 organisations operating in China. Although the sample was predominantly Chinese state-owned and privately-owned firms, almost 40 percent of the sample were joint-ventured and foreign owned companies in the service sector, similar to Australian SMEs operating in China. The authors found the positive effects of both commitment-oriented and collaboration-oriented HRM systems on firm innovation. The commitment-oriented HRM system consists of 15 areas of HRM practices such as diversity-oriented selective recruitment, job enrichment, self-managed teamwork, egalitarian participation, extensive training, job rota-tion, information sharing, result-based appraisal, development-oriented feedback, skill-based pay, high remuneration, promotion from within, employment security, employee proposal mechanism and overarching goal setting. The collaboration-oriented HRM practices include six items which include a formal external learn-ing program with business partners, consulting service buy-in, flexible partner-ship with autonomous external professionals, long-term personnel alliance with external academic institutions, building extensive social networks and profes-sional HRM outsourcing. Specifically, the commitment-oriented HRM systems help enhance employee creativity and cohesiveness to exploit knowledge, thus positively associate with firms' internal innovative capability. On the other hand, collaboration-oriented HRM systems stimulate open innovation by building social networks with external sources, which in turn help explore new knowledge and assist firm innovative performance. The interesting result of this study is that there exist significant negative interactions between the two HRM systems on both firm innovation and performance. This suggests that the firm, especially those small companies with limited resources, might be better off to stick to one set of bundled HRM practices, instead of two HRM systems that may lead to negative organisational outcomes.

Other scholars (e.g. Jiménez-Jiménez and Sanz-Valle, 2008; Prieto et al., 2010; Chowhan, 2016) use different terminologies to represent a bundle of HRM practices and test their effects on innovation, though not in the specific context of SMEs, and with inconclusive results. For instance, Jiménez-Jiménez and Sanz-Valle (2008) find that a bundle of HRM practices such as flexible job design and empowerment, team working and skill-oriented staffing is positively associated with product, process and administrative innovation (see also Shipton et al., 2017, p. 250). Prieto et al. (2010) allude to 'high involvement' HRM practices and examine three factors representing ability-enhancing, motivation-enhancing and opportunity-enhancing, but the results show that motivation-enhancing HRM practices (incl. direct compensation, promotion opportunities and benefits) is not statistically related to innovative work behavior. Chowhan (2016) applies the similar ability-motivation-opportunity (AMO) model, and tests the effects of a bundle of HRM practices on innovation and performance. The findings indicate that skill (ability)-enhancing HRM practices (i.e. intensive selection and hiring procedures, effective training) induce employee creativity and innovative action, which in turn positively affect organisational performance. Opportunity-enhancing practices (i.e. autonomous work, self-directed work groups, flexible job design and information sharing) were found to enhance employee innovative thinking and activities, but motivation-enhancing HRM practices (e.g. individual and group pay for performance schemes) do not relate to innovation. However, scholars tend to unanimously agree that bundled HRM practices contribute to overall organisational performance (Allen, Ericksen and Collins, 2013; Zhou, Hong and Liu, 2013; Chowhan, 2016), and that innovation achieved from enhancing human and social capitals mediate the relationship between HRM and innovation (Donate, Peña and Sánchez, 2016; with Shipton et al., 2017).

Reliance of CEO and business owners/managers on SME innovation

Whilst the bundle of HRM practices tends to focus on employees' contributions to innovation and performance in large and small organisations, a group of scholars (e.g. Lynskey, 2004; De Winne and Sels, 2010; Andries and Czarnitzki, 2014), with the support of upper echelon perspective, argue that small firms rely mainly on the CEO's individual knowledge for developing innovations. The upper echelon perspective emphasises the role of top management's skills and knowledge for firms' innovative performance, and that organisational outcomes – both strategies and effectiveness – are viewed as reflections of the values and cognitive bases of powerful actors, such as CEOs, business owners and managers in the organisation (Andries and Czarnitzki, 2014). Again because of the size and resource constraint of small firms, it is likely that small firms' leaders and managers would regard their own activities as sufficient and seldom involve employees in unique and valuable activities such as developing innovations (Klaas et al., 2010).

However, the results from empirical studies supporting this line of argument based on the upper echelon perspective tend to be mixed. For example, Lynskey (2004) does not find any link between the CEO's human capital and new product development in new ventures. Klaas et al.'s (2010) findings call for more utilisation of other employees' talents and knowledge than dependence on the CEO's individual knowledge for SME innovation. Furthermore, a study by De Winne and Sels (2010) in the context of Belgium SMEs finds that owners' and managers' human capital has no direct effect on new ventures' innovative output, but only an indirect effect in the sense that highly educated CEOs and managers tend to hire more highly educated employees and tend to use more human resource practices, which in turn increase the venture's innovation intensity. Andries and Czarnitzki (2014) confirm that not only CEOs' and managers', but also non-managerial employees' ideas contribute to small firms' innovation performance. The authors further state that firms' productivity and innovative performance is related to high degrees of decentralisation and involvement, which are facilitated by a set of HRM practices that include employee participation in decision making, delegation of responsibilities, job designs with formal or informal work teams and/or quality circles and employee communication via proposals and feedback (Andries and Czarnitzki, 2014).

Summary

Based on the resource/knowledge-based view and institutional theory, it is important that innovative SMEs pursue a distinctive (strategic) set of bundled HRM practices that would not only internally encourage employee creativity and new knowledge generation, but also externally build partnership and networks for open innovation and further knowledge creation in order to achieve sustaining business performance. There exist a different set of HRM practices that would help generate different types of innovation activities. Both commitment-based and high-performance work practices were identified to have contributed to both employees' innovative capabilities and organisational performance. However, within the context of small business operation in China, collaboration-oriented HRM practices characterised by work autonomy, broad flexible job design, empowerment, teamwork and group-oriented incentives (Donate et al., 2016) as well as utilising HRM outsourcing, external learning programs and consulting services buy-in, building extensive social networks and business partnership with professional bodies and academic institutions (Zhou, Hong and Liu, 2013) may be better considered by Australian SMEs in order to achieve innovative performance outcomes. Lastly but not the least, it is possible that entrepreneurial small business owners, managers and CEOs play a significant role in accepting, adopting and executing appropriate HRM practices suitable for SME innovation. Therefore, their skills and knowledge and ability to execute HRM practices to implement innovation-oriented SME business strategy need to be acknowledged.

Research method and data analysis

To answer the research questions related to a set of HRM practices adopted by SMEs, we conducted an exploratory study of 35 Australian SMEs operating in China. The detailed research paradigm and methods chosen for the current study have been justified in the earlier chapter. Essentially, the grounded theory is used to explore the data with an intention to build a theory. An exploratory method such as grounded theory can be used as a general method to analyse any form of data collection such as survey, experiment or case study with interviews. It is regarded as very flexible in terms of data, however, more stringent on theoretical sampling and saturation of both data and theory (Morse et al., 2016). In order to examine the three sets of theoretically supported relationships between HRM and innovative SMEs, especially between different sets of HRM and different innovative types, the grounded theory is adopted. Nvivo v.11 was employed to conduct open, axial and selective coding first. Nodes and themes are created for subsequent analysis.

One of the challenges of understanding the grounded theory approach to data analysis is to do with the abstract nature of the explanation. Thus, the use of open coding helps the researcher to create tentative labels for chunks of data that may summarise what can be seen. This may not be based on existing theory, but the meaning emerged from the data. Axial coding consists of identifying relationships among the open codes, and exploring the connections among the codes. To eventually create a useful theory, we need to identify key variables in the model that will be developed. Therefore, selective coding is also used to figure out the core variables that are embedded in all of the data (Creswell, 2013).

To explore what would be the most important issues related to Australian innovative SMEs operating in China, we conducted a word frequency search in Nvivo as the first step for open coding. As shown in Figure 8.1, among 20 most frequently used words, 'China', 'Think', 'Business', and 'People' stand out clearly, followed with some strategic HR-related words such as 'different', 'work', 'time', 'things', 'know', 'need' and 'want'. We conceptualise the word 'think' as related to innovation, critical thinking and/or creativity, and 'people' to human resources, employees and workers as well as the management of the SME workforce. Thereafter, a text search for words (included stemmed words) related to various types of innovation (i.e. product, process, market, organisational, technological and technical) and HRM practices such as job design, recruitment, selection, training, development, pay, appraisal and work autonomy etc. was conducted. Features related to SMEs' owners/managers such as 'skills', 'knowledge' and 'education' are also used in text search. After extensively checking the related contents in line with each specified text, nodes were created to reflect various themes.

At the end, it was clear that a total of three themes can be aggregated as in line with the previous literature review. These themes are presented in Table 8.2. To examine the possible relationship between HRM and SME innovation, we implemented the text search for two or three more words in combination within a 100-word range (Adu, 2016). For example, if we would like to see whether training as a part of the bundled commitment-based HRM practices is related to process innovation, we typed "training process innovation ˜100" in the text box and run query. Consequently, paragraphs were identified to see the link between these words that would enable further analysis of key relationships as suggested in the research propositions.

Figure 8.1 Frequently used words related to HRM of Australian SMEs in China

Discussion of findings

The results show strong evidence of HRM practices among Australian SMEs operating in China, similar to those functions displayed among Australian domestic SMEs in a large-scale study by Innes and Wiesner (2012). Various types of innovation activities (Ceylan, 2013) were also demonstrated. There is also a clear role played by CEOs, entrepreneurs, managers and business owners who, with networking skills and industry specific knowledge, have helped Australian SMEs successfully do business in China, in addition to the contribution made by the overall SME workforce. Several relationships between HRM and SME innovation are also identified. We start the discussion of key findings in this section by first looking at various HRM practices. This is followed by illustrating possible bundled HRM practices that were adopted by Australian SMEs, as in line with different types of innovation. The relationship between the role of CEOs and innovation, with a unique HRM system of Australian SMEs is then discussed.

HRM practices of Australian SMEs

Participants from all 35 Australian SMEs have indicated that their companies have adopted some form of HRM practices with these specific terms mentioned 181 times. The majority of respondents spoke about the key HRM functions of

Table 8.2 Key themes/nodes and number of sources cited with corresponding number of references

Nodes and themes	Number of sources	Number of references
Human Resource Practices	35	181
Job Design	30	456
Team Work	34	1104
⇒ Work	34	994
⇒ Team	22	110
⇒ Group	25	108
⇒ Individual	11	26
⇒ Responsibility/Autonomy	17	44
Pay, Benefits, Compensation, Rewards and Social Security	29	384
Performance Appraisal/Review	12	25
Recruitment and Selection	24	45
• Hiring	14	42
• Staffing	25	33
Training and Development	35	376
Possible bundled HRM practices		
✓ Collaboration-based	10	35
✓ Commitment-based	9	23
✓ Performance-based	12	23
✓ Strategic/selective	20	37
Innovation	35	544
Market	24	78
Product	18	34
Process	31	182
Organisational	35	768
Technical	20	63
Technological	24	112
CEOs	11	12
Entrepreneurs	7	17
Owners	8	18
Managers	19	49
Education	22	106
Knowledge	26	64
Skills	25	60
Employees	24	52

Note: Administrative innovation was not mentioned at all among all interviewees in the current study. Despite 'education' was mentioned by the participants with most references, when combined with 'manager', 'innovation' and 'training' etc. it returns with no single reference, so it is omitted in the analysis.

pay, benefits, compensation, rewards and social security, job design, recruitment and selection, training and development. A low number of responses were placed on HRM functions such as performance appraisal, career development, strategic hiring, work autonomy and/or responsibility.

Interestingly, it is found that teamwork was mentioned most frequently with a total of 1104 references. This is understandable as China represents a society with a high index of collectivism different from Australian individualistic society (Hofstede, 2017). Australian businesses operating in China would need to adapt to China's business culture and design corresponding organisational structures and group work. Thus, teamwork, instead of individual-based work as an effective job design method would have been adopted to suit the Australian SMEs operating in China's context. This phenomenon is best illustrated by the following quote:

> I think with us having all these serviced offices across nine locations in China and our teams are not huge. We've got teams of five to seven people . . . and management of the team members and this is quite a small group to build a good rapport with everyone. . . . We make a big deal out of that, we really have regular meetings in which we're saying this should never be a surprise. . . . Everyone always says everything is different in China but it really isn't if you keep your eyes open, maybe just a different culture, but the emotions of people, I think that's not so hugely different.
>
> (Case 14: Office Co)

Pay is the second item in this theme that attracts the most responses, together with benefits, compensation, rewards and social security. It appears that Australian SMEs need to use attractive compensation packages to secure talents in the China market. Menzies and McDonnell (2012) argue that financial motivation is a critical factor for staff retention among Australian multinational companies operating in China. Similar findings in the current study show that employees in China have not only looked for more money but also cared a lot about non-monetary rewards, such as flexible work, training, benefits and workplace safety – the last one is a luxury commodity in China. For instance, one of the interviewees stated:

> . . . . because that (i.e. safety) affects our image and our branding. But sometimes with day to day management stuff you have people who are trying to get the job done to be more flexible because they're not used to . . . it's like a cultural difference. Chinese safety isn't up to international quality because they're not educated in that way. But a lot of what we do is try to educate the workers on the ground so we have workshops, we have different toolbox meetings about safety and why. . . . What we're doing is we're training the workers. They're not taking these skills and taking them anywhere else where they'll be valued. For our own staff I think that our training plus reasonable compensation, remuneration, keeps them and not leaving.
>
> (Case 18: Build Co)

Pay systems of foreign companies operating in China also are subject to the influence of institutional factors, such as tax and government regulations on social security as well as housing. Thus, the design of appropriate pay systems is a challenging task for SMEs, as the following two quotes suggests:

> We're disadvantaged I suppose to some extent in that we have a lot of foreign designers therefore we have higher salaries. We also pay full tax so

everybody's salaries are double what they actually are. For example, if some-body is paid 10,000 in the hand, we end up paying I think in Shanghai it's 67 percent add-ons, social security, housing, all that and tax. So instead of getting 10,000, they're actually getting 16,700.

(Case 34: Architect Co 3)

Yes, they're totally unrealistic. It doesn't affect us as much as other people but they impose things as a sweeping rule and usually there's no notice so it'll change from one day to the next, requirements on how much you have to pay for social security, changes in a moment's notice. . . . A couple of years ago they (Chinese government) basically blissfully announced we are improving the working conditions of the thing so every employer has to pay a 5,000 RMB social security bonus.

(Case 34: Architect Co 3)

Training and development was also regarded as very important by Australian SMEs operating in China, as this is the third highest item responded by the interviewees with a combined total of over 376 references. Earlier studies (e.g. Kotey and Slade, 2005; Zheng, Morrison and O'Neill, 2006, 2009) suggest that innovative SMEs focus on employee training and development as this would help them generate employee creativity and develop organisational capability and competency (Shipton et al., 2006; Tan, Smyrnios and Lin, 2014; Donate, Peña and Sánchez de Pablo, 2016). Additional challenges may exist for Australian SMEs to train and develop Chinese employees, due to cultural and institutional influences. Firms may need to rigorously consider how to train employees and what skills to develop in response to the host country's (China) cultural and institutional differences. Two interviewees illustrate this point as follows:

So I think guanxi (social network skills) is just another name for what I've spent a lot of time researching and developing for myself as a sales professional, it's just relationship building and it's exactly . . . again people are people and I'm now of the absolute, firm belief that there is absolutely no difference in what people want it to achieve in business, what they want in their personal life, everything is the same in Australia, it's just the piece in the middle that you need to adapt which is the believability, the credibility, just I guess making sure that you don't waste too much time and money targeting in the wrong way.

(Case 13: Vehicle Co)

I'm still figuring out what the business model will be, if it will be based exactly like we do in China which is essentially developing their staff. One of the failures of their society is the education system, it hasn't really done much, it hasn't changed much in 30 years, maybe even longer. They're still producing a lot of note takers and order takers. They're not producing critical minds and creative thinkers.

(Case 26: HR Consulting Co)

Recruitment and selection which also relate to strategic hiring and staffing constitute relatively less responses, nonetheless are also considered important for Australian SMEs operating in China. Because of size and resource constraints, SMEs often focus more on strategic staffing and selective recruitment to source needy talents (Jiang, Wang and Zhao, 2012; Menzies and McDonnell, 2012; Zhou, Hong and Liu, 2013; Donate, Peña and Sánchez de Pablo, 2016). The findings from the current study confirm this line of observation, as the following quotes aptly illustrate:

> probably one of our biggest risks is that we don't want to be a training ground. While we're giving back to the industry by training these individuals, ultimately we go through a very rigorous recruitment process that we really understand that their (employees') aspirations match our aspirations and it's up to us as good business leaders that we keep them motivated and engaged in business.
>
> (Case 16: Processing Co)

> I would say it goes back a long way, maybe some SMEs aren't as honest as me about this point, I would say that selection is an issue for SMEs. We tend to rush selection compared to say a big business that goes through a fairly reasonable process. I always said Drucker said it really well in his book on management. He said it's about one third, one third, one third. One third absolutely excellent, one third just OK and one third just don't fit. I don't think that small business gets quite those numbers. I think they don't do quite as well and I think part of the problem is we rush selection because we don't have such a big gene pool to choose from and so sometimes we just go yes you, a friend said you're good so can you start on Monday. So some of the retention issues are just around competency of staff.
>
> (Case 28: Consult Co 1)

Coupled with this challenging issue of strategic recruitment and selection, Australian SMEs in China also tend to focus on discriminative selection of Chinese employees based on young age, energetic outlook with high level of English proficiency. This is largely because Australian SMEs consciously pursue innovative ways of doing new things, of which assumingly only young people are capable. The participants had the intention of training regional managers from a young talent pool so as to assist Australian SMEs with their ambition to further successfully internationalise their businesses to the greater China region, as the following quote illustrates:

> Basically (we select) a younger team. Like we've got a couple of senior principal Chinese engineers but definitely the team here is younger and that was a conscious decision. One was for (English) language, one was also for that they are probably willing to accept new ideas and new ways to take things on and it won't just be the standard way, there's other ways to do things and I suppose the energy level. There is travel, we want them to go to Australia

and so forth but in return they get to work on projects all across the globe. This is not just a Chinese sort of focus, they get to work on jobs in Mongolia, South East Asia, Australia.

(Case 16: Processing Co)

Despite a strong emphasis on SME performance and further growth, there appears limited emphasis on employee performance evaluation and feedback; only 12 participants responded to performance appraisal with an additional 25 references. Again, this area of HRM practices among Australian SMEs operating in China is also subject to cultural and institutional influences, which require Australian companies operating in China to adapt and adjust, as illustrated by the following quote:

If someone doesn't perform on one of our projects, like the worst is you haven't performed, you're off, you're off the job, you're kicked off (in Australia), whereas the Chinese way is more they'll try and encourage them to get back on track and perform. It's a more tedious, patient process than doing business normally.

(Case 17: Metal Frame Co)

Performance review is better incorporated with other HRM functions to be effective, especially when it comes to consider its impact on overall SME innovation. Many SMEs have recognised the importance of taking a holistic view of adopting a HRM system which would help their firms sustain continuous growth (Hayton, 2003; Kotey and Slade, 2005; Sheehan, 2014). This point is well illustrated by an interviewee below:

Getting the right one with skills and training them to stay because if you train them you put a lot of energy into growing that knowledge and we do have a system that we work towards that is the same all over the world, so training schedules, performance reviews, salary reviews and what not, so that's always . . . I think that helps, having that sort of organised structure in place helps.

(Case 14: Office Co)

From the above discussion, it could be summarised that Australian SMEs operating in China have adopted a set of HRM practices, such as team-based job design, pay and benefits, training and development, and recruitment and selection, though they are less focused on effective performance appraisal and review because of cultural and institutional factors. Therefore, we offer the following proposition:

Research proposition 1:

Australian SMEs have implemented a set of HRM practices to facilitate their innovative business operation in China.

Bundled HRM practices and innovation
for Australian SMEs

All 35 participants in the interview indicated one form or another of innovation among Australian SMEs operating in China, with a total of 544 times of mentioning the word 'innovation'. When the text search combined two words with various types of innovation, such as 'market innovation', 'process innovation', 'product innovation' etc. within a parameter of <10 words, it was found that 'organisational innovation' was mostly referenced, with 768 times. Administrative innovation often discussed in the literature (e.g. Ceylan, 2013) was not found to be mentioned at all by any respondent in this study. Perhaps the excessive use of 'organisational innovation' would have covered the aspect of administrative innovation, as two concepts were often used interchangeably (see Damanpour and Evan, 1984; Seeck and Diehl, 2017).

As mentioned earlier, we extended the search for the link between innovation and HRM practices, using a parameter of <100 words to combine three key words. It is found that some evidence of bundled HRM practices characterised with collaboration, commitment and performance among Australian SMEs was investigated. Furthermore, Australian SMEs in China were found in the current study to be strategic and selective in pursuing different innovation strategies.

Both commitment and performance-based HRM practices (such as high pay, reasonable benefits, flexible job design with work-life balance and volunteering program, training and career development and safety etc.) adopted by Australian SMEs operating in China tend to link to process and organisational innovation. An example illustrated earlier by Case 18, Build Co, who spoke about the importance of having a set of commitment-based HRM practices that would affect his company's "image and branding" (see Section 4.1) – which is clear evidence, showing a need of the company to focus more on organisational innovation by changing the organisational culture and structure, in order to "keep employees from leaving". A similar example was demonstrated by Case 16, Processing Co, whereby the interviewee simply placed down the importance of "following [the] hot market bubble outside", but focused on internal organisational innovation by "having a number of initiatives", which include "a fitness (work-life balance) program, environmental and community awareness (volunteering) programs", as well as a "no work on weekend" policy in addition to offering career development programs instead of paying more to people who often "jump around in the superhot (labour) market" with severe talent shortage. The result was that a greater number of employees were retained by the Case 16, Processing Co.

Being able to retain talent helps Australian SMEs achieve better performance outcomes in China. Therefore, high-commitment and high-performance work practices tend to be used interchangeably to also address the internal process innovation. For instance, an interviewee from a clothing factory (Case 23, Print Co) shows that:

> Yes. It's quite difficult, the sublimation process. People think it might just be something very simple printing on to garments but it's a very technical

process that if you're not doing it right you can have a lot of problems with it and actually lose a lot of money. So, yes, there's a lot of time and effort gone into operating the machinery and perfecting the performance to get it right. So that's our real major advantage I think as a clothing factory to be different from a million and one other clothing factories across Asia. . . . That's pretty much how our factory was born and we moved about six months ago and it was actually really good. The workers at first didn't want to move and we set up a nice facility for them and they've all come back and they're very happy and things are running smoothly now so it's quite good.

(Case 23: Print Co)

Making workers happy, utilising the right recruitment and selection methods, training and developing employee skills and involving them in the process of innovation is a typical set of commitment-based HRM strategies utilised by several Australia SMEs in China to address organisational change and process efficiency, as illustrated in a few short quotes below:

And then our motto is Evolving People and it's very much about developing those outside the organization but also developing ourselves, so what are you doing internally yourself to get better. So that involves continuous evolution and therefore continuous innovation without going into any specifics of the product.

(Case 26: HR Consult Co)

Having the right people is everything and hiring and training is huge . . . a lot of start-ups don't focus on it which is why a serviced office is perfect because they're able to utilise our trained human resources more efficiently.

(Case 14: Office Co)

The idea of the internal flexibility, you had to adapt because this is a big deal with companies and particularly process oriented companies, this is the way it's done and we really find it difficult to cope with the fact that you've got to change your essential management practices in different countries.

(Case 15: Resource Co)

These findings suggest that Australian SMEs operating in China have adopted the high performance/commitment work practices when they are pursuing internal processes and organisational innovation that facilitate employee creativity and enhance employee knowledge and skills. Thus, the following research proposition can be derived from this set of findings:

Research Proposition 2a:

If pursuing internal process and organisational innovation (that is with focus on enhancing employee knowledge and creativity), Australian SMEs would be more likely to adopt commitment-based HRM practices.

To illustrate a relationship between market (marketing) innovation and collaboration-based HRM practices, a short transcript of the conversation between the interviewee and interviewer of Case 10, Biotech Co 4 is used:

Interviewer: Do you have marketing activities in China? How do you market in China to find the clients?

Interviewee: . . . in China it's more like just like my personal relationship, use my personal network, use personal network to market rather than to do a proper business development in China.

Interviewer: OK. I think your business is not like marketing the products, you need some clients not the customers so it's not huge scale marketing anyway is it?

Interviewee: That's right.

Interviewer: If you have some connections, some network, just to find the people?

Interviewee: I think China is more like collaboration rather than [just connections] because I think China is still maybe five years [behind IT innovation]. . .

Interviewer: And this network is the main sort of marketing strategy? With the company or employees or managers?

Interviewee: Yes.

Interviewer: What are your future strategies in China? For the China market?

Interviewee: Yes. I mentioned about this before as well. The first one is to build up our own research IT in a sense of innovation, focus on the big target of China. The second one is we also want to build up relationship with other companies in China, similar like ours, that have this capacity to do innovation work. . . . so we can really begin to look in the China market.

The collaborative-based HRM system are those practices with broad job design, teamwork, employee empowerment and group-incentives (Donate, Peña and Sánchez de Pablo, 2016), which would appear to fit in the above Case 10, Biotech 4. Furthermore, Zhou, Hong and Liu's (2013) collaboration-oriented HRM practices include learning with business partners, which would be similar to the research activities likely to be conducted in the first step of innovation taken by the case company and the effort for building "up relationship with other companies in China, similar like ours" mentioned by the case interviewee. Although the case did not mention other aspects of collaboration-oriented HRM practices such as consulting service buy-in, flexible partnership with autonomous external professionals, long-term personnel alliance with external academic institutions and professional HRM outsourcing (Zhou, Hong and Liu, 2013), it did refer to "building extensive social networks" with use of "personal relationships" (guanxi) and "personal networks" by company employees and managers to implement the firm's marketing strategies. Similar cases with using teamwork, extensive relationships and networks were found in Cases 26, Human Resources Co, 30, Finance Co and 32, Marketing Consultants Co. In particular, the interviewee from Case

11, Recruitment Co made a good observation of "using certain business (including HR) practices" to generate "creativity within business in order to facilitate the development of guanxi networks". As the interviewee says reflectively, "more social mechanisms you develop, more innovation" (Case 11: Recruitment Co).

Australian SMEs in the high-tech industry are also more inclined to use the collaboration-oriented HRM practices to use radical innovation in generating new products (from Case 8, Biotech 1 interviewee working in the biotech sector). For instance, the interviewee spoke about building the long-term (almost 30 years) relationship between company researchers and colleagues in China and having "constantly been collaborating with Chinese colleagues" in order to create "new vaccines and drugs to address unmet health needs" in China. The case company also focused on teamwork and group-incentives, and working closely with various Chinese government agencies to ensure continuous innovation and smooth operations in China. This view was echoed by another interviewee from Case 30, Finance Co. Although in the finance sector, Case 30 has constantly brought in external partners to help create new financial products inside China with an aim of extending this to other Asian countries and building a truly global company worldwide.

The findings from several cases illustrated above suggest that a possible bundle with collaboration-focused HRM practices have been adopted by Australian innovative SMEs operating in China, which subsequently support their product and market innovation activities globally. These findings support the notion that:

Research Proposition 2b:

If pursuing external market innovation, with aim of branding innovative product and service among Chinese consumers (that is with focus on achieving organisational performance outcomes), Australian SMEs would be more likely to adopt collaboration-based HRM practices.

Because of different cultural and institutional factors between Australia and China, Australian SMEs have to be strategic and selective in choosing a suitable innovation strategy corresponded with an appropriate set of HRM practices that are in line with the Chinese culture and business context. Apart from culture, China's political system, education system and labor market conditions are very different from those in Australia. Therefore, as mentioned by an interviewee (Case 16, Processing Co), "there are strategic reasons for us to be in China to leverage the (labor) cost advantages" and to expand market in the beginning. However, cost competitiveness will eventually die away as the Chinese government has changed its industry policy from being 'a world factory' to becoming 'an innovative house'. Australian SMEs would be required to pursue other types of business strategies apart from cost innovation in order to sustain their long-term business operation in China.

Earlier it was illustrated by the SME, HR Consulting Co (Case 26) that China's education system did not help produce critical thinkers and innovative ideas.

This is echoed by another interviewee from Case 10, Biotech Co 4, who found it difficult to talk about real innovation in China as "a lot of people (in China) have no technical knowledge" for product innovation. That is why for Australian SMEs to be successful in China, they need to pursue a different business model that focuses on process and organisational innovation, which helps develop knowledge and talent; this has been emphasised more by the participants in the current study. In addition, technological innovation related to generating process efficiency was also found to be referred more often than technical innovation (Table 8.2).

However, there appear different arguments among the participants' responses to what role technical and technological innovation play. For example, a manager from Case 22, Medical Equipment Co argued that "technological innovation is very much to do with radical thinking about generating brand new products. . . . so knowledge and talents are important". Here it is believed that technological innovation embedded in process and organisational innovation could facilitate knowledge production and talent retention first, before having critical organisational capabilities to generate a new product with a radical step. In contrast, however, an interviewee from Case 15, Resources Co appeared to disagree with this line of argument, as showed below:

> for us innovation is not incremental changes, it's a leap. It's maybe even a new business or a game changer rather than just a 10 percent or a 15 percent improvement in operating costs or product quality or something like that. So, yes, it is an issue for us and we're very conscious of it and we know we need to improve.
>
> (Case 15: Resources Co)

Both interviewees appear to favor "radical innovation" without realizing that radical innovation can only happen when the incremental changes occur in the process and organisational structure. In particular, if they would like to stay in China for the long haul, Australian SMEs need to listen intensively and consider strategically which innovation strategy they should pursue, as two interviewees from the same case company illustrated below:

> we have personally had academic collaborations there for many, many years. . . . and we have relationships there with other technical agencies. There's a national centre there that's quite closely aligned with the work that we do in the public health space and. . . . That's very much in line with our strategic planning if you like that we've been doing for the China programme over the last four or so years. We realised very early on I think that China is changing so quickly. . . . China no longer requires the financial assistance and what that left was a gap around the sort of softer skill base, the know-how, the technical know-how and expertise, that China can throw enormous resources at the challenges that it has domestically but it doesn't necessarily have that softer side of innovation and the technical know-how. . . . So we've

been thinking about how to position ourselves for a long term presence in China because we're quite committed to being there long term. So for us we listened very carefully to our Chinese counterparts . . . it made a lot of sense for us to leave aside the bigger bio hubs and focus elsewhere in the country where we can make a tangible impact.

(Case 8: Biotech Co 1)

Reading the statement above leads one to attach the collaboration-based practices to technical innovation, and the commitment-based HRM practices to technological innovation. Yet it is also possible that the commitment-based HRM practices help develop skills and competencies that enable building external collaboration, strategic partnership and social networks. Therefore, in a long run, two sets of HRM strategies may need to be both in place to facilitate Australian SMEs' various innovation activities.

The role of CEOs/SME owners and business managers

The literature (e.g. De Winne and Sels, 2010; Andries and Czarnitzki, 2014) suggests that CEOs of SMEs and their owners or business managers play an important role for choosing the right innovation strategy and determining the organisational culture, structure and HRM policy and practice. The findings of the current study show that CEOs, entrepreneurs, owners and managers were mentioned by the participants, with most references (49) made for 'manager' by 19 interviewees (see Table 8.2). Further analysis of references indicates that CEOs, business owners and managers are regarded as very "hands-on" in every business decision (Case 1, Furniture Co), "very adamant all the time in promoting innovation" and were the ones who "sign off the company's policy and procedures (Case 4, Security Co), "build strategic partnerships with other companies" (Case 18, Build Co) and were "responsible to grow business" (Case 27). These few quotes demonstrate a clear evidence of the role played by owners, business managers and CEOs in implementing HRM practices and contributing to the firms' innovative performance among the Australian SMEs investigated.

To analyse the link between an individual manager's (CEO, entrepreneur) knowledge and skills and innovation, the approach of combining two words (e.g. "knowledge innovation" or "entrepreneur HR") within a parameter of 100 words, was adopted. It is found that being an entrepreneur is about knowing and 'doing all the things', for instance, a manager of Case 33, Investment Co, states that:

Innovation has turned around, it's really about being vigilant and being open to new ideas and being able to craft solutions for people and being agile in the market. Innovation is creating new things and solutions for people so I suppose we don't say no, let me see how I can sort that out. Then in some respects, it's like the Chinese saying it's a one dragon strategy, head to tail, so you pretty much do all the things that someone needs to be done. . . .

Filling in the gaps and different paradigm shifts or different needs. . . . So (as an entrepreneur), you do things that you're passionate about.

(Case 33: Investment Co)

As a business manager of SME, constant involvement in managing onsite staff and implementing several HRM practices in combination was also found as demonstrated in the following quote:

> So I think training just to come back to the question. Hiring people with great education and multinational experience, great English skills, training them, not letting them just run or do whatever. Really sitting down training, maybe checking back six months later what have they learnt, where have they developed themselves, regular performance reviews and providing a career opportunity, a brightness of future, that's all everyone wants whether they're Chinese or foreign. If there's no career opportunity, which to be fair in our sense, [it would be a failure for] management.
>
> (Case 14: Office Co; words in bracket were added).

The interviewee did not finish the last sentence, but it is assumed that there is a closer link between a set of good HRM practices and small business outcomes, and not managing employees well is indeed a failure of management. These findings lead us to propose that:

Research Proposition 3a:

Managers and business owners of Australian SMEs have unique education and sufficient individual knowledge and skills to develop innovative products and services in China. Thus,

Research Proposition 3b:

Managers and business owners of Australian SMEs are more likely to have implemented a set of HRM practices that would help facilitate their business operation in China.

Apart from the role played by CEOs/managers/owners in HRM and innovation, SMEs' general workforce have indeed also contributed to innovation. We ran a test of mentioning "employee innovation" within a parameter of 100 words, there were 24 participants who spoke about the link of employee to general innovation 52 times (see Table 8.2). However, specific contributions of general employees to different types of innovation were not clearly identifiable.

Summary and a conceptual model

The discussion of key findings from analysing 35 interview transcripts came to a clear conclusion that Australian SMEs operating in China have indeed put in place a unique HRM system that facilitates their pursuit of different innovation strategies. With different size, structure, culture and industry, Australian SMEs operating under the changing national and global labor, capital, environmental and legal environment would be required to focus on different innovation activities, such as product, process, market and organisational innovation, as well as technical and technological innovation.

Due to the cultural and institutional differences between home (Australia) and host (China) countries, Australian SMEs need to respond appropriately with the design and development of either commitment-based or collaboration-oriented HRM practices that would help implement their choice of innovation strategies. It was found that the set of collaboration-oriented HRM practices would be especially useful in facilitating the implementation of market, product and technical innovation, whilst the set of commitment-based HRM practices would help achieve process, organisational and technological innovation of Australian SMEs. However, in the long run, Australian SMEs may be required to develop a unique HRM system that blends the commitment-based with collaboration-oriented HRM practices in order to achieve their internationalisation goals.

The findings from the current study also show that CEOs/business owners and managers contributed to establishing a suitable HRM system and general employees to assist in implementing various innovation strategies. A conceptual model is thus derived from these findings and depicted in Figure 8.2.

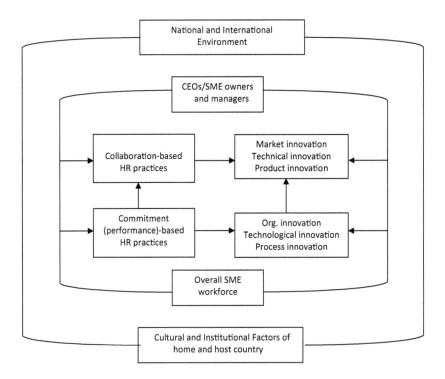

Figure 8.2 A conceptual model for testing the relationship between HRM practices and SME innovation

Conclusion, limitation and future research direction

The aim of the current chapter is to explore various HRM practices that might have been adopted by innovative Australia SMEs operating in China, and to answer the key research question on "what constitute specific and systematic HRM practices used by SMEs?". A qualitative research method, using the grounded theory approach was employed to conduct data analysis of 35 interview transcripts. Three sets of research propositions emanated from the data and findings of this examination of the HRM practices used by these innovative SMEs, which were strongly supported by our data. We then synthesise some additional findings, such as influence of national and international environment, cultural and institutional factors of home and host country, which were not extensively discussed in the prior studies, and include these factors in developing a conceptual model (Figure 8.2). It is believed that the model can be used for further testing the relationship between HRM and SME innovation, as established in the current study.

Noticeable findings of this current study are related to the identification of two HRM systems that have currently been adopted by Australian SMEs in China. These two HRM systems focus on either collaboration-oriented or commitment/performance-based HRM practices. Commitment-based HRM practices taken by Australian SMEs are related to high pay/salaries, reasonable benefits, flexible job design with work-life balance and community volunteering programs, training and career development and safety practices. This set of commitment-based HRM practices in the current study were also found to be related to high performance work practices adopted among SMEs in the earlier studies (e.g. Allen, Ericksen and Collins, 2013; Wu, Bacon and Hoque, 2014; Seeck and Diehl, 2017). The commitment-based HRM practices have enabled Australian SMEs' organisational, process and technological innovation. In contrast, the collaboration-oriented HRM system covers several practices such as broad job design, teamwork, employee empowerment, group-incentives, learning with strategic partners and extensive network and personal relationship building. The collaboration-oriented HRM practices were found to be associated with Australian SMEs' product, market and technical innovation. Australian SMEs in general are very strategic and selective – because of their different size, organisational structure and culture, and industry – in choosing and implementing their different innovation strategies.

Several theoretical and practical implications can be drawn from the current study. First, theoretically, our findings of Australian SMEs' adoption of a set of commitment/performance-based HRM practices support the resource/knowledge-based view that strategic values of enhancing employee knowledge and creativity via a HRM system are critical to sustain SMEs' innovative performance and business success. The evidence of using a set of collaboration-oriented HRM practices by Australian SMEs suggests that institutional factors, such as the Chinese culture of guanxi, association with local business groups to gain legitimacy, building strategic partnerships and utilising personal networks to link with government agencies (Zhou, Hong and Liu, 2013; Newman and Abdullah, 2014) are also considered to be important for Australian SMEs operating in

China, supporting the key propositions within the institutional theory. Despite how employees were also found to contribute to innovation, our data show that CEOs, business managers and SME owners played a weighty role in establishing the HRM system and leading the innovation; these results support the notion derived from the upper echelon perspective that innovation is tied to the top management team's education, skills and knowledge.

The second implication is related to management practices. It is believed that our findings would help existing Australian companies operating in China and those SMEs that intend to internationalise to China be more aware of cultural and institutional factors that may impact on their design and development of various HRM systems. In particular, for those leaders and managers responsible for SME business operation in China, time and energy invested into building personal relationships and networks (guanxi) and collaboration with strategic business partners would eventually pay off in the long run because these skills and knowledge ultimately contribute to create opportunities for market, product and technical innovation. Understanding the Chinese government's changing industry and taxation policies as well as their likely impacts especially on the commitment-based HRM practices is also important for SME managers and HRM practitioners, as they need to adapt and adjust their organisational structure and labour management processes aptly in order to keep up SME's technological innovation, process and organisational innovation in line with China's institutional environment.

Lastly, our findings show that if pursuing internal process and organisational innovation (that is with focus on enhancing employee knowledge and creativity), Australian SMEs would be more likely to adopt commitment-based HRM practices; however, firms pursuing external market innovation, with the aim of branding innovative products and services among Chinese consumers (that is with focus on achieving organisational performance outcomes), would be more likely to adopt collaboration-based HRM practices. Thus, if Australian SMEs intend to operate in China for the long haul, it is not sufficient to rely on the upper echelon management skills and knowledge. There is a great need to develop the SME workforce in China, not only with their innate capability, creativity and commitment, but also with abilities to venture outside, take initiatives and risks, build relationships, networks and strategic partnerships with business and academic institutions, continue learning and innovation. To achieve the overall quality enhancement of SME human and social capital (Donate, Peña and Sánchez de Pablo, 2016), a unique HRM system to blend both commitment and collaboration HRM practices should be in place for Australian SMEs operating in the greater China region as well as in the world.

Several limitations remain despite the contributions of the current study to the existing knowledge as outlined above. First, the results from the qualitative data analysis of only 35 SMEs operating in China may encounter the issue of generalisation to the other contexts. However, we were able to develop the conceptual framework that could be used for future research investigating the relationships between SME innovation and human resource practices in other contexts. In particular, future studies should aim to collect a large scale of quantitative data from different countries so as to facilitate the comparison of different cultures and institutions that may have mediating effects on the relationship between HRM and innovation, which have not been studied so far in the field. Second, although several items related to both commitment-based and collaboration-oriented HRM practices were identified to be associated with SME innovation, these may be far from the perfect representation of a truly unique HRM system for SME. Future studies should apply additional validated items from the prior studies, and develop a scale for differentiating a distinctive SME's HRM system from the prescribed set, and test its impact on various innovation activities. Furthermore, the findings from the current study with reference to HRM practices among SMEs tend to be general, as it is not overtly clear how different sets of HRM practices influence the overall SME workforce, and as a result, employees under the influence of different HRM systems could have contributions to different types of innovation. We suggest that future research look into this aspect, as the outcomes would be useful for SMEs to develop appropriate HRM and innovation strategies in order to further pursue their internationalisation goals.

References

Adu, P. (2016). Perfecting the art of qualitative coding, *QSR International*, www.qsrinternational.com/blog/perfecting-the-art-of-qualitative-coding, retrieved on 30 May, 2017.

Allen, M. R., Ericksen, J., and Collins, C. J. (2013). Human resource management, employee exchange relationships, and performance in small businesses. *Human Resource Management*, 52:2, 153–174.

Andries, P., and Czarnitzki, D. (2014). Small firm innovation performance and employee involvement. *Small Business Economics*, 43, 21–38.

Barney, J. B. (2001). Resource-based theories of competitive advantage: A ten-year retrospective on the resource-based view. *Journal of Management*, 6, 643–650.

Birkinshaw, J., Hamel, G., and Mol, M. J. (2008). Management innovation. *Academy of Management Review*, 33, 825–845.

Bondarouk, T., Looise, J. K. and Lempsink, B. (2009). Framing the implementation of HRM innovation: HR professionals vs line managers in a construction company. *Personnel Review*, 38:5, 472–491.

Bornay-Barrachina, M., De la Rosa-Navarro, D., Lopez-Cabrales, A., and Valle-Cabrera, R. (2012). Employment relationships and firm innovation: The double role of human capital. *British Journal of Management*, 23, 223–240.

Ceylan, C. (2013). Commitment-based HR practices, different types of innovation activities and firm innovation performance. *The International Journal of Human Resource Management*, 24:1, 208–226.

Chen, C., and Huang, J. (2009). Strategic human resource practices and innovation performance – the mediating role of knowledge management capacity. *Journal of Business Research*, 62, 104–114.

Chowdhury, S., Schulz, E., Milner, M., and Van De Voort, D. (2014). Core employee based human capital and revenue productivity in small firms: An empirical investigation. *Journal of Business Research*, 67, 2473–2479.

Chowhan, J. (2016). Unpacking the black box: Understanding the relationship between strategy, HRM practices, innovation and organizational performance. *Human Resource Management Journal*, 26:2, 112–133.

Cooke, F. L., and Saini, D. S. (2010). (How) does the HR strategy support an innovation oriented business strategy? An investigation of institutional context and organizational practices in Indian firms. *Human Resource Management*, 49, 377–400.

Creswell, J. W. (2013). *Qualitative Inquiry and Research Design: Choosing Among Five Approaches* (3rd ed.). Los Angeles, CA: Sage Publications.

Damanpour, F. (1991). Organizational innovation: A meta-analysis of effects of determinants and moderators. *Academy of Management Journal*, 34, 555–590.

Damanpour, F., and Evan, W. M. (1984). Organizational innovation and performance: The problem of organizational lag. *Administrative Science Quarterly*, 29, 392–409.

De Winne, D. and Sels, L. (2010). Interrelationships between human capital, HRM and innovation in Belgian start-ups aiming at an innovation strategy. *The International Journal of Human Resource Management*, 21:11, 1863–1883.

Della Torre, E., and Solari, L. (2013). High-performance work systems and the change management process in medium-sized firms. *The International Journal of Human Resource Management*, 24:13, 2583–2607.

Donate, M. J., Peña, I., and Sánchez de Pablo, J. D. (2016). HRM practices for human and social capital development: Effects on innovation capabilities. *The International Journal of Human Resource Management*, 27:9, 928–953.

Georgiadis, A., and Pitelis, C. N. (2012). Human resources and SME performance in services: Empirical evidence from the UK. *The International Journal of Human Resource Management*, 23:4, 808–825.

Gialuisi, O., and Coetzer, A. (2013). An exploratory investigation into voluntary employee turnover and retention in small businesses. *Small Enterprise Research*, 20:1, 55–68.

Grant, R. M. (1996). Towards a knowledge-based theory of the firm. *Strategic Management Journal*, 17, 109–122.

Halim, H. A., Ahmad, N. H., Ramayah, T., and Hanifah, H. (2014). The growth of innovative performance among SMEs: Leveraging on organisational culture and innovative human capital. *Journal of Small Business and Entrepreneurship Development*, 2:1, 107–125.

Hayton, J. C. (2003). Strategic human capital management in SMEs: An empirical study of entrepreneurial performance. *Human Resource Management*, 42, 375–391.

Huselid, M. A. (1995). The impact of human resource management practices on turnover, productivity, and corporate financial performance. *Academy of Management Journal*, 38, 635–672.

Innes, P., and Wiesner, R. (2012). Beyond HRM intensity: Exploring intra-function HRM clusters in SMEs. *Small Enterprise Research*, 19: 32–51.

Jiang, J., Wang, S., and Zhao, S. (2012). Does HRM facilitate employee creativity and organizational innovation? A study of Chinese firms. *The International Journal of Human Resource Management*, 23, 4025–4047.

Jiménez-Jiménez, D., and Sanz-Valle, R. (2008). Could HRM support organizational innovation? *The International Journal of Human Resource Management*, 19, 1208–1221.

Klaas, B. S., Klimchak, M., Semadeni, M., and Holmes, J. J. (2010). The adoption of human capital services by small and medium enterprises: A diffusion of innovation perspective. *Journal of Business Venturing*, 25, 349–360.

Kotey, B., and Slade, P. (2005), Formal human resource management practices in small growing firms. *Journal of Small Business Management*, 43: 1, 16–40.

Lynskey, M. K. (2004). Determinants of innovative activity in Japanese technology-based start-up firms. *International Small Business Journal*, 22, 159–196.

Mayson, S., and Barrett, R. (2006). The 'science' and 'practice' of HRM in small firms. *Human Resource Management Review*, 16:4, 447–455.

Menzies, J., and McDonnell, A. (2012). Talent in China: Exploring the issues of faced by Australian multinational enterprises. *International Journal of Chinese Culture and* Management, 3:2, 107–124.

Morse, J. M., Stern, P. N., Faan, N., Corbin, J., Bowers, B., and Clarke, A. E. (2016). *Developing Grounded Theory: The Second Generation.* New York: Routledge.

Newman, A., and Abdullah, Z. S. (2014). Determinants of best HR practices in Chinese SMEs. *Journal of Small Business and Enterprise Development*, 21:3, 414–430.

Rosi, M. M., and Mahnood, R. (2013). Moderating effects of human resource management practices and entrepreneur training on innovation and small-medium firm performance. *Journal of Management and Strategy*, 4:2, 60–69.

Seeck, H., and Diehl, M-R. (2017). A literature review on HRM and innovation – taking stock and future directions. *The International Journal of Human Resource Management*, 28:6, 913–944.

Sheehan, M. (2014). Human resource management and performance: Evidence from small and medium-sized firms. *International Small Business Journal*, 32:5, 545–570.

Shipton, H., West, M. A., Dawson, J., Birdi, K., and Patterson, M. (2006). HRM as a predictor of innovation. *Human Resource Management Journal*, 16, 3–27.

Tan, C. S. L., Smyrnios, K. X., and Lin, X. (2014). What drives learning orientation in fast growth SMEs? *International Journal of Entrepreneurial Behavior & Research*, 20:4, 324–350.

Tang, G-Y., Chen, Y., and Jin, J-F. (2015). Entrepreneurial orientation and innovation performance: Roles of strategic HRM and technical turbulence. *Asia-Pacific Journal of Human Resources*, 53, 163–184.

Verreynne, M-L., Parker, P., and Wilson, M. (2011). Employment systems in small firms: A multilevel analysis. *International Small Business Journal*, 31:4, 405–431.

Wu, N., Bacon, N., and Hoque, K. (2014). The adoption of high performance work practices in small businesses: The influence of markets, business characteristics and HR expertise. *The International Journal of Human Resource Management*, 25:8, 1149–1169.

Zheng, C., Morrison, M., and O'Neill, G. (2006). An empirical study of high performance HRM practices in Chinese SMEs. *The International Journal of Human Resource Management*, 17:10, 1772–1803.

Zheng, C., Morrison, M., and O'Neill, G. (2009). Enhancing Chinese SME performance through innovative HR practices. *Personnel Review*, 38:2, 175–194.

Zhou, Y., Hong, Y., and Liu, J. (2013). Internal commitment or external collaboration? The impact of human resource management systems on firm innovation and performance. *Human Resource Management*, 52:2, 263–288.

9   Conclusion

Overview

This book investigates the experiences of Australian small and medium-sized enterprises (SMEs) in their internationalisation to China. The limited resources and the constraints that investing in China creates for development in other markets makes their effect upon the participant's internationalisation success more clearly identifiable than in data collected from a large company. In large organisations, internal dynamics, international capabilities and aggregated international experience moderate and possibly obscure the effect of the local conditions on the Chinese operations. Collecting data from SMEs resulted in a less biased and more evidence-based data set than data collected from large organisations, which can aggregate both experiences and data, would provide.

The project collected data from 35 organisations using personal interviews with either the CEO or a senior representative of the organisation, conducted at their operations in China. The organisations came from a wide range of industries, including service, manufacturing, finance, consulting and agribusiness. They were all characterised by being innovative enterprises, relative to their industries. The interview data was thematically analysed and used to examine a range of different domains which were identified in the literature as having a significant effect upon the internationalisation experience. These domains were the internationalisation process, the role of innovation, the role of networks, the role of part entrepreneurship, the role of resources and capabilities, barriers and liabilities and the human resource practices of the participants. Each of these domains has been considered in detail, along with their contribution to the literature, in the preceding chapters of this book.

The findings also produced some universal observations that applied to all of the domains examined in the chapters. Firstly, all of the participants experienced a range of challenges and opportunities associated with internationalising to China. The challenges and the opportunities were, to some extent, unanticipated by every participant. The only exceptions came from participants with extensive knowledge of doing business in China, although these participants noted many limitations in the value of their past experience to contemporary conditions. Another universal finding was that the rate of change in the Chinese environment affected all of the domains at a fundamental level. Changes in cultural and business behaviours, changes in regulatory and infrastructure systems, changes in human resource capabilities, changes in market profile and the development of local industries affected the way in which the Chinese environment impacted upon internationalisation of the participants, from each of the domain perspectives.

These findings indicate that an SME internationalisation theory is needed to explain the experiences of the participants and the development of knowledge, resources, capabilities and the opportunities that they experienced. The rate of change in each of the domains, however, suggests that traditional theories, based on static perspectives, such as institutional theory or organisational learning theory may not be appropriate for describing the longitudinal experiences of SMEs in China. Instead, dynamic theories that incorporate the factors driving the Chinese business environment and the adaptation to the current conditions may be more appropriate. This is an important topic for future China internationalisation research.

One of the factors which contributes to the changes in the context for the experiences of the participants in the different domains is the rapid assimilation of international experience in China, flowing from government initiatives and commercial Chinese enterprise internationalisation (Zheng, Khavul and Crockett, 2012; Zhong, Peng and Liu, 2013). This knowledge has resulted in an increase in the focus on innovation, resource development and employee skills, as well as influencing Chinese management practices (Li, 2016; Wu and Boateng, 2010; Wu, 2015). This phenomena was evident in the data provided by the participants. It suggests that knowledge, strategic resource levels and innovation should be incorporated in theories developed in future research, which describe the behaviours in these domains in China's business environment.

Another dominant factor identified was the rapid development of the Chinese economy, which has affected China's infrastructure, demographics and local markets (Chiang, 2012; Qi, Yang, and Jin, 2013; Xiaohe Zhang, 2015; Yang, Xu and Long, 2016; Zhu, 2012). This has resulted in the rapid development of local organisations and changed the way in which institutional factors such as regulation, structural factors such as infrastructure and attitudinal factors such as employment loyalty affect foreign SMEs internationalising to China. This suggests that the level of economic development of China must be represented in theories of SME internationalisation to China for any of the domains considered in future research.

The remainder of this chapter will consider the key messages resulting from the evidence presented in the preceding chapters. It will conclude with a consideration of how the dynamics of knowledge, resources, innovation and economic development could be incorporated into future theories which explain the experiences of SMEs in China.

Internationalisation process

The SMEs who participated in the study were found to internationalise either by adopting the stages model or the born-global approach. The approach that they chose affected the level and rate of internationalisation as well as their behaviours and characteristics. The wholly owned foreign entities (WOFEs) were particularly likely to adopt the stages model, whilst the born in China (BIC) organisations internationalised via the born-global approach. The SMEs that chose to internationalise as WOFEs were also more likely to have higher levels of resources (enabling them to support both Chinese and Australian operations). By contrast, the organisations that internationalised to China as BICs invested all of their resources in their Chinese operations. The BIC participants were also more likely to have entrepreneurial owners with a Chinese background, experience and networks in international markets and were more likely to be established on the basis of an unexpected opportunity, rather than by a long-term strategic plan.

Increased time in the market knowledge and strengths of contacts were associated with the SME making increased levels of investment in the market and either internationalising as a BIC or a WOFE. Some participants were found to adopt a minimalist approach to internationalising, settling for importing products from China as a permanent business arrangement. There was some evidence to suggest that importer SMEs may expand their international investment using the stages approach if they detect opportunities in the foreign environment. The participants that exported products to China, however, acquired knowledge through this process and usually planned to move to a higher form of investment. They experienced the liability of smallness (LOS) as a major barrier to making this transition. Both the BIC and WOFE were termination points for the participants, with none of the participants indicating that they had plans to become large organisations, although several had adopted a business structure which allowed for continual expansion (e.g., through replication). Those organisations may become large organisations in time through natural growth, but this would not be a reflection of their market entry approach.

The role of innovation

The participants used innovation in their internationalisation to China to gain an advantage over domestic competitors. Not surprisingly, the participants indicated that internationalisation and innovation were closely related and interdependent. More surprisingly, perhaps, innovation sometimes created a liability for the internationalisation of these SMEs, because many segments of the Chinese market did not accept significant innovation due to uncertainty avoidance. They were also more interested in cost than innovative product and service features. The mismatch of product or service innovation to the market indicates a lack of market knowledge and integration and is a liability of foreignness (LOF).

The participants reported using innovation in their organisational design, products, services and processes to help internationalise. Organisational design innovation created new opportunities, whereas the value of product and service innovation was highly dependent on the market context. Process innovation, however, tended to lead to improved product value which gave the participants an advantage. The different innovation behaviours of the participants could also be categorised as the level of standardisation or adaption incorporated in their innovation and whether the innovation could be described as radical or incremental.

The resistance of many sectors of the Chinese market to significant product or service innovations led the participants to focus on standardisation of product and service features and adaptation of their innovations to these standard formats to try to create an intrinsic advantage, such as a cost advantage. Internal innovation focused on product and process also lead to the adoption of incremental innovation. The majority of the participants focused on incremental innovation, predominantly because of the cost and resource requirements associated with implementing radical innovation. This was also consistent with the adaptation innovation approach.

The externally focused organisations, however, applied innovations to their organisational design to create new opportunities for which there was also a market in China, rather than compete with existing products and services. This radical form of innovation required a more sophisticated understanding of the market and integration and was associated with more market experience. The participants in the service industry, in particular, adopted a radical and external market orientation to their innovation, whereas the nonservice organisations tended to adopt a process and product orientation and incremental innovation.

The role of networks

The internationalisation of SMEs is often limited by a shortage of resources. Networks, contacts and social capital are important mechanisms through which SMEs can access resources. The different entry modes and business structures adopted by the participants also drove them to focus on different networks. The participants importing products from China utilised fairly simple networks, mainly comprising local agents and local network services. These networks provided advice and the SME's objective was controlling costs and problem avoidance. The networks provided market information and so network trust was an important feature. Trade fairs were frequently used to establish the contacts necessary to establish these networks.

The participants that exported to China developed more sophisticated networks. They adopted a combination of formal and informal networks, built using existing connections and contacts made during trade missions. The primary objective of these networks was to gain access to information and trust was again an important feature, as was the use of trade shows and customer relationships to make initial contacts. Social capital was developed through potential relationships with institutional support, while some resources were provided through networks of customers and technology parks. The WOFE participants focused on building local network relationships. These organisations commenced their network development in a fairly formal manner by making contacts through Australian government support agencies and, to a lesser extent, through associations and some trade shows. The BIC participants also used government services and connected with Australian institutes and business associations located in China, entrepreneur associations and both local and global industry groups to establish their networks. They also established direct social connections. These SMEs connected with these networks at the senior level and reported high levels of support.

The role of entrepreneurship

The process of establishing SMEs and the process of internationalising an organisation both require entrepreneurial behaviours. The data was examined for evidence of autonomous behaviours, motivation, risk-taking, competitor orientation and proactiveness. These factors were considered from the perspective of how they affected the participant's entrepreneurial identity, motivation and internationalisation performance. Evidence was found for opportunistic motivation, proactiveness and competitor orientation, but limited evidence was found for risk-taking. The limited evidence for risk-taking was an interesting finding, however, as the initial plan to internationalise to China represented a significant risk, this may have dominated the participant's perspective of risk-taking. Evidence was also identified for creative behaviours, personal reward and the importance of entrepreneurial identity.

Part of the competitor orientation identified was the focus on planning, which included both the basis of business development, as well as how the organisation would continue to compete in the market as it developed. This planning and the maintenance of the plan required very up-to-date market knowledge. The participants indicated an association between the possession of market knowledge and the processes for responding to this knowledge, suggesting that they engaged in dynamic planning. There was also evidence to suggest that the participants engaged in long-term planning.

The service industry participants also appeared to place more emphasis on planning how their SME would be established in China than the participants from the nonservice industry participants, such as manufacturing. A difference in the pattern of innovation behaviours between the service and non-service companies was also identified. The participants from hard industries such as manufacturing usually entered the market with an innovative product and became less focused on innovation over time. The participants in the service industries, however, usually entered the market with a non-innovative product and became more innovative over time.

The role of resources and capabilities

Adopting an internationalisation strategy requires an adequate set of resources to be successful. Tangible resources identified included parent company support, presence, location in China and Hong Kong as a destination of interest. Intangible resources included brand, reputation, Australian origin, experience and knowledge. Human resources were also seen as imperative. Different types of human resources included Western educated Chinese staff resources (Haigui),

Chinese local staff, owners/managers/employees' capabilities, external consultants and the owners/managers' Chinese background. Organisational resources included technology/technical experience, online presence, Chinese language capability, flexibility/agility/size and the ability to think 'new'. Some resources were required for all entry modes (importer, exporter, WOFE and BIC), however, other types of resources were only required for some of these entry modes.

The internationalisation of SMEs can be considered as a process that combines different resources and capabilities utilised by the SME to develop strategies in the environment, take advantage of opportunities and minimise risk. Each enterprise has its own internationalisation process realised by the construction of resources and competences in different ways: some SMEs progressively combine resources and competences, entering foreign markets by steps, whilst others combine resources and competences at the outset and internationalise very rapidly. The application of resources and competences to internationalisation is dependent upon the resources available to the SME, the characteristics of the foreign market into which it internationalises and the competencies the organisation possesses to exploit its resources.

Barriers and liabilities

The most frequently identified barriers for the participants to internationalising to China were understanding local culture and language, adapting, achieving credibility, developing relationships and meeting expectations and regulations. These barriers created subsequent liabilities; mainly liabilities of foreignness and smallness, although there was some evidence of liabilities of outsidership (LOO) and newness as well. This finding was consistent with the experience of an SME in a developing foreign market described in the literature (Dominguez and Mayrhofer, 2017). These findings confirmed the value of liability theory for explaining the behaviours and experiences of SMEs internationalising to China. By contrast, the analysis only identified limited support for institutional theory explanations of the barriers experienced by the participants. The finding that foreignness and smallness were the most commonly identified liabilities suggests that SME internationalisation theory should focus on the reactions to these liabilities. It was also interesting that dynamic effects were apparent. Although LOF and LOO theory correctly predicted the effects reported by participants, the moderating effect of partnerships (also identified as a common liability response in the literature) was only considered by the participants to be effective as short-term solutions because of the organisational complexity and costs that it created.

Not all features of foreignness created liabilities. In some industries, businesses run by expatriates from home countries with good credentials, for example in the areas of finance or agriculture, actually experienced more trust than domestic organisations. Trust, transparency and understanding culture and language were otherwise found to create liabilities. This was particularly true for the smallest organisations in the study, whose limited trust in their customers was a LOS. The participants noted the rapid rate of change in each of these factors and their varying effects. This provides evidence for the proposition that theories of SME internationalisation to China need to account for changes the psychic distance represented by the foreign market. In a rapidly changing foreign market, responses to change in these factors should be the principal research and practice focus. It is unlikely that the Chinese market, economy or culture will reach an equilibrium in the foreseeable future. As China becomes the largest economy in the world, it will continue to develop its own unique characteristics and create new forms of psychic distance for foreign enterprises. This suggests that the change in key independent variables will not progress to a zero point, but possibly reduce and then expand again.

Putting these ideas together leads to the conclusion that liabilities are likely to continue to exist for foreign SMEs in China and particularly for small foreign organisations. The factors which create these liabilities, however, will change, so they need to be measured as the effect of a difference on the established operations, rather than as an external influence. It should be noted that the continuing resource, economic and social development occurring in China will mean that this difference could result in either a deficit or a surplus at different times. For example, in the case of LOS, a future Chinese market condition may demand a rate of innovation which an SME may be unable to achieve. This new condition would change customer expectations of innovation from creating an opportunity which the innovative SMEs in this survey had been utilising to become a requirement that the SMEs would be unable to meet and thus generate a LOS.

Human resource management practices

The participants were found to utilise one of two HRM systems: either commitment-oriented or collaboration-based HRM practices. Commitment-based HRM practices (i.e. high pay/salaries, reasonable benefits, flexible job design with work-life balance and volunteering programs, training and career development and safety practices) were found to facilitate the SMEs' organisational, process and technological innovation. Collaboration-oriented HRM practices (i.e. broad job design, teamwork, employee empowerment, group-incentives, learning with strategic partners and extensive network and personal relationship building) were associated with product, market and technical innovation.

The findings indicate that for a foreign SME in China, cultural integration, cooperation with local associations, building strategic partnerships and personal networks would be critical factors for developing a performance oriented HRM system when the HRM practices are based on collaboration. Foreign SMEs in China that focus on the use of internal processes and organisational innovation to compete, such as the service industry participants in this study, needed to adopt commitment oriented HRM practices. The nonservice industry participants offering innovative products and an external perspective were more likely to adopt collaboration-based HRM practices because of the important role of accessing and utilising market information as part of the HRM practices. As most of the participants exhibited evidence of slowly shifting from externally focused to internally focused bases of innovation, it is likely that their HRM practices orientation will also change over time. The most competitive position, however, would be to improve performance through both innovative project products and an external perspective while still taking advantage of internal processes and organisational innovation, which suggests that a combination of commitment and collaboration oriented HRM practices is required for long-term success.

A unified SME internationalisation model for China

The findings presented in the previous sections describe the participants' experience in China, from the perspective of seven different research domains. These perspectives resulted in the identification of a number of important relationships, all of which connected through the pluripotent characteristics of entry mode, entrepreneurship behaviours, innovation type and organisational size. A key feature of the findings from all the perspectives was the need to measure the factors (independent variables) in terms of psychic differences between China and the SME's home country, as well as the fact that this difference could create either an opportunity or a limitation. The magnitude of the difference and the conditions in China determined whether the current state of the factors represented an opportunity, created a liability or had little effect. A number of the findings from the different perspectives indicated that the direction of change in China reduced the psychic distance and so many sources of liability and opportunities will disappear as the psychic distance diminishes. The dynamic nature of these factors is also a key feature, which is a reflection of the economic, resource and infrastructure development in China. These observations lead to the model shown in Figure 9.1.

The model shows how the inputs of human resource management, home country characteristics and Chinese conditions affect the process of resource allocation, innovation and the subsequent internationalisation success for these organisations. The figure also indicates that the process of entrepreneurship affects both resource development as well as innovation, that barriers and liabilities affect the process of innovation and internationalisation success and that networks affect resources, innovation and internationalisation success. The model also identifies the nature of the contributions of these effects.

The model indicates that there are compounding effects due to the multiple relationships between the factors and the three sequential activities of resources, innovation and internationalisation success. For example, Figure 9.1 shows that HRM practices have a direct effect on resources, which is dependent on the type of HRM practice adopted and affect the networks which can be created. The networks which can be created affect which resources are available to the SME (see Chapter 8). The combined direct and indirect effect on resources is a compounding of the two pathways in which HRM practices affect resources. In a similar way, entrepreneurship affects the resources that are available which, in turn, affects the innovation achieved, however, entrepreneurship also directly

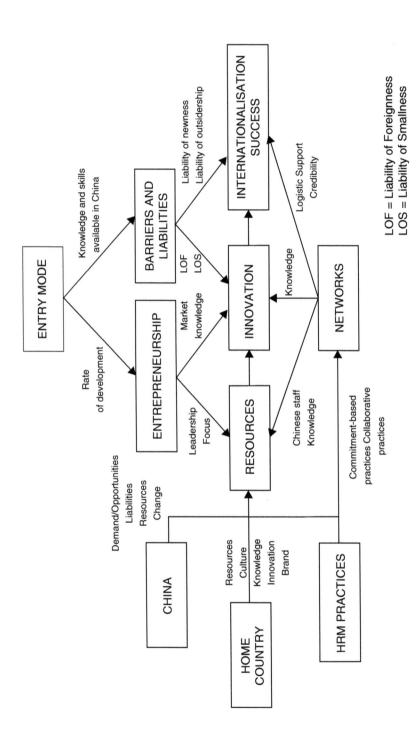

Figure 9.1 Factors affecting SMEs internationalising to China

affects the innovation achieved. Thus the effect of entrepreneurship on innovation is compounded by its indirect effect on resources.

A typology of SME internationalisation to China

The following typology represents a static perspective on the characteristics of foreign SME internationalisation to China shown in Figure 9.1. The typology shown in Figure 9.2 draws out other dimensions which were identified in the findings, but were less evident in the flow model presented in Figure 9.1. The three important dimensions which the typology introduces are the level of complexity or investment in the foreign SME, the level of intensity or creativity of the foreign SME and the effect of the entry mode selected. The high intensity/

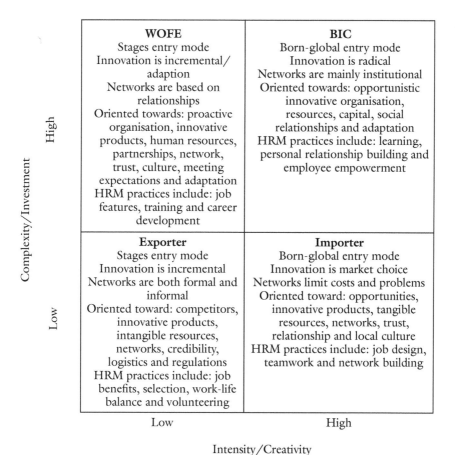

Figure 9.2 Complexity/Intensity matrix for SME internationalisation

creativity perspective can be considered to be a strategic perspective. This is evident in the entry mode which relies on the local conditions and the opportunistic and innovative organisational behaviours of the SMEs. The low intensity/creativity mode can be considered to be structural. This is evident in the incremental approach to establishing the foreign SME activities, the incremental approach to innovation and the focus on innovative products (rather than organisation), logistics and meeting customer/partner expectations entry modes.

From the complexity/investment perspective, the high complexity investment modes included both greater investment in networks and an orientation towards maximising the return that the organisation achieved through innovation, resources, relationships and collaboration with staff. High levels of complexity/investment can be considered to reflect transformational approaches in the management of foreign SMEs in China. The low levels of complexity/investment were associated with process-oriented networks, a focus on responding to competitors and building internal resources, but still gave attention to product innovation and creating commitment in the workforce. Low levels of complexity/investment can be considered to reflect in transactional management approaches to the management of SMEs in China.

Application to contemporary research

The relations represented in the model in Figure 9.1 can be represented as propositions which could be used for the design of future research. These propositions are as follows:

P1: The conditions in China affect the resources available to foreign SMEs by creating demand, liabilities, offering resources and creating change.

P2: The home country conditions for foreign SMEs in China influence the resources available to the SME on the basis of the home country resources, culture, knowledge, innovation and brand.

P3: HRM practices influence the resources available to foreign SMEs in China differently depending on whether the practices are commitment or collaborative based.

P4: HRM practices influence the networks of foreign SMEs in China differently depending whether the practices are commitment or collaborative based.

P5: Entrepreneurship affects the resources available to foreign SMEs in China through leadership and focus.

P6: Entrepreneurship affects the innovation process of foreign SMEs in China through market knowledge.

P7: The networks of foreign SMEs in China affect the resources that are available through the capabilities of their Chinese staff and environmental knowledge.

P8: The networks of foreign SMEs in China affect the innovation process through the technical and market knowledge that they provide.

P9: The networks of foreign SMEs in China affect their innovation success through the logistical support and credibility that they provide.

P10: The barriers and liabilities that foreign SMEs experience in China affect the innovation process on the basis of foreignness and smallness.

P11: The barriers and liabilities that foreign SMEs experience in China affect the internationalisation success on the basis of newness and outsidership.

P12: The type of entrepreneurship exhibited by a foreign SME in China will be affected by the rate of development which the selected entry mode allows.

P13: The barriers and liabilities that a foreign SME in China experiences is affected by the home country knowledge and skill transfer to China that the selected entry mode allows.

P 14: The type and amount of resources available to a foreign SME in China will affect the type and amount of innovation that occurs.

P 15: The type and amount of innovation that occurs in a foreign SME in China will affect its internationalisation success.

Future research

The findings of this project indicate that future research into the internationalisation of SMEs into China must incorporate dynamic effects. As the market develops, examinations of innovation intensity and type would make a significant contribution to the literature. Examining the process of internationalisation from different countries to China, which would introduce different psychic distances in the key independent variables would have the effect of varying the levels of psychic distance on internationalisation outcomes to be identified. Future research projects should test the propositions represented in this chapter, as well as their application to SMEs originating from different cultural backgrounds. Examining these effects on SMEs from different foreign cultural backgrounds and longitudinally will provide these tests with greater variation in the key independent variables, such as understanding of the Chinese culture. It will also test their application to different relational (intercultural) contexts.

Conclusion and limitations

This project included a number of limitations. Firstly, the research only considered the effect of the various perspectives on Australian foreign SMEs in China. As indicated in Chapter 1, this group of foreign SMEs have proven to be fairly successful in their internationalisation. This would have reduced the variation in some of the factors and disguised some relationships which may otherwise have been apparent. Future research needs to consider the effect of these perspectives on foreign SMEs in China from different countries. In addition, the research identified temporal effects in several of the perspectives. The data collected, however, only considered a single timeframe. Future studies should examine the longitudinal effects of these perspectives. Finally, the findings of this research were based on interviews conducted with representatives of 35 SMEs. Larger and single industry studies will provide more confirmatory evidence for the relationships proposed above.

This research has identified a large number of potential relationships for foreign SMEs in China. The effect of the rapid rate of development in China was evident in the identified relationships for many of the perspectives, but this effect was generally absent from the extent literature on these perspectives. This indicates that internationalisation of SMEs to rapidly changing foreign environments, such as China and many other countries in Asia, needs to be viewed from a different theoretical lens. We hope that some of the insights presented in this book will spark the interest of other researchers and engage them in this fascinating area. In addition, we hope that the practical insights contained in this book will assist managers already operating in China to more deeply understand the conditions that they experience. We also hope it will inform managers contemplating working in China in a foreign SME about the factors they will need to deal with, as well as their causes and potential solutions. We sincerely hope that you have enjoyed this book and wish you a prosperous future, however you choose to engage with China.

References

Chiang, M.-H. (2012). The changing role of tourism in China's economy. *Journal of China Tourism Research*, 8:2, 207.

Dominguez, N., and Mayrhofer, U. (2017). Internationalization stages of traditional SMEs: Increasing, decreasing and re-increasing commitment to foreign markets. *International Business Review*.

Li, Y. (2016). Rethinking organizational change: Implications from the Chinese Shi 势. *Frontiers of Philosophy in China*, 11:4, 540–555.

Qi, Y. J., Yang, Y., and Jin, F. J. (2013). China's economic development stage and its spatio-temporal evolution: A prefectural-level analysis. *Journal of Geographical Sciences*, 23:2, 297–314.

Wu, J., and Boateng, A. (2010). Factors influencing changes in Chinese management accounting practices. *Journal of Change Management*, 10:3, 315–329.

Wu, S. J. (2015). The impact of quality culture on quality management practices and performance in Chinese manufacturing firms. *International Journal of Quality & Reliability Management*, 32:8, 799–814.

Xiaohe Zhang, J. (2015). Is China's economic growth sustainable? A general equilibrium analysis. *Journal of Developing Areas*, 49:4, 407–414.

Yang, R., Xu, Q., and Long, H. (2016). Spatial distribution characteristics and optimized reconstruction analysis of China's rural settlements during the process of rapid urbanization. *Journal of Rural Studies*, 413.

Zheng, C., Khavul, S., and Crockett, D. (2012). Does it transfer? The effects of pre-internationalization experience on post-entry organizational learning in entrepreneurial Chinese firms. *Journal of International Entrepreneurship*, 10:3, 232–254.

Zhong, W. G., Peng, J. S., and Liu, C. L. (2013). Internationalization performance of Chinese multinational companies in the developed markets. *Journal of Business Research*, 66:12, 2479–2484.

Zhu, X. (2012). Understanding China's growth: Past, present, and future. *Journal of Economic Perspectives*, 26:4, 103–124.

Index

For Product Safety Concerns and Information please contact our EU
representative GPSR@taylorandfrancis.com
Taylor & Francis Verlag GmbH, Kaufingerstraße 24, 80331 München, Germany

www.ingramcontent.com/pod-product-compliance
Ingram Content Group UK Ltd.
Pitfield, Milton Keynes, MK11 3LW, UK
UKHW020959180425
457613UK00019B/749